Management for Professionals

Sanjay Mohapatra

Business Process Reengineering

Automation Decision Points in Process Reengineering

 Springer

Sanjay Mohapatra
Xavier Institute of Management
Bhubaneswar, Orissa, India

ISSN 2192-8096   ISSN 2192-810X (electronic)
ISBN 978-1-4614-6066-4   ISBN 978-1-4614-6067-1 (eBook)
DOI 10.1007/978-1-4614-6067-1
Springer New York Heidelberg Dordrecht London

Library of Congress Control Number: 2012954051

Printed on acid-free paper

Springer is part of Springer Science+Business Media (www.springer.com)

Dedicated to Late Parmananda Mishra
Late Dr. Sushila Mishra
Dr. B C Mohapatra
and
Mr. H K Mohapatra
Mrs. K K Mohapatra

Preface

Business Process Re-engineering (BPR) is a powerful approach to bring in extraordinary improvements in the output of an organization. This is achieved through radical changes in the processes which are keys to the success of the firm. Many organizations have benefited from this approach. In today's world where the market dynamics change quite often, organizations need to work harder to remain competitive. In a globally competitive market these companies need to improve the outputs from their processes dramatically and at a fast pace. This can happen by automating the re-engineered processes. This helps in sustaining implementation of the re-engineered processes, increasing consistency of the output as well as making processes result oriented and transparent through work flow management.

With the rapid penetration of Internet, information technology has become all pervasive. From being an enabler of business in the past, it now partners with business strategy to provide direction to the business. Automation using technology has become critical organization asset, source of strategic advantage. Increasingly, success of an organization depends on its ability to gather, produce and disseminate knowledge through a systematic process orients approach will be key to success of business. Using re-engineering approach, processes can be redesigned and streamlined so that roles can be assigned to different processes as owners. Using the work flow method, service-level agreements can be defined for internal and external customers so that effectiveness of different outputs from the process can be measured. Automating the work flows and re-engineered processes can increase consistency of process performance with increase in sustainability in implementing processes so that interpretation of processes across the organization is same. Thus, role of automation for re-engineered processes play a vital role.

To compete in an ever-changing business environment, it is essential that the managers have adequate information about the parameters that impact global competitive environment. These changes require efficient, accurate information to flow seamlessly to the managers. With rapid advancement of Internet, extranet and intranet, technology has increased the capabilities of an organization in terms of its reach for information from different geographies. With availability of information through technology from different remote locations, managers can respond to different problems and situations faster and with increased efficiency and capitalize on market opportunities. By using technology-based online analytical engines, business intelligence and knowledge management practices, managers can get better returns on investment from its investment in re-engineered processes. This will help them to retain competitive advantage.

Mere definition of processes will not be enough. The processes need to be implemented with correct intent and proper alignment of business goals with objectives of the processes. The biggest stumbling block in this alignment is the resistance offered by the practitioners who are quite familiar with the current processes. As the law of inertia implies (Newton's law of inertia), there will be a challenge for the employees to change the present state of behaviour to a new state of behaviour in the context of new processes. A framework-based scientific approach will help in reducing mistakes while implementing new processes. Chapters 7 and 8 talk about the framework and cases that can help readers understand the nuances of behavioural aspects in change management.

This book attempts to show decision points where re-engineered processes need to be automated so that a firm can get maximum returns on investment. All the re-engineered processes cannot be automated as it would lead to high investment making the investment a white elephant. Through framework and case studies, the book will guide its readers on how to re-engineer processes and when to automate these processes. The book can be used by students in management schools who are specializing in General Management, Strategic Management, Information System, and Operations Management. The book can be used also by consultants who are in Management Consulting, Technology Consulting and who are playing the role of Business Analysts.

I hope the readers would like the contents and style of writing and would be happy to receive feedback for further improvement.

Bhubaneswar, Orissa, India   Sanjay Mohapatra

Acknowledgements

The production of any book of this magnitude involves valued contributions from many persons. I would like to thank Amboy Matthew for providing continued editorial support and making this project a reality. His association and patronage has become a motivational factor for me to write and publish with Springer.

The manuscript has been class tested. It has undergone 2 years of discussions and reviews in the class, and I thank my students who have helped me in reviewing and providing feedback so that I could complete the manuscript. I would like to mention the names of the following students whose efforts shaped the final manuscript: Swavab Sourav Moharana, Priyabrata Das, Rabindra Jena, Purbesh Mahapatra, Hemant Sharma, Anuj Das, Shilpi Sandwar, Bagdevi Panda, Abhijeet Das, Binay Prasanna Jena, Tuktuk, Kanmaani, Anindita Patnaik, Pinakini Mohanty, Ashutosh Didwania, Ashish Kailash Sharma, Rani Jain, Sameer Sawant, Sudip Ghosh, Kanti Prakash Brahma, Sandeep Swain, Suchismita Gupta, and Aurelie Tockqueville.

Last but not the least, I would like to thank Dr. Bharati (my wife) for helping me in taking decisions at a critical stage of the manuscript.

Bhubaneswar, Orissa, India   Sanjay Mohapatra

Contents

Chapter 1
Business Process Reengineering: A Consolidated Approach to Different Models

1.1 Background

The beginning of the concept of business process reengineering dates back to at least a decade ago when the realization of the success of the synergy between process focus and just-in-time techniques employed by Japanese organizations (especially in the manufacturing sector) was recognized and appreciated. This kind of an approach reduced work-in-progress, improved the rate of workflow, and thus affected lead times as well, which reduced by giving better customer service. During this time, the concept of *Quality Circles* came into being which held the separate work cells responsible for their work rather than departments. Thus due to such decentralized quality control, better customer service could be provided as well as multiskilled work could be performed. This reduced costs as well as made the quality control tasks dynamic and dealing with customer satisfaction easier as, instead of knowing the customer's discomfort at the end, it could be identified early and requisite action could be taken.

1.2 Introduction

In today's world, three Cs have become very important for organizations: customer, competition, and change. Business process reengineering (BPR) is a kind of solution based on the latter. Reengineering refers to the fundamental rethinking and radical redesign of business processes to achieve rapid improvements, keeping in mind performance, cost, quality, responsiveness, and service. A business process is a series of steps which if implemented lead to a product or service. Through these business processes, organizations endeavor to add value for the customers, both internal and external. But the plot is lost when individual departments think only about their own department's efficiency and not the process efficiency as a whole. Process mapping is an important tool which suggests a methodology for identifying

S. Mohapatra, *Business Process Reengineering*, Management for Professionals,
DOI 10.1007/978-1-4614-6067-1_1, © Springer Science+Business Media New York 2013

the current As-Is processes and can be used to provide To-Be processes after reengineering the product and service business enterprise functions. But the choice of processes to be reengineered is made based on the following criteria: *dysfunction*, identifying the processes that are functioning the worst; *importance*, identifying the most critical and influential processes on the basis of customer satisfaction; and *feasibility*, identifying the processes that are most likely to be reengineered successfully.

1.3   Office Process Reengineering and Change Management

1.3.1   Traditional Businesses and Problems

1.3.1.1   Traditional Businesses

Traditionally, businesses are divided into divisions and/or departments. Each division is responsible for certain product lines, services, or other sets of responsibilities, for example an insurance company may have different divisions for each product. These divisions could be divided into departments, which are responsible for key functions in the division. Within these departments, different tasks can be identified, which are performed by certain employees.

This concept was built for almost two centuries on the principles of Adam Smith's insight about fragmenting work into its component tasks. In itself, the idea is simple, being that several highly specialized workers performing single elementary tasks would produce more efficiently than the same number of generalists each engaged in performing the whole work.

1.3.1.2   The Problem Traditional Businesses Experience

The result of the Adam Smith-module is that you divide employees into small compartments. You teach them to do their portion of the work, and only their portion, very well, while nobody explains to them the objective of the process and where their small portions fit into the process. This results in bad customer service, mainly due to two reasons discussed below.

1. *Many organizations are not customer focused*
   They provide products/services to customers, but not solutions to their problems. Besides the fact that companies are not customer focused with regard to products, many companies are also not customer focused with regard to customer service. Michael Hammer describes the reason for this as being employees' lack of knowledge with regard to processes. Every employee is only interested in his/her part of the responsibility, which includes individual tasks. Nobody is interested in the process, which will ensure customers are satisfied at the end of the day.

   Another reason why an organization is not customer focused is that processes tend to be fragmented among each of a dozen business units and departments. As a result, each department treated the customer differently and according to its own standards. The customer on the other end had to deal with multiple unites of the company in trying to solve a problem.

2. *Too much time and resources spent on non-value-added activities*
   Michael Hammer classifies activities into three types:

   Value-adding work, or work for which the customer is willing to pay
   Value-adding work, or work for which the customer is willing to pay
   Non-value-adding work, which creates no value for the customer but is required in order to get the value-adding work done

Waste, or work that neither adds nor enables value

   Waste work is pointless work whose absence would, by definition, not be noticed by the customer. This includes activities such as producing reports that no one reads, doing work erroneously so that it needs to be redone, and redundant checking activities. These activities should be eliminated from processes.

   The Delphi Consulting Group estimates that up to 90 % of the time needed to complete typical office tasks is a result of gathering and transferring paper documents. Develin & Partners pointed out in their research that the proportion of time normally taken up by diversionary activities in a business is 35 %, which is the same as support activities, while time spent on the core business is only 30 %.

   Michael Hammer also gives examples where organizations spent too much time on waste activities:

- Aetna Life & Casualty took 28 days on average to process applications for homeowner's insurance, only 26 min of which represented real productive work.
- Chrysler incurred internal expenses of $ 300 in reviews, sign-offs, and approvals when buying anything through their purchasing organization, even small stationery items costing less than $ 10.
- Texas Instruments' Semiconductor Group took 180 days to fill an order for an integrated circuit while a competitor could often do it in 30 days.
- GTE's customer service unit could only resolve customer problems on the first call for less than 2 % of the time.
- Pepsi discovered that 44 % of the invoices that it sent retailers contained errors, leading to enormous reconciliation costs and endless squabbles with customers.

   According to Hammer, the reason why managers are unable to solve problems is because they apply task solutions to process problems. The reason why services are delivered slowly is not because employees perform their individual tasks slowly, but because they have to perform tasks that need not be done at all. Another reason is because of delays in getting the work from the person who does the one task to the person who does the next task. As a result, customer service contains errors, not because people perform their individual tasks inaccurately, but because people misunderstand each other while performing one task after another.

Organizations are inflexible not because individuals are locked into fixed ways of operating, but because no one understands how individual tasks are combined to create an end result that satisfies the customer's need. Unsatisfactory service is provided due to a lack of knowledge and perspective to explain the status of the process to customers. Costs are high not because individual tasks are expensive, but because so many employees have to be employed to combine these individual tasks into one process in order to add value to customers.

Although other reasons for bad customer service could be added, most of them remain related to the fact that a *company is not process driven*.

1.4 History and Development of Business Process Reengineering

The beginning of business process reengineering goes back at least a decade, when Western companies realized why the Japanese used the concept of processes together with *just-in-time* principles for manufacturing. By applying these principles, they introduced a product-oriented factory layout. This involved partitioning of activities into separate cells organized by type of machine instead of the traditional functional departments. This had remarkable benefits for manufacturing within Japanese companies. These benefits included improving coordination of the rate of workflow and reducing work-in-progress. As a result, lead times had been reduced dramatically and the customer received a much better service. The concept of cells instead of departments led to multiskilled workforces, who were responsible for their own quality inspections. Due to this fact, the Japanese companies moved away from centralized control which was a feature of hierarchical organizations, and created semiautonomous cells with substantial decision-making power to direct and control their own activities.

Together with just-in-time principles, Japanese companies introduced *Quality Circles*. This was an introduction not only to total quality control but also to the principles of working in teams to streamline processes and reduce costs. While the tendency of companies in the United States was to check product quality at the final inspection, Japanese companies performed quality control as part of the total production process. US companies used their quality control departments to identify reject products at the end of the production process. However, as these products were only identified at the end of the production process, related costs and customer dissatisfaction were unacceptably high. Japanese companies on the other hand did not use a quality control department, but included quality controllers as part of the project teams. They identified reject products at a much earlier stage. Costs were reduced and better yields, greater efficiency, and higher productivity were some of the results.

As a result of the success achieved by Japanese manufacturing companies, organizations elsewhere started to show an interest in these innovative techniques. In the later half of the 1980s and early 1990s companies in the United States of America introduced *business process reengineering programs* to improve performance. European companies soon followed. These companies were so successful that business process reengineering became a vast global business movement.

1.5   What Is Business/Office Process Reengineering?

Reengineering Defined

> Reengineering is the fundamental rethinking and radical redesign of business processes to achieve dramatic improvements in critical, contemporary measures of performance, such as cost, quality, service, and speed.
>
> > (Hammer and Champy 1993)

> *The definition for business process reengineering according Du Plessis: "Business process reengineering is the fundamental analysis and radical re-design of every process and activity pertaining to a business — business practices, management systems, job definitions, organisational structures and beliefs and behaviours. The goal is dramatic performance improvements to meet contemporary requirements — and IT is seen as a key enabler in this process"*
>
> > (Du Plessis 1994:39–42).

From the above and other available definitions, the following key elements are identified as essential for business process reengineering:

- *A radical change.*
- *Change in orientation.*
- *Redesign business processes.*
- *Change organizational structure.*
- *Technological improvements.*
- *The objective is the improvement of customer service and reduction of costs.*

The National Academy of Public Administration of the USA recasts this definition for the Government:

> *Government business process reengineering is a radical improvement approach that critically examines, rethinks, and redesigns mission product and service processes within a political environment. It achieves dramatic mission performance gains from multiple customer and stakeholder perspectives. It is a key part of a process management approach for optimal performance that continually evaluates, adjusts or removes processes.*
>
> > (NAPA 1995)

As *BPR* enters a new century, it has begun to undergo a resurgence in popularity. Organizations have seen real benefit in evaluating processes before they implement expensive technology solutions. By deconstructing processes and grading them in terms of whether they are value-added or non-value-added activities, organizations are able to pinpoint areas that are wasteful and inefficient.

1.6   Understanding Office/Business Process Reengineering

BPR relies on a different school of thought than continuous process improvement. *In the extreme*, reengineering assumes the current process is irrelevant—it doesn't work, it's broke, forget it, start over. Such a clean slate perspective enables the designers of business processes to disassociate themselves from today's process, and focus on a new process. In a manner of speaking, it is like projecting yourself into the future and asking yourself: What should the process look like? What do my customers want it to look like? What do other employees want it to look like? How do best-in-class companies do it? What might we be able to do with new technology?

Such an approach is pictured below. It begins with defining the scope and objectives of your reengineering project, and then going through a learning process (with your customers, your employees, your competitors and noncompetitors, and with new technology). Given this knowledge base, one can create a vision for the future and design new business processes. Given the definition of the *To-Be* state, one can then create a plan of action based on the gap between your current processes, technologies, and structures and where you want to go. It is then a matter of implementing one's solution.

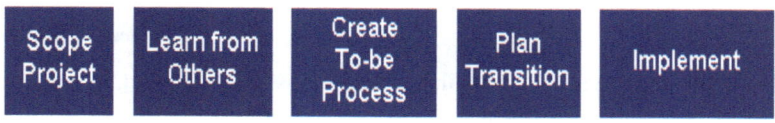

Breakthrough Reengineering Model

Over time many derivatives of radical, breakthrough improvement and continuous improvement have emerged that attempt to address the difficulties of implementing major change in corporations. It is difficult to find a single approach exactly matched to a particular organization's needs, and the challenge is to know what method to use when and how to pull it off successfully such that bottom-line business results are achieved.

The question arises what are the characteristics of a reengineered company. In addition one should consider how organizational structures would differ in traditional and reengineered companies. The answer is difficult, as none of the reengineering solutions is identical. The objective is to find the best possible solution for a business although there are no prescribed rules on how to structure the new business. From the examples given by Hammer and Jacobson there are a few common trends on how to restructure the business, which are discussed below.

1. *Processes replace individual tasks and departments*
   The first option is to divide the company into *processes instead of individual tasks and departments*. That does not mean a company will no longer have departments, but the way in which these departments operate will change. This

concept can be applied with great success where complex skills are required. An example is the financial function (accountants and financial analysts) or the IT support function.

2. *Complex jobs and simple processes replace simple jobs and complex processes*
   The second solution is to replace simple jobs and complex processes with *simple processes and complex jobs*. An employee will no longer be responsible for only one simple task, but by understanding the total process, he/she should be able to perform multiskilled tasks in a process.

3. *Work in teams*
   A third solution to the restructuring of a business is to organize the workforce into *teams*, whose goal is to satisfy customers' needs. Each team member understands the process, and not only his/her own task. Complex business processes are most often divided and assigned to several independent teams, who work in parallel with each other until their tasks have been completed. These tasks are then integrated with each other.

   Cross, Feather, and Lynch argued that the new organization should include *small self-managed teams*. They suggest that everyone in the team should be *business orientated* and employees should be turned "…into mom-and pop enterprises, into real… business persons" who are responsible for customers from receiving the order till the goods or services are delivered.
   The following elements should be included in teams:

   (a) Cross-training between employees.
   (b) Teams should be responsible for their customers and if services cannot be performed personally, the help of an expert or senior should be called.
   (c) Teams should have access to financial information and expert systems to evaluate performance and to take the necessary actions.
   (d) Teams should have access to the *Global University*, which means that they should have access to all the information needed to support them in performing their tasks.
   (e) Teams should be responsible for their own budgets. That means that they will have the power to act on their own initiative without prior approval.
   (f) Teams should be owners of their assets, which means it is their responsibility to obtain the required return on these assets.
   (g) Teams should have substantial spending authority.
   (h) Teams should be responsible for quality assurance.

4. *A process owner replaces the manager*
   A fourth methodology that can be applied in restructuring the business is to replace managers with process owners. A process owner will be responsible to ensure customers' needs are satisfied and to manage the team. This person will act as the contact between the customer and the company.

   An advantage of replacing managers with process owners (*interface objects*) is that customers only deal with one contact person who is responsible for all aspects of their business. Problems can easily be referred to the process owner and customer relationships will improve.

1.6.1 A Different Approach in the Government

Some have argued that government activities are often policy generators or oversight mechanisms that appear to add no value, yet cannot be eliminated. They question how reengineering could have applicability in the public sector. Government only differs from the commercial sector because it has different kinds of controls and customers. It still utilizes a set of processes aimed at providing services and products to its customers.

Transitions that must take place in any government reengineering approach

Transition from—	Transition to—
Paper driven	Electronic based
Hierarchical	Networked
Power by hoarding information	Power by sharing information
Appropriations funding	Leveraged-cost funding
Stand-alone	Virtual and digital
Compliance oriented	Performance oriented
Control oriented	Benchmark oriented
Sole resident experts	Teams by talent
Stovepipe organizations	Honeycombed organizations
Oversight agencies	Coaching agencies
Single-agency projects	Cooperative projects
Information-limited environment	Information unlimited environment
Delayed access	Instant access
Slow response	Prompt response
Data entered more than once	Data entered once
Technology fearful	Technology savvy
Business as usual	Routinely improving
Decisions pushed to top of the agency	Decisions pushed to the customer transaction
People do processing; limited time for critical thinking	People do critical thinking; smart technology does processing

Reengineering is also consistent with the new form of governance that has emerged during the Information Age—one that favors mission-driven, result-oriented activities.

Even with this new focus, there are some elements of the public sector that will not change and remain challenging for reengineering implementers. For instance, government agencies are subject to greater political executive management and oversight. Election cycles and administration changes at least every 4 years also impact reengineering efforts. In addition, governments cannot revise or depart from their missions and operations, whereas in the private sector there is much greater discretion to change business orientations. Legislation, taxpayer accountability, competition for funding and resources, continuous change, as well as partnerships with international, state, and local governments will continue to challenge government agencies as they reengineer.

Perhaps the most critical challenge for government lies in the area of risk-taking. Historically the culture of government has been to avoid risk. Any successful reengineering effort will need to embrace change and negotiate some degree of risk.

1.7 The Reengineering Vision

BPR is based on a horizontally structured enterprise organized around key business processes. The following are features of the BPR vision:

- *Shared information*
  Information must be maintained, managed, and made available when it is needed for critical decision making.
- *Mission support*
  When business processes are redesigned they should strengthen mission support. Those that do not add value to mission achievement should be eliminated.
- *Functional leadership*
  Reengineering can be risky. Recent surveys estimate the percentage of BPR failures to be between 50 % and 70 %. If there is one message that has been reinforced over and over, it is the need for executive-level leadership and commitment to the process. All federal agency heads must participate in and take responsibility for the management of his or her agency's core processes. Without leadership throughout the department, process improvement efforts will falter.
- *Reduced costs*
  Activities that increase the cost of doing business but provide no benefits to stakeholders are to be reduced or eliminated.

1.7.1 Reusable Technology

There should be a shift from custom-developed, unique information management systems to the use of off-the-shelf technologies that support standard business processes.

- *Single interface*
  Federal agencies should have to master only one system interface for accessing their agency's information resources.
- *Just-in-time*
  Information, training, and support should be delivered electronically to the work site at the precise time they are needed.

1.8   The Principles of Reengineering

In Hammer and Champy's original manifesto reengineering was by definition radical; it could not simply be an enhancement or modification of what went before. It examined work in terms of outcomes, not tasks or unit functions, and it expected dramatic, rather than marginal improvements.

The following are seven principles of reengineering, suggested by the authors, that would streamline work processes, achieve savings, and improve product quality and time management.

1. Organize around outcomes, not tasks.
2. Identify all the processes in an organization and prioritize them in order of redesign urgency.
3. Integrate information processing work into the real work that produces information.
4. Remove non-value-added activities, undertake parallel activities, and speed up response and development times.
5. Link parallel activities in the workflow instead of just integrating their results.
6. Put the decision point where the work is performed, and build control into the process.
7. Capture information once and at the source.
8. Give customers and users a single and accessible point of contact through which they can harness whatever resources and people are relevant to their needs and interests.
9. Encourage learning and development by building creative working environments. This principle has been almost forgotten in many organizations, the current emphasis being to squeeze more out of people and working them harder, rather than improving the quality of work life and working more cleverly.
10. Avoid over-sophistication. Don't replace creative thinking with software tools.
11. Network related people and activities. Virtual corporations are becoming commonplace in some business sectors.
12. Treat geographically dispersed resources as though they were centralized.
13. Build learning, renewal, and short feedback loops into business processes.
14. Ensure that continuous improvement is built into implemented solutions. Experience of business reengineering can reawaken interest in TQM (Total Quality Management); both are natural complements. This is widely overlooked.
15. Ensure people are equipped, motivated, and empowered to do what is expected of them.

1.8.1   Process Reengineering Methodologies

1. *The Hammer/Champy methodology*
Hammer/Champy popularized business reengineering. Their business reengineering methodology, which was fine-tuned by Champy's consulting company, breaks into six steps.

The Hammer/Champy methodology	
Project steps	Objectives
Introduction into business reengineering	The CEO initiates the project. His/her describes briefly and pragmatically the current business situation to start actions. She introduces her vision to the employees of the company
Identification of business processes	This step looks at the broad picture of how processes interact within the company and in relation to the outside world. One deliverable is a graphical display of all processes
Selection of business processes	The third step serves to select such processes, which—once reengineered—will lead to high value for the company's customers. Also processes that lend themselves to easy reengineering are being selected
Understanding the selected business processes	This step does not dwell on a detailed analysis of the functioning of the selected business processes, rather concentrates on the performance of the current processes as opposed to what is expected from them in the future
Redesign of the selected business processes	The fifth step is according to Hammer/Champy the most creative of all. It is characterized by imagination, lateral thinking, and some sort of craziness
Implementation of redesigned business processes	The last step covers the implementation phase of the business reengineering project. Hammer/Champy do not talk about implementation as much as about project planning. They believe in the success of the implementation, once the five preliminary steps have been properly performed

2. *The Davenport methodology*
Davenport puts information technology at the heart of business reengineering. For Davenport, information technology possesses the most important role for innovating business processes. Despite his emphasis on innovation and technology, Davenport states that organizational and human resource issues are more central than technology issues to the behavior issues that must occur to within a business process. Davenport sees culture as a constraint, when there is a poor process innovation to cultural fit. With regard to managing the change, Davenport emphasizes traditional management functions, like planning, directing, monitoring, decision making, and communicating.

Davenport is convinced that business reengineering should better integrate with the other nonrevolutionary (incremental) process approaches, like Total Quality Management. His methodology covers six steps.

The Davenport methodology

Project steps	Objectives
Visioning and goal setting	The first step is needed to focus all subsequent actions on company visions and process goals. Cost reduction is considered an important goal, yet Davenport warns against concentrating too much on cost cutting, because other goals, such as worker satisfaction, reduction of time requirements, and improvement of process performance, might be discriminated against
Identification of business processes	This step identifies the business processes, which should be reengineered. Davenport advises business reengineering teams to concentrate on a few important, not more than 15 core processes
Understand and measure processes	The third step studies the exact functioning and performance of the selected business processes. This differentiates Davenport from the Hammer/Champy approach. Davenport in particular wants to make sure that during the process redesign old practices are not being *reinvented* and performance benchmarks for the redesigned processes are being set up
Information technology	The fourth step serves to study the applicability of information technology tools and applications for the newly designed work processes
Process prototype	This step covers the design of a functioning prototype of the new business process. People in the company study this prototype, develop ideas for enhancements, and make themselves comfortable with the redesign of their work processes
Implementation	The last step serves to implement the tested prototype on a company-wide basis. Davenport considers this step crucial to the success of the overall effort, since implementation takes roughly double as long (minimum 1 year) as the foregoing steps

3. Andrews and Stalick (1994) (Nissen, Quality Management Journal, Number 3, 1996)

(a) Frame the project.
(b) Create vision, values, and goals.
(c) Redesign business operations.
(d) Conduct proof of concept.
(e) Plan implementation.
(f) Get implementation approval.
(g) Implement redesign.
(h) Transition to CPI environment.

1.8.1.1   The Kodak Methodology

The international Kodak organization developed a business reengineering methodology that is being applied to Kodak facilities around the world. Similar to other practitioner approaches, has the Kodak methodology been influenced by Hammer/Champy. The Kodak methodology breaks into five steps:

The Kodak methodology

Project steps	Objectives
Project initiation	The first step is considered key. It covers project planning and definition of all project administration rules and procedures
Process understanding	This step sets the project team up, designs a comprehensive process model for the organization, and assigns process managers, who will be responsible for the redesigned process after implementation
New process design	The third step covers the redesign of selected business processes, taking into account the potentials of information technology. This step ends with the planning of a pilot implementation of the redesigned processes
Business transition	The fourth step is focused towards the implementation of the newly designed processes within the organization. Part of this step is the adaptation of the organization's infrastructure to the requirements of the newly designed processes
Change management	The last step is being performed parallel to the first four steps. The project team handles barriers, which crop up during the course of the business reengineering project

1.8.1.2   The Manganelli/Klein Methodology

Manganelli/Klein argue to only concentrate on those business processes that directly support the strategic goals of the company and customer requirements. Product development (a knowledge process) is such a preferred business process. They see organizational impact, time, risk, and cost as obstacles to success. They claim business reengineering to be more successful than incremental change initiatives, which tend to fail more often.

The Manganelli/Klein business reengineering methodology Rapid-Re (TM), which is supplemented by the Rapid-Re Reengineering Software toolset for Microsoft Windows (TM), breaks into five steps.

The Manganelli/Klein methodology

Project steps	Objectives
Preparation	The first step asks all directly involved persons to define goals and to prepare for the business reengineering project
Identification	This step defines a customer-oriented process model of the organization, as well as selects key business processes for redesign
Vision	The third step serves to define at which performance level the processes currently deliver and which higher level is required for the future

(continued)

(continued)

Project steps	Objectives
Redesign (i) Technical design (ii) Social design	This step breaks into two parallel sub-steps. The technical design deals with information technology design to support the new processes. The social design step serves to design new work environments for the people, including organizational and personnel development plans
Transformation	The fifth step is meant to implement the redesigned processes and work environments within the organization

1.8.1.3   Conceptual Model as per Carr and Johansson and Krieter

Project steps	Objectives
Leadership team	In both Carr and Johansson's and Krieter's research executive-level support was shown to be an important factor for the success implementation of BPR. The leadership team should consist of the top managers of the organization. The responsibility of the leadership team is to define the vision, establish improvement objectives and metrics, communicate the need for change, and establish the process redesign team(s)
Listen to the voice of the customer	Most business processes were never designed or engineered; they evolved over time. At the root of their evolution is the industrial revolution, which resulted in the breakdown of business processes into specialized tasks divided among unconnected departments. It is little wonder that business processes today are not customer focused. The lack of connection between tasks and communication between departments makes it impossible to hear the voice of the customer. To understand our current business processes, from the customer's perspective, we must seek their input on how well we currently meet their needs and where we fall short. A variety of methods can be used to collect customer data including surveys, focus groups, and site visits. Only when we look outward and answer the Champy's question "How do we want to be perceived by our customer?" can we begin to look inward and build a long-term strategic vision for the future or a constancy of purpose
Develop a long-term strategic vision for the organization	To chart a new course, an understanding of the ultimate destination is necessary. The strategic visions help to define and identify opportunities for improvement. A long-term strategic vision also answers the question "How are we going to distinguish ourselves from our competitors." The vision provides the organization with a long-term perspective and does not focus on short-term profits. The vision also provides a compass to judge improvement progress against

(continued)

(continued)

Project steps	Objectives
Establish improvement objectives	The leadership team should perform a gap analysis to establish improvement objectives. The gap analysis should assess the difference between the strategic vision and how our customer perceives our current process performance. Developing improvement objectives in this manner ensures they are linked to the strategic vision. In both research projects cited, the linkage of improvement goals to the strategic vision was important. The linkage of improvement goals to the vision provides constancy of purpose and long-term thinking
Establish metrics for improvement objectives	The leadership team should establish performance metrics for each improvement objective. The metrics should reflect how the process needs to operate so that the strategic vision and customer needs are fulfilled
Communicate the need for change	Once the improvement objectives are established, it is the responsibility of the leadership team to communicate the *need for change* to the organization. Communication of the need for changes helps to alleviate fear and provides an understanding of why the change is being made. If the organization understands the change, they are more likely to accept it. Both Carr and Johansson's and Krieter's research points out that effectively communicating the need for change is important for successful BPR implementation
Establish a cross-functional design team	The use of a cross-functional team is important for BPR success. The team should have members who represent the current task owners and important stakeholder of the process to be redesigned. The leadership team needs to provide the process redesign team with the information used to establish the improvement objective and performance metrics. The leadership team and process redesign team should agree on the scope of the improvement objective and performance metrics identified
Gain an understanding of the need for change	The process redesign team needs to review the data provided by the leadership team and ask for clarification in necessary. It is the team's responsibility to ensure they understand the customer's perception of the current process, how the process falls short of the strategic vision; the improvement objectives identified; and the performance metrics chosen by the leadership team
Come to a basic understanding of the process	The process redesign team needs to have a basic understanding of how the process operates and how the process components interact. A process map showing all the different departments involved in completing the work task and how they interface with each other should be sufficient. Too much detail here will slow down the redesign process. The team also needs to understand how the current process performs using the metrics established by the leadership team

(continued)

(continued)

Project steps	Objectives
Use a structured approach to develop redesign alternatives	The process redesign team should select or establish a methodology for developing redesign alternatives. This will provide structure and ensure the team does not flounder or get offtrack. When developing alternatives, the team should explore various transformation and enabling technologies including information technology, machine automation, and human resource empowerment. The team should use caution when evaluating different technologies. Transformation and enabling technologies should be evaluated based on their ability to increase the performance of the redesigned process, not used as a driving force for change
Develop an implementation plan	Process redesign efforts are of little value, unless the proposed change can be implemented successfully. The process redesign team should develop an implementation plan. Piloting or prototyping the change on a small scale as part of the implementation plan can help to identify any technical or organizational problems. Problems identified can be addressed by the team prior to implementation of the change throughout the organization
Develop a continuous improvement plan for the process	Process improvement does not stop once the process redesign has been implemented. To ensure the process continues to be aligned with the strategic vision and fulfills customer needs and requirements, the process must be maintained. Regular review of the process performance metrics will help identify necessary corrective action

The comparison of the selected methodologies shows many similarities. First, the overall approach business reengineering projects take is of a linear nature. Further, business reengineering projects take a similar route as information technology implementation projects. Within the three consecutive steps, the individual approaches differ in the scope of project preparation. Davenport asks for a complete preparation including visioning, whereas the other methodologies contrast by hands-on approaches right from the project start. Davenport, Manganelli/Klein, and Kodak also address the people side of business reengineering, but only as far as implementation issues are concerned. Taking the conclusion further and applying it to the sources of existing methodologies, then consultants appear to see business reengineering as yet another systematic and marketable approach for fast and cost-efficient implementation of planned change. Technically oriented academics take a broader view, yet shy away from really integrating social psychology into their linear approaches, because this might be considered nonscientific by colleagues. Users prefer an eclectic approach. They take proven elements both from consultants and academics and apply them as needed.

1.8.2   Selecting Methodology for Process Reengineered RTI

1.8.2.1   Recommended Approach

The recommended approach for a business process reengineering project includes the following phases:

1. *Project planning and launch* (leadership team formation, objective setting, scope definition, methodology selection, schedule development, consultant selection, sponsor negotiations, change management planning, team preparation)
2. *Current state assessment and learning from others* (high-level process definition, benchmarking, customer focus groups, employee focus groups, technology assessment)
3. *Solution design* (innovative methodologies, administrative reform, process design, enabling technology architecture, organizational design, job design)
4. *Business case development* (cost and benefit analysis, business case preparation, presentation to key business leaders)
5. *Solution development* (detailed process definition, system requirements writing and system development, training development, implementation planning, operational transition plan, pilots and trials)
6. *Implementation* (larger-scale pilots and phased implementation, measurement systems, full implementation)
7. *Continuous improvement* (ongoing improvement and measurement of new processes and systems, six sigma capability, performance audit)

1.8.3   Role of Information Technology in BPR

Reengineering and automating a process are not the same thing. As Hammer and Champy point out, automating is often little more than *paving the cow paths* of processes that are redundant or inefficient. This is not what reengineering is about.

Many organizations have spent millions of dollars on information technology, automating existing processes, without determining whether or not those processes were even necessary. Only after business processes have been streamlined and redesigned should automation be applied.

Reengineering must work hand in hand with information technology to consider cutting-edge innovations—things never attempted before. In a reengineering project, IT is an *essential enabler*. Many processes cannot be reengineered without it. In keeping with reengineering's *ambitious* approach, information technology should be anticipatory; it should answer problems the consumer does not know his/her has yet.

In order to more effectively respond to BPR demands, IT must play a more active role throughout a BPR project. IT must:

- Increase their level of participation in all areas of a BPR initiative
- Provide key information regarding automated processes to business analysts
- Build a transition strategy that meets short- and long-term retooling requirements
- Enforce the integrity of redesigned business processes in the target system
- Reuse business rules and related components that remain constant in a target application

1.8.4 Change Management Intervention Models

> Any single change in the existing system affects all parts of the system; a complex change, such as may be needed to meet competitive challenges, has virtually unlimited ramifications. Any program that seeks to introduce change into an organization will fail if it is not grounded in this system wide view of the organization.
>
> (Mink/Esterhuysen/Mink/Owen, Change at Work 1993)

Change involves moving from the known to the unknown. Because the future is uncertain and may adversely affect people's competencies, worth, and coping abilities, organizational members generally do not support change, unless compelling reasons convince them to do so.

Similarly, organizations tend to be heavily invested in the status quo, and they resist changing it in the face of uncertain future benefits. Consequently, a key issue in planning for action is how to motivate commitment to organizational change, such as business reengineering. This requires management attention to two related tasks: creating readiness for change and overcoming resistance to change. Change management focuses on these two tasks by proposing, designing, and subsequently executing effective interventions at individual, group, organizational, and environmental levels. It should not be overlooked, though, that the environment often is more powerful than the organization itself, while the psyche, the most personal category, is too deep-seated to external change initiatives. All other categories between these macro and micro aspects are directly controllable by managers and consultants.

Interventions refer to a set of planned change activities performed by internal or external people, intended to help an organization increase its effectiveness. Interventions, which assist in improving productivity and the quality of work life, have three characteristics: (1) they are based on valid information about the organization's functioning; (2) they provide organizational members with opportunities to make free and informed choices; and (3) they gain member's internal commitment to these choices. Valid information is the result of an accurate diagnosis of the firm's functioning. It must fairly reflect what organizational members perceive and feel about their primary concerns and issues. Free and informed choice suggests that organizational members are actively involved in making decisions about the changes that will affect them. It means that they can choose not to participate and that interventions will not be imposed upon them. Internal commitment means that organizational members accept ownership of the intervention and take responsibility for implementing it. In fact, if interventions are to result in meaningful changes, management must be committed to implementing them.

Business reengineering methodologies do not take people much into consideration, even that there exists a vast amount of literature on change management. Business reengineering is dealing more with information technology aspects of reorganizing the way corporations work. Change management deals with how people are being affected by an organizational change of any kind, and what interventions have to be undertaken to make the change effort a success for the customers, the company owners, and the people working for the company. The large number of change management approaches available can be classified into six categories.

Classification of change management approaches

	Individuals	Groups	Organization	Environment
1. Psychology of the individual	■			
2. Social Psychological approaches	■	■		
3. Cultural approaches	■	■	■	
4. Innovation approaches			■	■
5. Global change approaches			■	■
6. Practitioner approaches	■	■	■	■

The black blocks indicate the potential impact of the respective interventions (rows) on the domains (columns) individual, group, organization, and environment.

1. *Psychology of the Individual Change Approaches*
   Psychology of the individual deals with the individual person. The character and the process of individual change are at the heart of psychological research. Individual psychology is relevant to business reengineering, since project initiators, project team members, and affected people in the organization are individual people with individual characters and behaviors. Dr. Johnna Shamp, a licensed organizational psychologist, remarks that most consultants focus on organizational change, but don't pay enough attention to the impact change has on the individual worker. She encourages consultants to intervene at the level of the individual affected by change. Relevant authors to the field of individual change are listed in Table.

Relevant authors of individual change

Individual change approaches	Author
Reengineering yourself	Aaroz/Sutton (1994)
Stewardship	Block (1993)
The seven habits of highly effective people	Covey (1989)
The evolving self. a psychology for the third millennium	Csikszentmihalyi (1993)

(continued)

(continued)

Individual change approaches	Author
How to stubbornly refuse to make yourself miserable	Ellis (1988)
The tactics of change	Fisch/Weakland/Segal (1982)
Masterful coaching	Hargrove (1995)
Thriving in transition	Perkins-Reed (1996)

2. *Social psychological change approaches*

Social psychological change is a wide field of study. It is based on the works of Kurt Lewin, who fled Nazi Germany to become the founder of field theory, action science, group dynamics, socio-technical science, and organizational development. Lewin himself was influenced by Gestalt psychology. Lewin's basic idea was that the individual person is more shaped by his/her social environment (groups) than by his/her genes. Relevant authors to the field of social psychological change are listed.

Relevant authors of social psychological change

Social psychological change approaches	Author
Knowledge for action	Argyris (1995)
Changing the essence	Beckhard/Pritchard (1992)
Leading self-directed work teams	Fisher (1993)
Organization development	French/Bell Jr. (1973)
Groups that work (and those that don't)	Hackmann (1990)
Changing behavior in organizations	Judson (1991)
Field theory	Lewin (1982)
Change at work (action science approach)	Mink/Esterhuysen/Mink/Owen (1993)
Designing effective organizations (sociotechnically)	Pasmore (1988)
Competitive advantage through people	Pfeffer (1994)
Driving fear out of the workplace	Ryan/Oestreich (1991)

3. *Cultural change approaches*

Cultural approaches look at change from the perspective of the culture of an organization. Organizational culture is a much-discussed topic and will emerge as a pivotal frame of reference for many leaders or managers in any organization. Culture of an organization or group of people can be defined as:

"A pattern of shared basic assumptions that the group learned as it solved problems of external adaptation and internal integration, that has worked well enough to be considered valid and, therefore, to be taught to new members as the correct way to perceive, think, and feel in relation to those problems."

Culture is mostly unconscious to the members of the organization and is able to control the behaviors of organizational change, even when the project plan calls for new behaviors. This is one of the reasons why new leaders introducing change in an organization sometimes replace key positions with new people external to the organization.

Relevant authors of cultural change

Cultural change approaches	Author
Corporate cultures	Deal/Kennedy (1982)
Working the shadow side	Egan (1994)
Corporate assessment (A company's personality)	Furnham/Gunter (1993)
Organisations on the couch	Kets de Vries (1991)
How leadership differs from management	Kotter (1990)
Corporate culture and performance	Kotter/Heskett (1992)
Organizational behavior	Organ/Bateman (1991)
Organizational culture and leadership	Schein (1992)
The reengineering alternative	Schneider (1994)
Unwritten rules of the game	Scott-Morgan (1994)

4. *Innovation approaches*

   Innovation approaches look at change from the perspective of the diffusion of a new idea or practice. Diffusion is a process by which an innovation is communicated through various channels over time among the members of a social system. Resistance to process innovation can be defined as late or no adoption by members of the organization undertaking a business reengineering project. Relevant authors of innovation change approaches are listed in Table.

Relevant authors of innovation change approaches

Innovation approaches	Author
Innovations management	Hauschildt (1993)
Polarity management	Johnson (1992)
Diffusion of innovation	Rogers (1983)
Mastering the dynamics of innovation	Utterback (1994)

5. *Global change approaches*

   Global change approaches look at organizational change from a very broad perspective. They focus on global transformations, based on life-threatening changes dictated by the whitewater-type changes happening in an organization's environment. Not only processes, but structures, strategies, values, and basically all variables of a business are subject to change.

Relevant authors of global change approaches

Global change approaches	Author
Turning points	Fombrun (1992)
The unshackled organization	Goldstein (1994)
Diagnosis for organizational change	Howard (1994)
Organizational change and redesign	Huber/Glick (1993)
The challenge of organizational change	Kanter/Stein/Jick (1992)
Corporate transformations	Kilman (1988)
Transforming organizations	Kochan/Useem (1992)
Discontinuous change	Nadler/Shaw/Walton (1995)
Creative destruction	Nolan/Croson (1995)

(continued)

(continued)

Global change approaches	Author
The fifth discipline (learning organization)	Senge (1990)
Breakpoints	Strebel (1992)
Rethinking the organization	Tomasko (1993)
Sculpting the learning organization	Watkins/Marsick (1993)

6. *Practitioner approaches to change*

Practitioners (consultants and managers) typically take an eclectic approach to organizational change. They combine various aspects of the available theoretical approaches they know about, as well as add practical experiences with real change processes. Practitioner approaches typically intervene at all levels.

Table Relevant authors of practitioner approaches to change

Relevant authors of practitioner approaches to change

Practitioner approaches to change	Author
Road map to corporate transformation	Berger/Sikora/Berger (1994)
Managing at the speed of change	Conner (1995)
Managing organizational change	Connor/Lake (1994)
People ware	DeMarco/Lister (1987)
The limits of organizational change	Kaufmann (1995)
Changing the way we change	LaMarsh (1995)
Beyond the wall of resistance	Maurer (1996)
Change management	McCalman/Paton (1992)
Better change—best practices	Price Waterhouse (1995)
Taking charge of change	Smith (1996)
Handbook for revolutionaries (Jack Welch's Story)	Tichy/Sherman (1993)
Reward systems for the changing workplace	Wilson (1994)

7. *Suitable intervention models*

From the vast amount of available approaches in the literature, there are several models which suit the practical requirements of business reengineering projects regarding interventions to change, targeting the individual, the group, the organization, and the environment.

Selected intervention models

Change management category	Intervention models (IM)
1. Individual change interventions	IM 1.: Turning stress into energy
	IM 2.: The flow concept
	IM 3.: Personal coaching (new leadership)
2. Social psychological change interventions	IM 4.: The Lewin model of change
	IM 5.: The resistance formula
	IM 6.: Drive out fear
3. Cultural change interventions	IM 7.: Becoming an effective behind-the-scenes manager

(continued)

(continued)

Change management category	Intervention models (IM)
4. Innovation interventions	IM 8.: The roles of the change agent
5. Global change interventions	IM 9.: Breakpoints
	IM 10.: The learning organization
6. Practitioner interventions	IM 11.: Workout
	IM 12.: Working with resistance
	IM 13.: Levers for minimizing resistance to change
	IM 14.: Alignment of reward systems

1.8.5   Change Management Process

The change management process is the sequence of steps or activities that a change management team or project leader would follow to apply change management to a project or change. Based on Prosci's research of the most effective and commonly applied change, most change management processes contain the following three phases:

Phase 1—Preparing for change (preparation, assessment, and strategy development)
Phase 2—Managing change (detailed planning and change management implementation)
Phase 3—Reinforcing change (data gathering, corrective action, and recognition)

These phases result in the following approach, as shown below in Fig. 1.1.

1.8.5.1   Readiness Assessments

Assessments are tools used by a change management team or project leader to assess the organization's readiness to change. Readiness assessments can include organizational assessments, culture and history assessments, employee assessments, sponsor assessments, and change assessments. Each tool provides the project team with insights into the challenges and opportunities they may face during the change process.
Assess the scope of the change, including

How big is this change?
How many people are affected?
Is it a gradual or radical change?

Assess the readiness of the organization impacted by the change, including
What is the value system and background of the impacted groups? How much change is already going on? What type of resistance can be expected?
Assess the strengths of your change management team.
Assess the change sponsors and take the first steps to enable them to effectively lead the change process.

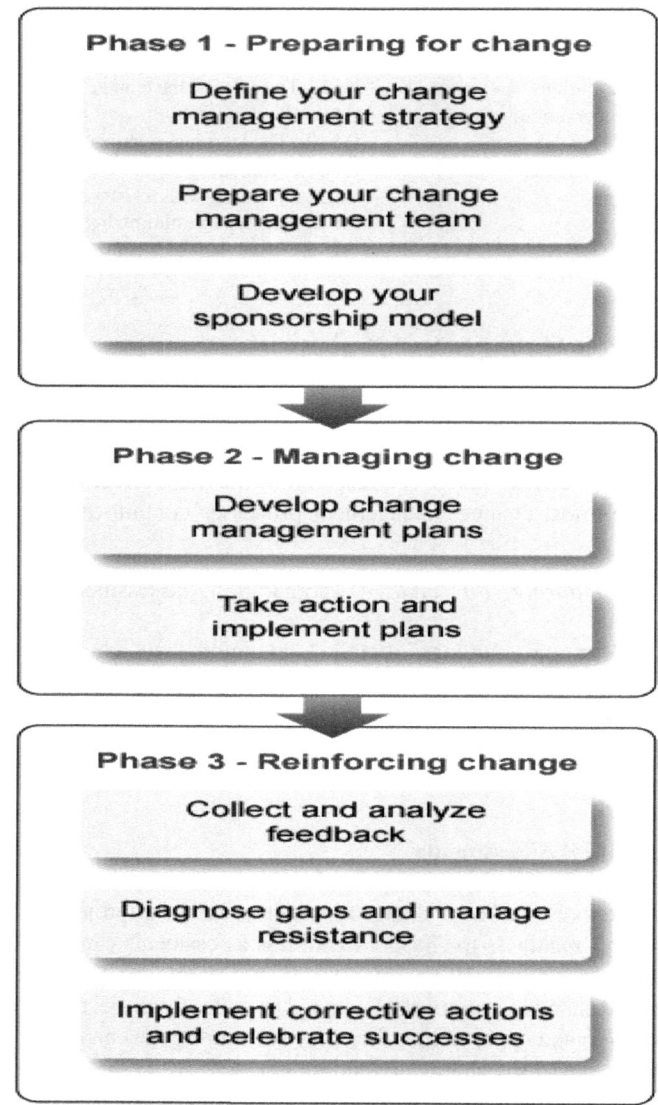

Fig. 1.1 Change management process

1.8.5.2   Communication and Communication Planning

Many managers assume that if they communicate clearly with their employees, their job is done. However, there are many reasons why employees may not hear or understand what their managers are saying the first time around. In fact, you may have heard that messages need to be repeated six to seven times before they are cemented into the minds of employees. That is because each employee's readiness to hear depends on many factors. Effective communicators carefully consider three components: the audience, what is said, and when it is said.

For example, the first step in managing change is building awareness around the need for change and creating a desire among employees. Therefore, initial communications are typically designed to create awareness around the business reasons for change and the risk of not changing. Likewise, at each step in the process, communications should be designed to share the right messages at the right time.

Communication planning, therefore, begins with a careful analysis of the audiences, key messages, and the timing for those messages. The change management team or project leaders must design a communication plan that addresses the needs of front-line employees, supervisors, and executives. Each audience has particular needs for information based on their role in the implementation of the change.

1.8.5.3 Coaching and Manager Training for Change Management

Supervisors will play a key role in managing change. Ultimately, the direct supervisor has more influence over an employee's motivation to change than any other person at work. Unfortunately, supervisors as a group can be the most difficult to convince of the need for change and can be a source of resistance. It is vital for the change management team and executive sponsors to gain the support of supervisors and to build change leadership. Individual change management activities should be used to help these supervisors through the change process.

Once managers and supervisors are on board, the change management team must prepare a coaching strategy. They will need to provide training for supervisors including how to use individual change management tools with their employees.

1.8.5.4 Training and Training Development

Training is the cornerstone for building knowledge about the change and the required skills. Project team members will develop training requirements based on the skills, knowledge, and behaviors necessary to implement the change. These training requirements will be the starting point for the training group or the project team to develop training programs.

1.9 Sponsor Activities and Sponsor Roadmaps

Business leaders and executives play a critical sponsor role in change management. The change management team must develop a plan for sponsor activities and help key business leaders carry out these plans. Sponsorship should be viewed as the most important success factor. Avoid confusing the notion of sponsorship with support. The CEO of the company may support your project, but that is not the same as sponsoring your initiative.

Sponsorship involves active and visible participation by senior business leaders throughout the process. Unfortunately many executives do not know what this sponsorship looks like. A change agent's or project leader's role includes helping senior executives do the right things to sponsor the project.

1.10   Resistance Management

Resistance from employees and managers is normal. Persistent resistance, however, can threaten a project. The change management team needs to identify, understand, and manage resistance throughout the organization. Resistance management is the processes and tools used by managers and executives with the support of the project team to manage employee resistance.

1.11   Data Collection, Feedback Analysis, and Corrective Action

Employee involvement is a necessary and integral part of managing change. Managing change is not a one-way street. Feedback from employees is a key element of the change management process. Analysis and corrective action based on this feedback provide a robust cycle for implementing change.

1.12   Celebrating and Recognizing Success

Early successes and long-term wins must be recognized and celebrated. Individual and group recognition is also a necessary component of change management in order to cement and reinforce the change in the organization.

The final step in the change management process is the after-action review. It is at this point that you can stand back from the entire program, evaluate successes and failures, and identify process changes for the next project. This is part of the ongoing, continuous improvement of change management for your organization and ultimately leads to change competency.

1.13   The Benefits of Reengineering

The rewards of reengineering are many including

- Empowering employees
- Eliminating waste, unnecessary management overhead, and obsolete or inefficient processes

Table 1.1 Comparison of US and Japanese firms

	US firm	Japanese firm
Volume of products manufactured	10,000,000	3.500,000
Product types	11	38
Units per worker	43,100	61,400
Total staff	*242*	*57*
Direct staff	107	50
Support staff	135	7
Cost per unit in $	100	49

- Producing often significant reductions in cost and cycle times
- Enabling revolutionary improvements in many business processes as measured by quality and customer service
- Helping top organizations stay on top and low achievers to become effective competitors

Michael Ballé used an example to illustrate the difference between Japanese firms, which apply process-focused strategies, and a similar US firm in which process-focused strategies were not applied. This example is shown in Table 1.1.

1.14 Ensuring Reengineering Success

> Automating an already bad process just makes it easy to do the wrong thing faster.

The following are six critical success factors that ensure government reengineering initiatives achieve the desired results:

Understand reengineering.

- Understand business process fundamentals.
- Understand reengineering.
- Differentiate and integrate process improvement approaches.

Build a business and political case.

- Have necessary and sufficient business—mission delivery—reasons for reengineering.
- Have the organizational commitment and capacity to initiate and sustain reengineering.
- Secure and sustain political support for reengineering projects.

Adopt a process management approach.

- Understand the organizational mandate and set mission-strategic directions and goals cascading to process-specific goals and decision making across and down the organization.
- Define, model, and prioritize business processes important for mission performance.

- Practice hands-on senior management ownership of process improvement through personal involvement, responsibility, and decision making.
- Adjust organizational structure to better support process management initiatives.
- Create an assessment program to evaluate process management.

Measure and track performance continuously.

- Create organizational understanding of the value of measurement and how it will be used.
- Tie performance management to customer and stakeholder current and future expectations.

Practice change management and provide central support.

- Develop human resource management strategies to support reengineering.
- Build information resources management strategies and a technology framework to support process change.
- Create a central support group to assist and integrate reengineering efforts and other improvement efforts across the organization.
- Create an overarching and project-specific internal and external communication and education program.

Manage reengineering projects for results.

- Have a clear criteria to select what should be reengineered.
- Place the project at the right level with a defined reengineering team purpose and goals.
- Use a well-trained, diversified, expert team to ensure optimum project performance.
- Follow a structured, disciplined approach for reengineering.

1.15 Possible Impediments to Success

Apart from lack of top-level leadership, some of the problems that have plagued BPR efforts are related to the lack of performance measurement information, the lack of cost drivers, and the insufficient process mapping. The following are a number of other factors that can hinder BPR success:

1. Try to fix a process instead of changing it.
2. Do not focus on business processes.
3. Ignore everything except process redesign.
4. Neglect people's values and beliefs.
5. Be willing to settle for minor results.
6. Quit too early.
7. Place prior constraints on the definition of the problem and the scope of the reengineering effort.

8. Allow existing, corporate cultures and management attitudes to prevent engineering from getting started.
9. Try to make reengineering happen from the bottom up.
10. Assign someone who does not understand reengineering to lead the effort.
11. Skimp on the resources devoted to reengineering.
12. Bury reengineering in the middle of the corporate agenda.
13. Dissipate energy across many great reengineering projects.
14. Attempt to reengineer when the CEO is 2 years away from retirement.
15. Fail to distinguish reengineering from other business improvement programs.
16. Concentrate exclusively on design.
17. Try to make reengineering happen without making anybody unhappy.
18. Pull back when people begin to resist making reengineering changes.
19. Drag the effort out.

The traditional organizations believe in dividing the work among departments according to the functional areas of a division. Within these departments, also different tasks are allocated and most of them are only aware of their own small piece of task allotted and not how the holistic fabric of the project is served by the portion of work allotted to them. This kind of a structure was provided by Adam Smith. But due to such shortsightedness, the customer service deteriorates mainly due to:

1. *Organizations not being customer focused*: Products or services are provided to customers but no solutions to their problems are offered. This occurs only because of lack of knowledge on the part of the employees regarding the processes prevalent in the organization. Since the process focus is lacking, and there is lot of fragmentation among business units and departments, the customer is treated differently in different business units, which in turn breeds customer dissatisfaction.
2. *A lot of time and resources being spent on non-value-added activities*: There are three classifications for activities proposed by Michael Hammer:

   (a) Value-adding work, which refers to the work for which the customer is willing to pay.
   (b) Non-value-adding work, which no value in itself but supports the value-adding work for getting the value-added activity being performed.
   (c) Waste; this kind of work neither adds value nor enables any other activity to add value.

According to Hammer, the reason why managers fail to solve problems or identify the core issues in an organization is that they apply task-based solutions to problems in the processes. There are anomalies in the customer service not because of low efficiency performance of individual tasks but because of deficient assimilation of the tasks through a process integrating all the related tasks. The problem arises when individuals are skilled and knowledgeable enough about the task at hand but not aware of the holistic picture wherein how their particular task plays a role in the working of the organization. The cost to the company increases in this case as the firm has to hire lot of manpower to integrate the disjoint tasks in the organization and focus their efforts towards enhancing the processes of the organization.

1.16   Business Process Reengineering

Some of the key elements essential for business process reengineering are

- A radical change in the business processes
- Change in orientation of the organization
- Change in the organizational structure
- Improvements in technology
- Improvement in customer service and cost reduction

The benefits of reengineering are slowly becoming evident as organizations are going in for reengineering rather than technical solutions which are expensive as well. So, by reconstructing the processes and classifying them as value added or non-value added, organizations are able to resourcefully identify the areas that need attention.

Business process reengineering is based on a thought process different from continuous process improvement. It dismisses the current processes and suggests a rethinking of the processes and proposes a complete overhaul of the current processes and asks for a more customer-oriented perspective. This kind of approach can be explained as:

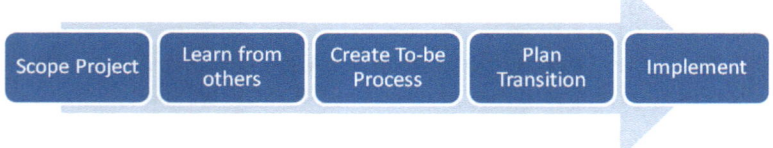

The process begins with defining the scope of the project as well as the objectives of the reengineering project. Then the learning from others' aspect takes into account the learning from customers, competitors, and noncompetitors as well. Using the data obtained, the To-Be processes need to be defined and then the gap between the current processes and the To-Be state can be bridged. The plan then needs to be finalized and implemented.

Some of the ways in which businesses can be restructured are the following:

1. *Processes replacing individual tasks and departments*: This approach suggests that different departments and tasks operate in a way such that there is an alignment of processes as well. This concept can be applied when complex skills are required such as the financial function or the IT function.
2. *Simple processes and complex jobs*: Only understanding one's own task at hand would not suffice and a complete view of the whole process is needed as well as multiskilled manpower.

3. *Teamwork*: Complex business processes are divided into teams and there has to be a synergy among the tasks performed by the independent teams, which work in parallel for the final result to be obtained. The tasks need to be integrated for a perfect end result. Also everyone in the respective teams must be business oriented.
4. *Process owner replacing the manager*: A process owner will be responsible to ensure that customers' needs are identified and duly satisfied through the team performance. His/her acts as a bridge between the company and the customer and the customer also has a single contact point in case of any anomalies.

1.17   Principles of Reengineering

Some principles of reengineering that would streamline work processes as well as achieve savings and also improve upon the product quality are:

1. Organizing around outcomes and not tasks
2. Identifying and prioritizing processes in an organization on the basis of urgency
3. Capturing information at source
4. Information processing and integrating all data for the organization's data warehouse
5. Removing non-value-added activities and undertaking parallel activities for better customer service
6. Linking parallel activities rather than just pipelining the results
7. Avoiding over-sophistication; not relying too much on technology
8. Considering geographically diverse resources as centralized
9. TQM and BPR as natural complements must be identified as a strength for both to work well together

1.18   A Consolidated Framework

The process of BPR can be mapped under five major methodologies or stages:

1. *Preparation for reengineering*: This asks questions to the organization about the necessity and the benefits of BPR to the organization. A cross-functional team is necessary to kick-start the process of reengineering. There is a need to identify the customers as well as understand the objectives of BPR with a customer focus. The business goals to be achieved are defined along with the changes that are proposed in organizational structure as well as a strategic direction to the company. Having defined customer-oriented objectives and formulating a vision and mission statement, the strategic goals can be defined by the top management. These would provide for a benchmark to the existing processes as well as the reengineered processes.

2. *Map and analyze As-Is process*: There are two different schools of thought in this stage; one feels that doing an As-Is process inhibits the creative thinking of the individuals involved in designing the To-Be processes. But unless there is enough information about the aspects which the customers want to be changed or which breed customer dissatisfaction, there cannot be a To-Be process which provides dramatic improvement. The resources need to be allocated according to the output of this process; which identifies the bottlenecks of the current value-adding processes.

3. *Design to-be process*: The first step of this stage is benchmarking, wherein ideas are borrowed from companies in the same industry for process improvements and implemented. These organizations may or may not be competitors as processes can be improved upon by observing completely disconnected organizations as well as the focus here is innovativeness in processes and creativity. Then a trade-off analysis is done on the feasibility of all the alternatives that are found, and the best alternative gets the go-ahead. Activity-based costing (ABC) is an important tool in deciding which alternative to choose.

4. *Implement reengineered process*: This is the most difficult stage and faces a lot of resistance from concerned employees. A culture change program helps in these matters by making the employees aware of the improvements in the processes of the organization and thus the growth of the organization. Then a transition plan has to be developed to migrate from the current As-Is processes to the designed To-Be processes. The organizational structure, IT infrastructure, business policies, and procedures, all should be aligned to the implementation. Alternately a work breakdown structure (WBS) can also be designed to help the organization move to the desired To-Be processes. This defines the causal and time sequential relationships between different activities that are planned and through a process modeling environment, it ensures smooth transition to the desired processes as well.

5. *Improve process continuously*: The first step in this stage is monitoring the processes and recording the progress of the activities and actions. The fallout of the reengineering can be gauged from metrics like measuring employee attitude, customer perceptions, and supplier responsiveness. So by taking customer feedbacks, employee attitude surveys and reviewing performance progressively against clearly defined targets can help in improving the processes continuously.

1.19   Pictorial Representation of Different Methodologies

• *The Hammer/Champy Methodology*

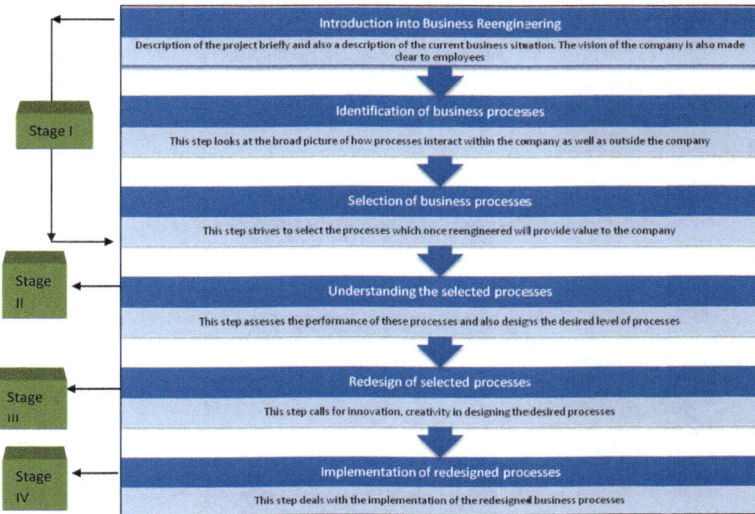

The above processes in the suggested methodology are mapped onto the different stages of the BPR stated in the consolidated framework above.

• *The Davenport Methodology*

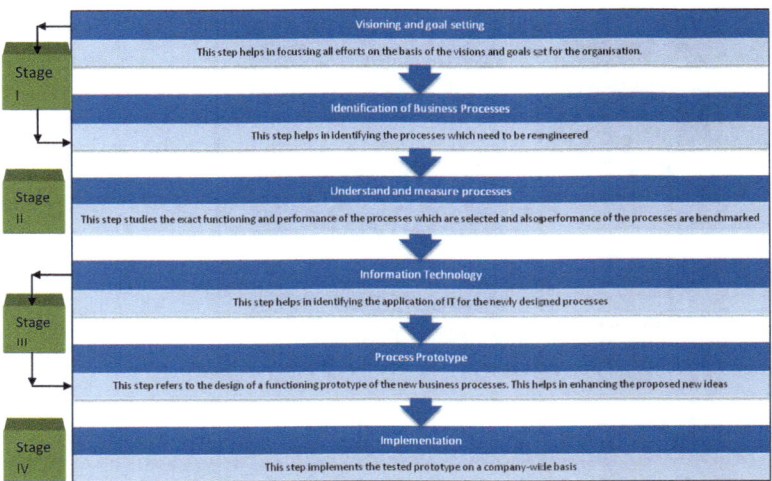

Davenport puts information technology at the heart of business reengineering. In this model, the emphasis is on innovation in technology and innovation. But along with the technology focus, the organizational and human resources side of the BPR is also not neglected by Davenport. He suggests a cultural change even before the technology is in place. In this case also the stages are mapped onto the steps identified in the consolidated framework.

• *Andrews and Stalick Methodology*

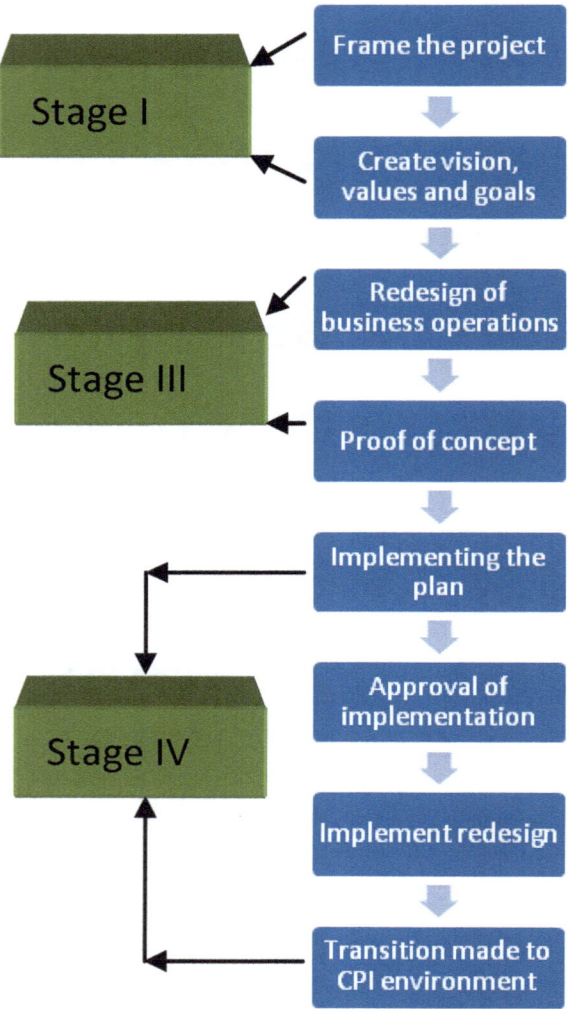

The above depiction maps the stages onto this methodology of BPR.

- *The Kodak Methodology*

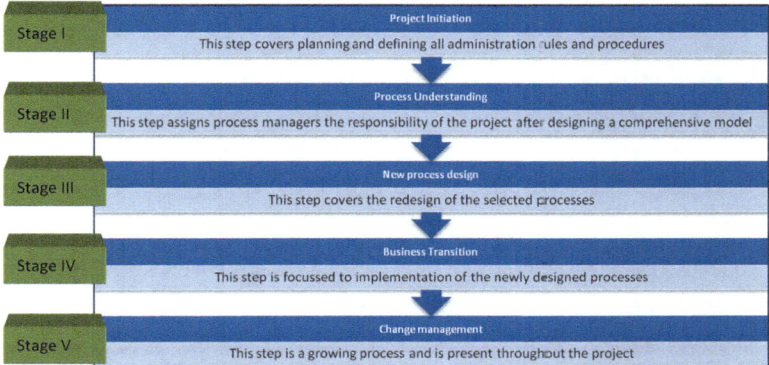

- *The Manganelli/Klein Methodology*
  This methodology concentrates on those processes which directly support the strategic goals of the company, keeping customer requirements in mind. The steps below are again classified into the stages mentioned in the consolidated BPR framework.

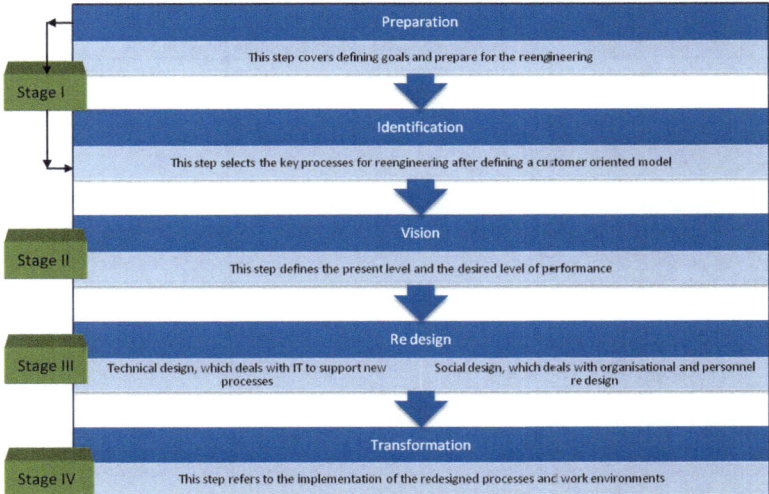

The Conceptual Model (Carr and Johansson, and Krieter)

> **Leadership Team**
>
> Executive/Top management support is extremely essential for the successful implementation of BPR. The responsibility of this team is to define the vision, establish objectives and metrics for improvement and the need to communicate the need for change and make process redesign team:

> **Listen to Voice Of Customer**
>
> There should be a customer focus in all the iness processes and there should be a link between the tasks and communicatio. ween between departments such that
>
> **Develop a strategic vision for the organisation**
>
> give us this information.
>
> The strategic vision helps in defining the ultimate destination and identifying the opportunities for improvement. It is a source of competitive advantage for the organization. It give a long term view and vision for the organization.

> **Establish improvement objectives**
>
> A gap analysis has to be done to establish these objectives. This analysis evaluates the difference between the strategic objectives and the customer's perception of process performance. Thus improvement objectives are also linked with the strategic vision of the organization.

> **Define metrics for measuring the objectives**
>
> The leadership team should establish metrics for each process on which improvement can be measured. This will be a mirror of the bridge between the strategic vision and the customer needs.

> **Communicate the need for change**
>
> The leadership team should communicate the need for change in the organization. This helps to allay fears and provide an understanding for the change. This helps in generating acceptance for the change brought about by BPR.

> **Create a cross-functional Design Team**

(continued)

Understanding of the need for change

The process re design team needs to review the information and ask for any clarification from leadership team if required. The whole process of improvement guidelines being set, alignment to strategic vision, designing performance metrics and customer's requirements should be well understood   he team.

Basic understanding of process

The process re design team needs to have a basic understanding of the processes and the way the processes interact with each other as well. A process map would establish the general working of different departm   and the synergies nvolved in the final outcome being obtained.

Structured approach to develop re design alternatives

The team should select and establish a methodology for developing re design alternatives. A structural approach ensures the team maintains its focus and does not waiver. Different combinations of IT, human resource empowerment and automation should be explored. The caution here wo   be to choose a technology which works well as an enabler for change and not being th   ange in itself.

Develop an implementation plan

The team should develop an implementation plan after proper piloting or prototyping the change on a small scale as part of the implementation plan. This also brings forth any technical or organizational glitches. These glitches can be addressed before implementing on a large scale.

Develop a continuous improvement plan for the processes

To ensure the processes continue to be aligned with the strategic vision as well as fulfill customer requirements, this step needs to be pro active. Regular review of the process performance metics will help enable corrective action.

1.20 Summary

The comparison of the different methodologies shows many similarities as well as differences. The use of BPR as a methodology can be gauged from the above varied illustration of the methodologies. But at the same time they can be mapped onto a particular broad consolidated framework as has been done for some of the methodologies. Though the focus of different methodologies has been different, still the holistic focus has been process oriented and deriving efficiency and effectiveness from the framework for better growth of an organization.

Bibliography

Muthu S, Whitman L, Hossein Cheraghi S. Business process reengineering: a consolidated methodology. Dept. of Industrial and Manufacturing Engineering Wichita State University, Wichita, KS-67260 0035, USA

Chapter 2
The Need for BPR and Its History

2.1 Executive Summary

Business process reengineering (BPR) is a very relevant term in today's world. It is widely used in organizations to inflict radical changes to the entire organization, the existing functional hierarchies, and the fragmented staff roles.

The origins of BPR can be traced back to early 1970s when the Japanese ways of working took the American business world by storm. It led to serious introspection in the minds of managers and hence, new management paradigms like Total Quality Management (TQM), Six Sigma, and Process Improvement Process (PIP) started taking shape. While 1980s saw the introduction of the above-mentioned paradigms in management, 1990s saw a new radical change brewing, with an eye to take organizations to the next level. As organizations reached the maturity phase, PIP was not able to sustain these organizations any more, and hence a new management paradigm became essential which could take radical steps to bring the organizations back on track of high growth.

BPR can be effectively used to develop the business process and vision objective and also identify the business processes that need to be redesigned. BPR can be useful in understanding and measuring the existing processes and also in identifying the IT levers. Also, it can be effectively used to build the prototype of the new processes that would be put up in place of the As-Is process. The need for BPR has been explained through the medium of two ideal cases which happened in real world. A case of business process redesign at Ford Motor Company and a similar case at IBM Credit have been discussed to explain how organizations have time and again felt the need for a radical change in their business processes, and hence have eventually adopted BPR. PIP and BPR are two polar management methodologies and the differences between the two have been aptly pointed out in this report. However, BPR is not merely an automation of whatever already exists. It acts as a natural precursor to the development of new systems or enhancement of existing ones.

S. Mohapatra, *Business Process Reengineering*, Management for Professionals, 39
DOI 10.1007/978-1-4614-6067-1_2, © Springer Science+Business Media New York 2013

2.2   Objective

This chapter strives to understand the origins of BPR and how it has evolved from the need of the organizations to bring about a drastic change in the way they work in order to be competitive in the global economy. We shall also see the transition from TQM and the philosophy of PIP to the more comprehensive business process management (BPM). It will be our endeavor to make the reader appreciate the differences between PIP and BPR and how these changes were necessitated by the changing business scenario over the years. Finally, we will try and put the things in perspective via two small case-lets.

2.3   Introduction

It has been a constant human desire to be dissatisfied with the status quo—we always need to improve upon the way we do things. It is this very desire which has seen the humankind develop from being cave-dwelling food gatherers to the present-day creators of megacities and a sprawling industrial civilization. There hasn't been a single aspect of the human story which has not been affected by this natural urge to grow and change into something better than it was before.

It is this urge which has brought about a sea change in which business is carried out in the modern world. Technology has become the very bedrock on which the multimillion dollar businesses are run and information technology has become a magician's wand which keeps the wheel of global economy turning. We have indeed covered a long way from the days of Charles Babbage's "Analytical Engine" to the present-day Internet age where efficiency and collaboration are keywords. Many eminent pioneers the world over have been trying to find new ways to run business operations, pushing the limits to efficiency more and more.

In last few years, one such business paradigm which has gained a lot of traction in recent years is BPR. Whole lot of organizations, big or small, are either undergoing the BPR exercise or are looking at awe with the kind of results their peers and competitors have been able to achieve as a result of BPR.

This sudden rush for BPR is not something which has happened out of the blue, but rather is a culmination of a chain of events which started with the assault by Japanese auto companies in the US market, which gave rise to business paradigms like TQM, and rapid improvements in the information technology and automation techniques over the years.

Let us analyze the process as it unrolled step by step.

2.4   TQM, Six Sigma, and PIP: The Precursors

The decade of 1970s saw the American auto industry witness an onslaught by the Japanese automakers which shook it to its very foundations. The Japanese were able to supply high-quality cars at prices much cheaper than what were being offered by the American giants like Ford and Chrysler. Suddenly the big auto behemoths realized there was something Japanese players like Toyota and Nissan were doing different which was making them so very competitive. This danger of being displaced as the market leader from their very own home turf led to a severe introspection which resulted in many management paradigms like Six Sigma, TQM, and PIP, which forced the managers around the world to take a nice hard look at their business and to explore possibilities to change the processes in a fundamental way.

2.4.1   Total Quality Management

The website *searchcio.techtarget.com* defines TQM as

> Total Quality Management (TQM) is a comprehensive and structured approach to organizational management that seeks to improve the quality of products and services through ongoing refinements in response to continuous feedback (http://searchcio.techtarget.com/definition/Total-Quality-Management).

The philosophy was first proposed by W. Edwards Deming and is founded upon the principles of reducing the errors produced during the manufacturing or service process, increasing customer satisfaction, streamlining supply chain management, and aiming for modernization of equipment and processes.

Deming crystallized these concepts in terms of the famous PDCA cycle:

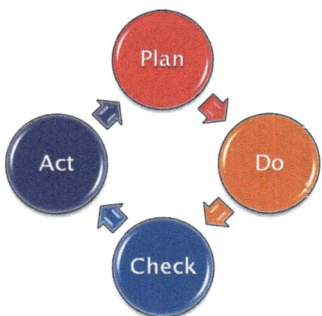

"Plan" stage involves the defining of the business problem, collection of relevant facts and data and an attempt to understand the root cause of the problem. A comprehensive solution is developed and implemented in the "Do" stage, along with the metrics which is used to evaluate the solution. In the "Check" stage, results are confirmed from before and after implementation, and in the "Act" stage, results are documented and communicated, and recommendations are made for further improvements in the next cycle of PDCA.

Hence, this is an incremental process where small changes are made to improve the processes continuously from one cycle to the other.

2.4.2   Six Sigma

Six Sigma was developed and popularized by Motorola Corp. in late 1980s. This is
how GE describes Six Sigma:

> Six Sigma is a highly disciplined process that helps us focus on developing and delivering
> near-perfect products and services (http://www.ge.com/en/company/companyinfo/quality/
> whatis.htm).

This ideology also strives to measure the defects and minimize them as much as
possible—ideally an organization should systematically try and achieve the "zero
defect" stage.

> To achieve Six Sigma Quality, a process must produce no more than 3.4 defects per million
> opportunities. An "opportunity" is defined as a chance for nonconformance, or not meeting
> the required specifications. This means we need to be nearly flawless in executing our key
> processes (http://www.ge.com/en/company/companyinfo/quality/whatis

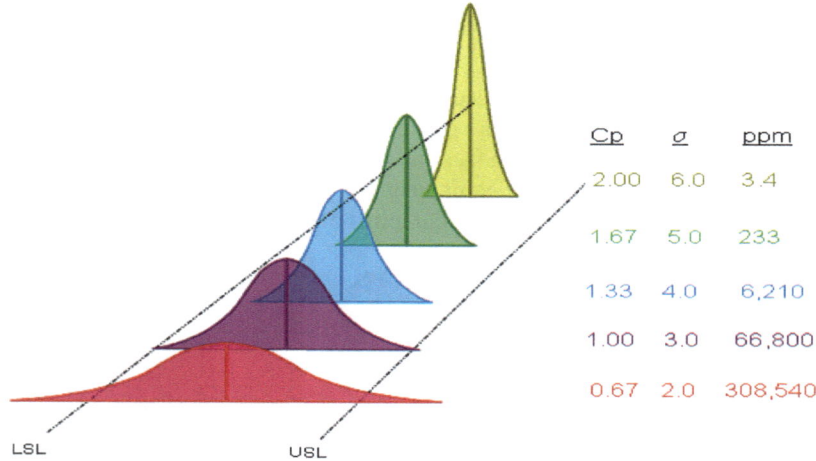

Cp	σ	ppm
2.00	6.0	3.4
1.67	5.0	233
1.33	4.0	6,210
1.00	3.0	66,800
0.67	2.0	308,540

The pillars on which the concept of Six Sigma stands are define, measure, analyze, improve, control (DMAIC).

Define • What problem needs to be solved

Measure • What is the capability of the process

Analyze • What and where do defects occur

Improve • What actions must be taken to eliminate defects and root causes?

Control • What controls must be implemented to sustain the improvements?

The key concepts of this ideology, as given by GE, are (http://en.wikipedia.org/wiki/Process_improvement).

Critical to quality	Attributes most important to the customer
Defect	Failing to deliver what the customer wants
Process capability	What your process can deliver
Variation	What the customer sees and feels
Stable operations	Ensuring consistent, predictable processes to improve what the customer sees and feels
Design for Six Sigma	Designing to meet customer needs and process capability

2.4.3   Process Improvement Process

PIP can be defined as

> Process Improvement is a method to introduce process changes to improve quality, reduce costs, or accelerate schedules (http://en.wikipedia.org/wiki/Process_improvement).

It can be thought of as "a series of actions taken by a Process Owner to identify, analyze and improve existing processes within an organization to meet new goals and objectives. These actions often follow a specific methodology or strategy to create successful results" (http://en.wikipedia.org/wiki/Process_improvement).

Therefore, in essence, both TQM and Six Sigma are both examples of PIP where the results obtained and the changes made in the process are incremental rather than dramatic, which is what sets them apart from the more radical BPR, as we shall see ahead.

2.5   Business Process Reengineering: A New Paradigm

While the 1980s saw the advent of various management paradigms like the ones described above, by 1990s it was becoming evident that something new, more radical was required to take the business to the next level of efficiency. Most of the organizations were reaching or were already at the maturity stage and PIP was not able to sustain these organizations anymore. It was becoming a matter of survival for the organizations to look for some solution, some framework which can make them return back to the trajectory of high growth, failing which they would have become too difficult to manage, eventually leading to loss of leadership and profitability and consequent undoing.

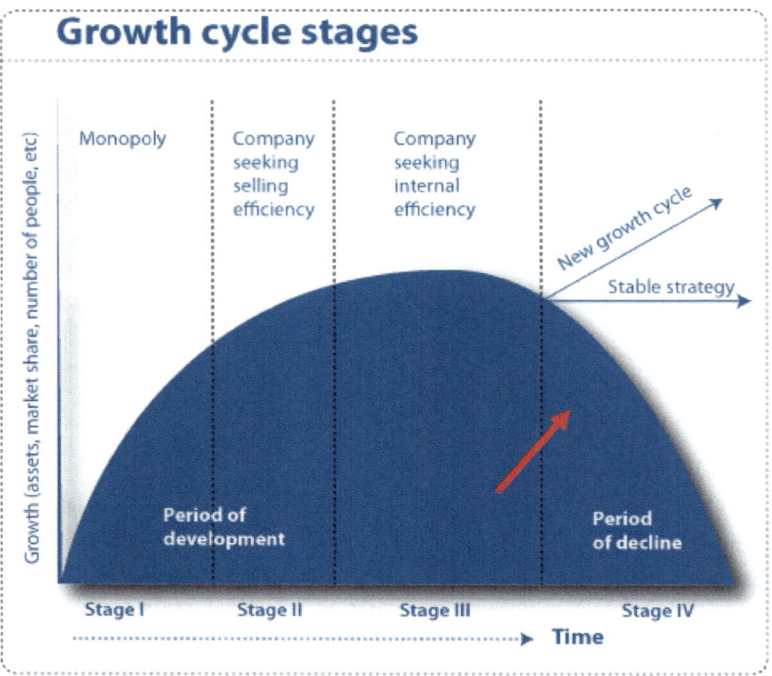

It was in such a scenario that Prof. Michael Hammer wrote his seminal article for the Harvard Business Review—"Reengineering Work: Don't Automate, Obliterate."

In this chapter, Hammer argued that "…the major challenge for managers is to obliterate non-value adding work, rather than using technology for automating it" (http://en.wikipedia.org/wiki/Business_process_reengineering#cite_note-1).

Similar views were expressed by Thomas H. Davenport and J. Short from Ernst and Young Research Center in their article "The Fad That Forgot People" (http://www.rotman.utoronto.ca/~evans/teach363/fastco/reengin.htm) which was published in the Sloan Management Review.

The idea was defined formally by Hammer and Champy in 1993 as

> …the **fundamental** reconsideration and **radical** redesign of the organizational process, in order to achieve **drastic** improvement of current performance in cost, service and speed (http://www.valuebasedmanagement.net/methods_bpr.html).

Davenport as an early proponent of the ideology gave his five-step approach to the BPR model:

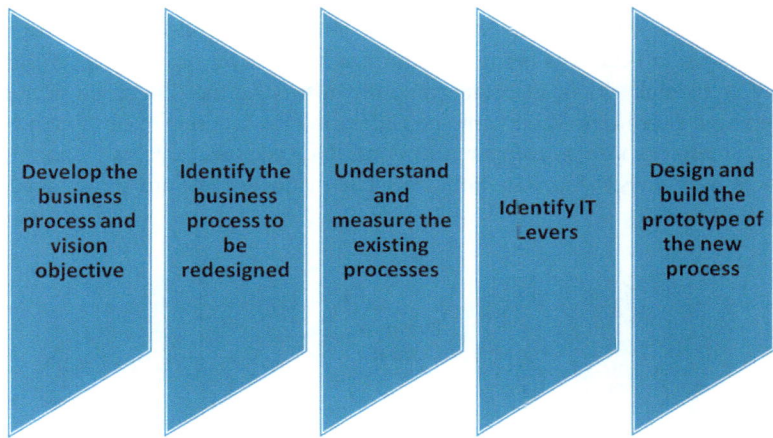

2.6   Why BPR?

The first half of the last decade of the twentieth century saw a lot of organizations adopt the BPR philosophy. The following questions were raised by the business managers as a justification for BPR:

- Is the competition outperforming the company by factors?
- Are there many conflicts in the organization?
- Is there an extremely high frequency of meetings? (Indicative of lack of clear direction at a macro level)
- Is there an excessive use of nonstructured communication?
- Have the continuous improvement processes stopped yielding meaningful business results?

The following few cases, which happened in the early 1980s and 1990s, would be helpful in explaining why and how organizations started feeling the need for complete reengineering of their business processes. The cases in point are two classic cases of BPR, one at Ford Motor Company and another at IBM Credit.

2.6.1   Two Cases

2.6.1.1   Ford Motor Company

In the early 1980s, Ford Motors, America's leading motor company, put its Accounts Payable Department under the scanner. The department employed around 500 employees, only in the North America itself. The senior management wanted to reduce the head count by around 20%, by installation of new IT systems. A group of managers from Ford visited the Mazda office in Japan and found that the work done by 500 people in Ford was being done by just 5 employees in Mazda. While Ford was trying to make its head count come down to 400, the difference in absolute numbers was enormous. Taking into consideration the fact that even though Mazda is much smaller in size as compared to Ford, the Accounts Payable Department of Ford was five times the size it should be. The managers of Ford started analyzing the *As-Is* process.

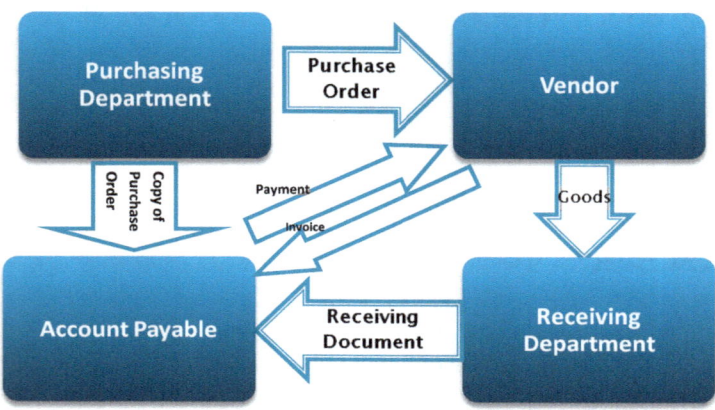

The As-Is process is shown in the figure above. The purchasing department sends the purchase order to the vendor, and also sends a copy of the same to the accounts payable department. When the goods are received by the material control department, it sends a copy of the receiving document to the accounts payable department. The vendor sends an invoice to the accounts payable department, which then matches the purchase order against the invoice and the receiving document, which is known as three-way matching. In case they match, the accounts payable department made the payment. In case of a mismatch, a clerk from the accounts payable department investigates the discrepancy, holds up payments, generates documents, and carries out all other necessary responsibilities. Under the As-Is process, it was the responsibility of the accounts payable department to match 14 data items between the invoice, the receipt record, and the purchase order, before the payment could be sent to the vendor.

When Ford management sat down to discuss the possible scope of process improvement, they contemplated a more efficient check by the accounts payable clerk. However, it was decided that preventing the mismatches is a better option. The *To-Be* process was designed and Ford instituted a process called "invoice-less processing." Here the purchasing department would enter information into an online database as soon as an order is initiated. In the To-Be process, the copy of the purchase order would no longer be sent to anyone. As soon as the goods arrive at the receiving dock, the receiver clerk would check the online database and match if the received goods correspond to any outstanding purchase order. If it matches, the clerk would accept the consignment and would enter the transaction into the database. However, in case of a mismatch, i.e., if there is no corresponding database entry existing for the received goods, then the clerk would return the order.

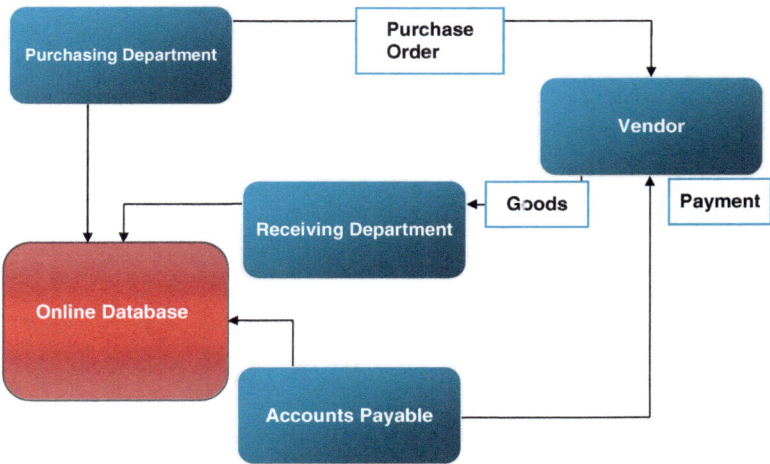

The To-Be process would require matching of three items, namely, the part number, supplier code, and unit of measure, between the receipt record and the purchase order. The matching would be done automatically and the check would be prepared by the IT system and the accounts payable department would send the check to the vendor. Ford Motor Company would request its vendors not to send any invoices, so that all the time and cost incurred on matching could be removed and an invoice-less process could be launched.

Ford implemented the To-Be process and thus achieved a head count reduction of 75%, as compared to the 20% that it would have achieved through a conventional process improvement. The new process would also ensure data consistency across all the departments, as all of them would be using the same online database.

2.6.1.2 IBM Credit

The process for approval of financial requests was very slow and bureaucratized at IBM Credit. An analysis of the *As-Is* shows that process had to go through five separate departments and an average of six working days to close a deal. The employees were extremely frustrated with the process, as during the course of these 6 days, while IBM Credit processed the approval of the deal, some customers used to switch their business to some other service provider. All attempts to streamline the process failed.

Two senior managers then decided to analyze the As-Is process by walking through a typical claim process themselves. The managers could find out that the entire process could actually be completed in 90 min, instead of 6 days. The management then decided to do away with the As-Is process and decided to go ahead with the To-Be process, which made one generalist responsible for completing the entire process of credit approval. The process would no longer be a tedious process involving five departments and 6 days, and would be taken out of the purview of specialists. The average time for the completion of the process came to around 4 h, which resulted in a 100% increase in the productivity of the entire system. New technology was extensively used for implementing the To-Be process and a small group of skilled employees was used as a backup for the generalist's responsibilities. The managers, thus, found a way to break the bureaucratic stalemate, thus opening the doors for the entire organization to go for a series of key improvements.

Both these cases amply show how breakthroughs have been achieved in the industry by rethinking and reshaping the entire business processes, while maintaining a customer-centric approach at all times.

2.7   Difference Between PIP and BPR

The table below provides a comparison between the implementation criteria of PIP and BPR. Both BPR and PIP have evolved over the years as two polar management methodologies, which are characterized by gradual and incremental improvements, as compared to radical innovation.

Primary criteria	PIP (process improvement)	BPR (process innovation)
Change level	Incremental	Radical
Starting point	Existing process	Clean slate
Frequency of change	One-time/continuous	One-time
Time required	Short	Long
Participation	Bottom-up	Top-down
Scope	Narrow, within functions	Broad, cross-functional
Risk	Moderate	High
Primary enabler	Statistical control	Information technology
Type of charge	Cultural	Cultural/structural

2.8   Conclusion

BPR is a creative process, which does not guarantee a certain successful outcome. A few basic steps need to be followed which can be immensely helpful in restructuring work. However, the key to success in a BPR lies in imagination, insight, and a willingness to challenge the regularly trodden path. BPR simplifies work. Rather than eliminating steps or specific tasks, BPR questions the whole process and contemplates radical changes at a much higher level. After a process has been justified, it needs to be redesigned with the power of IT. In the not-so-distant past, all information used to be on pieces of paper and every stakeholder in the process had to keep waiting till the information travelled all over the organization for approval. This caused inevitable delays, leading to immense time and cost overruns. However, things changed gradually as information technology found its way into most of the organizations which started redesigning their processes, keeping IT in mind. Today, with shared access to databases all across the world, there are hardly any acceptable delays in processes.

BPR is not merely an automation of whatever already exists. It acts as a natural prelude to the development of new systems or enhancement of existing ones. Many organizations consider it to be a natural step which needs to be taken when planning for enhancement in its IT systems. However, for BPR to succeed in its true meaning, it is very important to make a fundamental change. This need for fundamental change can be felt through some business challenge like high overhead costs, new competition, inferior quality, or some other source of dissatisfaction. If BPR is viewed as a regular exercise which every organization religiously needs to undergo, irrespective of its abilities, then it will be difficult to sustain the same energy level and intensity.

The purpose of BPR is to achieve radical changes. It is a high-risk–high-return strategy and it cannot be accomplished in small steps. A vision for a major transformation, in line with the vision and strategy of the organization, needs to be followed. A successful BPR can indeed work wonders for the fortunes of an organization.

Bibliography

Reengineering work: don't automate, obliterate, by Michael Hammer, Harvard Business Review, July–August 1990

Chapter 3
Business Process Reengineering: Framework and Approach

3.1 Learning Objective

- To study reengineering and its need
- To study the various reengineering approaches
- To compare these approaches and analyze the similarities and differences between these approaches
- To form a reengineering framework based on these analyses

3.2 Introduction

> Reengineering is the fundamental rethinking and radical redesign of business processes to achieve dramatic improvements in critical, contemporary measures of performance such as cost, quality, service and speed.[1]

BRP advocates in "reinventing the wheel," i.e., this approach encourages an organization to start from scratch and work towards reinvention, thus leading to manifold improvements in performance and revenue. BPR focuses on processes where it works to redesign the strategic and value-added processes which transcend the organizational boundaries.

It's a cross-functional approach and requires support from almost all the departments of the organization. Managerial support is prime for the approach to be a success, which also involves a tactful and well-planned culture change management program.

Business process reengineering cycle can be represented as follows[2]:

---

[1] http://www.enotes.com/management-encyclopedia/business-process-reengineering.

[2] http://en.wikipedia.org/wiki/Business_process_reengineering.

S. Mohapatra, *Business Process Reengineering*, Management for Professionals, DOI 10.1007/978-1-4614-6067-1_3, © Springer Science+Business Media New York 2013

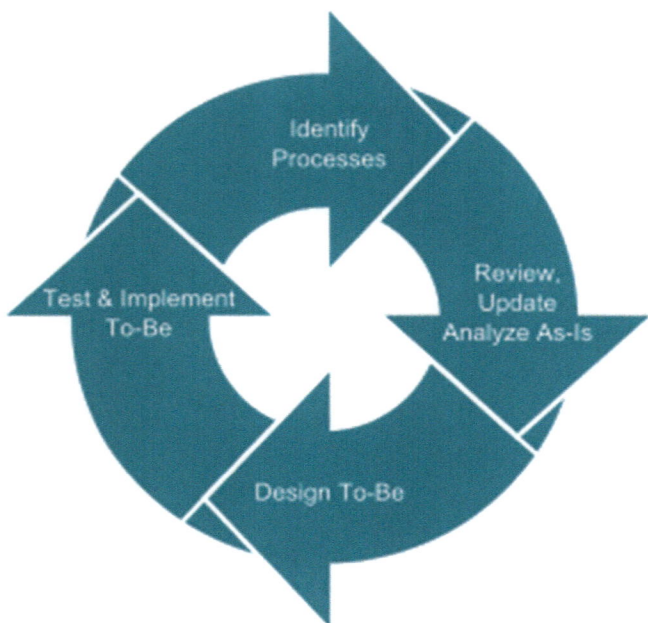

It involves identifying the processes first and then doing a thorough and in-depth As-Is analysis. Once it's done, the processes can be identified for update or review. Then a To-Be analysis is done and designed so that the organization knows where it has to go and what it has to achieve. Benchmarking is an important step here. Once the plan is in place, the reengineering process is implemented and continuous improvement is aimed at.

3.3 BPR Framework

A very basic framework for reengineering is shown below. An organization can add or skip a few steps based on any specific requirements. However the sequence more or less remains the same.

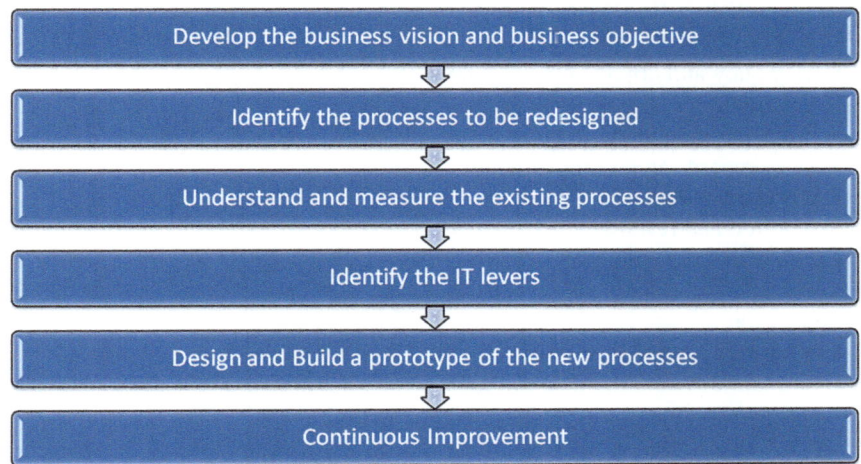

3.4   Develop the Business Vision and Business Objective

The object of reengineering is to provide competitive advantage of enterprise. This step of visioning has to take place at a senior enough level in an enterprise where the business is perceived as an integrated whole, rather than a sum of departmental or functional activities with conflicting interests and objects within enterprise.

Developing vision essentially recognizes the following:

- Business vision and goals are necessarily market/customer driven and contain in them the survival values and critical success factors of the enterprise.
- Achievement of business vision may involve reengineering of more than one process.
- Process attributes and process measures need to be derived. They form locomotive force by providing the right direction and speed to reengineering project.

Thus at the end of this step, one would be clear on the following aspects:

- What are the key processes?
- How will reengineered process perform qualitatively and quantitatively?

3.5   Choosing the Process to Be Redesigned

Once the company's business vision and objectives are clear, it should identify the processes that need to be redesigned. This can be done by two ways:

The *priority approach*: This involves identification of all the processes within an organization and the assignment of priority for redesign.

Some important processes along with the subprocesses are listed below:

3.5.1   Human Resource Function

- HRD policy and organization culture
- Recruitment
- Joining and induction
- Service records and establishment
- Performance appraisal
- Promotion and reward
- Conduct and discipline
- Training
- Separation
- Pay allowances and other perks
- Loans and travels
- Leave processing
- Recreation activity
- Self-development of employees

3.5.2   Finance and Accounts Function

- Budgeting and costing
- Payroll
- Staff payment and reimbursement
- Staff loans and advances
- External payments
- Imports
- Account maintenance , journal adjustments, and auditing
- Bank liaison and reconciliation of accounts
- PF and statutory deposits processing
- Financial reporting and MIS
- Investment planning

3.5.3   Material Management Function

- Vendor development
- Scrutiny of indents
- Inquiry processing
- Processing of quotations and placement of purchase orders
- Dispatch follow-up
- Inland clearance
- Customs clearance

- Receipt of purchased material
- Inspection stock charging and bill processing
- Payments
- Storage and issue of purchase material
- Handling of rejected material
- Stores accounting
- Asset identification and traceability
- Asset verification
- Scrap disposal as per asset management procedure
- Packing, forwarding, and dispatch
- Database management and report generation
- Maintenance of inspection, measuring and test equipment, and corrective action

3.5.4   Office Automation and MIS Function

- Identification and planning areas for computerization
- Develop automation tools and packages
- Develop information systems
- Testing and validating in-house and external packages
- Integration of stand-alone packages
- User training

3.5.5   Administration Functions

- Administration purchase and stores
- Transport
- Leased accommodation
- Canteen and catering
- Security and reception
- Housekeeping
- Maintenance functions

These processes can then be classified into interorganizational, inter-functional, and functional processes. Now prioritization can be done by taking into account the following:

1. Business division and corporate policy
2. Core competency of organization
3. Relative importance currently being given to the processes

This approach is particularly suitable when the company is simultaneously interested in TQM/ISO 9000. This enables the company to demarcate greater resources and time for BPR and the exercise also helps in the entire effort for Total Quality Management.

The *critical success process approach*: This involves the redesign of processes which are critical to the success of the organization. In this first the mission of the organization is defined. Then a study of critical processes is carried out at three levels:

- Industry
- Organization
- People

    The next step is the constitution of a corporate team of senior people who would have overall responsibility for the BPR. The team should have members from the various divisions of the organization. This team will coordinate the entire redesign of the interorganizational and inter-functional processes. Each member will be responsible for the BPR of the processes which predominantly involve his/her division/function.

    The main advantage of this approach is that it results in a set of critical business processes which can be redesigned within the limited resources and time available in the organization. However the disadvantage here is that some important processes might not be covered and get missed out.

3.6   Understanding and Measuring the Existing Processes

In order to understand each process, a separate team has to be formed which will be responsible for understanding and redesigning a particular process. Its first job is to define the beginning and end point of the processes. A convenient way to define process boundaries is to define the deliverables of the process.

    The next step is to make a block diagram of the process, identifying the various departments and individuals involved. This helps in a structured walk-through of the processes. The objective is to identify the various customers and suppliers (both internal and external) associated with the process without going into the modality of the process.

    A process can be specified by identifying the following:

- Inputs and outputs of the process
- Suppliers both internal and external
- Customers both internal and external
- Owners
- Internal deliverables at each stage of the process

    There are three major process measurements:

- *Effectiveness*: It is the extent to which the deliverables of the process at each stage of its customer supply chain meet the needs and the expectations of its customers.
- *Efficiency*: This measures the extent to which the resources have been utilized and rework and waste has been reduced. Main efficiency measures are cycle time, resources expended per unit of output, value-added cost per unit of output, defect rate, revenue per employee, time to market, etc.
- *Adaptability*: It is the extent of flexibility of processes to enable it to adapt to the future changing customer expectations. Though difficult to measure, it is imperative to obtain superiority over competitors in market share. A measure of adaptability of processes gives an idea of the responsiveness of the organization to the external environment.

3.7   Redesigning the Processes

Once an organization has selected business process to be redesigned, it can do so in these steps:

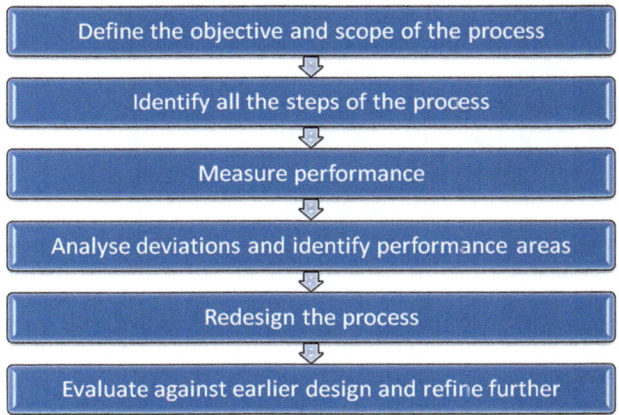

For redesigning processes, tools such as flowcharts, histograms, Pareto charts, control charts, scatter plots, and fishbone diagrams can be used. The above-mentioned steps come under PDCA framework, i.e., plan–do–check–act.

3.8   Information as Technology Enabler

The role of IT is of paramount importance in any redesign process. Some examples of how it can be used are given below:

	Use
Transactional	Information technology can transform unstructured processes into routinized transactions
Communication	IT can transfer information rapidly across large distances often geographically dispersed
Tracking	IT allows the detailed tracking of the performance of processes
Control	IT can help in implementing management and control system on processes
Poka-Yoke	IT can redesign processes in such a manner that they become mistake-proof

IT capabilities involve improving coordination and information access between internal departments, across organizational units, and between organizations, thereby allowing for more effective management of tasks.

Apart from its use in redesigning, IT can be used to make a prototype of the redesigned process and help in its automation.

Here it is important that a process-oriented approach is followed for the design of Information System Architecture. This means computerization coupled with business process redesign which includes all functions and helps realizing returns on IT investment fully.

But, even though information technology can be an enabler, it must not necessary drive change. When looking on the impact of IT development on organizational change, the period from implementation to change can vary significantly in time. It may be concluded that IT is only one of an assembly of change enablers. Beyond that, technology must be applied in an understandable way when trying to link IT capabilities to organizational objectives.

The following chart shows how IT can be used for business process innovation:

Earlier	Technology enabler	Now
Information can appear in only one place at one time	Shared databases	Information can appear simultaneously in as many places as needed
Only experts can perform complex work	Expert systems	A generalist can do the work of an expert
Business must choose between centralization and decentralization	Telecommunication networks	Business can simultaneously reap the benefits of both
Managers make all decisions	Decision support tools	Decision making is everybody's job
Field personnel needs offices where they can receive, store, retrieve, and submit information	Wireless data communication and computers	Field personnel can send and receive information wherever they are
The best contact with a buyer is personal contact	Interactive videodisk	The best contact with a buyer is effective contact
You have to find things where they are	Automatic identification and tracking	Things tell you where they are
Plans get revised periodically	High-performance computing	Plans get revised instantaneously

The rapid development of IT requires a permanent reevaluation of a company's IT use in order to sustain competitiveness permanently. But, looking ahead for new technology does not mean to find technologies looking for uses. IT opportunities should be monitored in terms of business applicability and process support and improvement. Information technology is no self-purpose, but a means to achieve a better competitive position by yielding purposeful application on business problems.

3.9 Prototyping

A prototype is a working model of the reengineering that is to be done. It is initially built as a baseline and then refined successively until the final output satisfies all business requirements. It provides an instant feedback to the reengineering on the progress and acceptance of the reengineering effort. It also provides opportunities for simulating and evaluating reengineering potentials within the organizational, as well as the system development area. Continuous prototyping enables the reengineering team and management to make necessary adjustments before a final process design is chosen. For example, it helps in understanding:

- Whether the engineered business operations will meet the production goals
- Whether there are any hidden bottlenecks or any other problem that must be fixed
- What transactions it can handle, including exceptions and error processing, effectively
- If any organizational issues or problems exist that were previously ignored
- Mistaken assumptions about how the business actually operates

3.9.1 Pilot Test

This is an actual live demonstration of the redesigned business process and creates the reengineered business operation in a controlled small-scale environment. It should run for a limited amount of time (e.g., a single business cycle), and involve a limited amount of people, with easily controlled interfaces. A successful pilot test requires accurate "before" and "after" benchmark data from the test environment and measurement process. The pilot test provides several benefits not attained through simulation. These include:

- Actual benefits that can be realized
- Helps people know how to ensure orderly change and avoid mistakes during implementation
- Understand training, materials, job structuring, and business practices testing requirements
- Refines processes, business policies, and practices based on actual use
- Cultural change experience, so expectations and resistance to change can be addressed during full-scale implementation
- Builds organizational awareness

When the pilot test is successfully over, the test environment should be able to continue the reengineered operation. As a pilot test can take up to 6 months to produce solid results, pilots should be conducted after implementation planning to avoid significant delays on the project.

3.10 Continuous Improvement

All the above-mentioned steps won't reap significant benefits unless the improvement is continuous. The first step in this activity is monitoring. Two things have to be monitored—the progress of action and the results. Action can be monitored by seeing how much informed people are, the commitment of management, and how well the change is received in the organization. As for monitoring the results, this should include such measures as customer perceptions, employee attitudes, supplier responsiveness, etc. This results in strengthened communication throughout the organization and reviewing of performance against earlier defined targets. Thus a feedback loop is setup wherein the process is remapped, reanalyzed, and redesigned. Thereby continuous improvement of performance is ensured through a performance tracking system and application of problem-solving skills.

Given below is an example of BPR implementation phases:

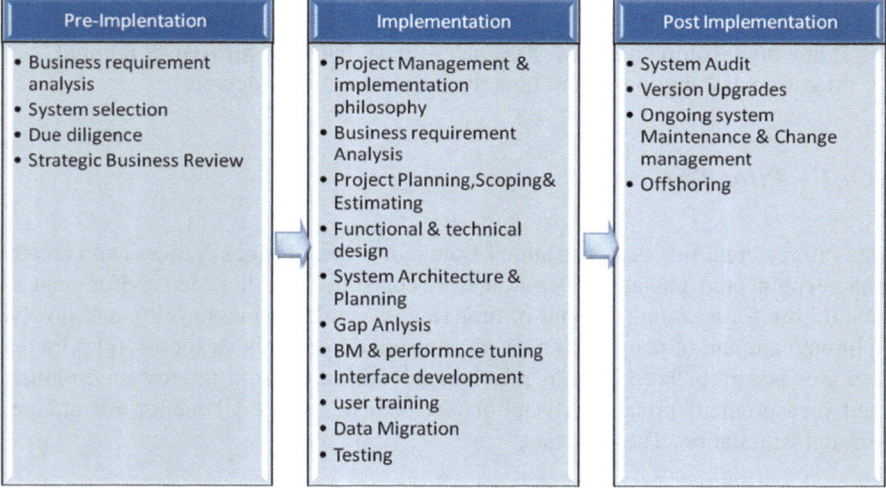

3.11 Reengineering Methodologies

Based on this basic framework we can develop a few approaches which can be implemented depending on the exciting processes in an organization and the organization culture. It will also depend on the extent to which reengineering is needed and the resources that can be dedicated for the same. Some of the common attributes that need to be taken care of are

- The project has to be defined first
- Cost–benefit analysis has to be done
- The whole process has to be planned first and then implemented
- A method has to be defined for measuring the performance change and for continuous improvement

However based on the above-mentioned organizational differences some unique features can be included in the various approaches which will vary in the steps that are involved in implementation. Some of these are

- Creation of a vision before the planning for the redesign work
- Need of As-Is study
- To what extent the processes need to be studied and the tools that are to be used
- Incorporating a desired culture in the organization depending on specific needs
- Extent of modification of the existing processes
- Solution planning and transition activities

Once the project area has been identified, there are various methodologies which can be followed for reengineering business processes.

The following are the different methodologies:

3.11.1 BPR Implementation Approach 1

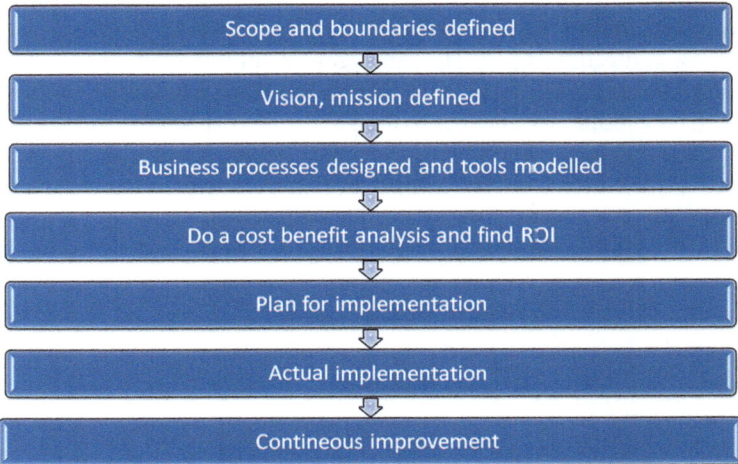

In this approach of reengineering, the objectives, values, and the vision get defined before the learning process which might act as an impediment in attaining final results. Creating a vision, goals, and values without the knowledge of competitors and noncompetitor capabilities leads to uncertainty of results. In this case it is important to understand the competitive advantage created by defining vision, the customer needs fulfilled, and the advantages of the new technology implemented. However to understand these factors, a prior customer and competitor analysis needs to be done.

3.11.2   BPR Implementation Approach 2

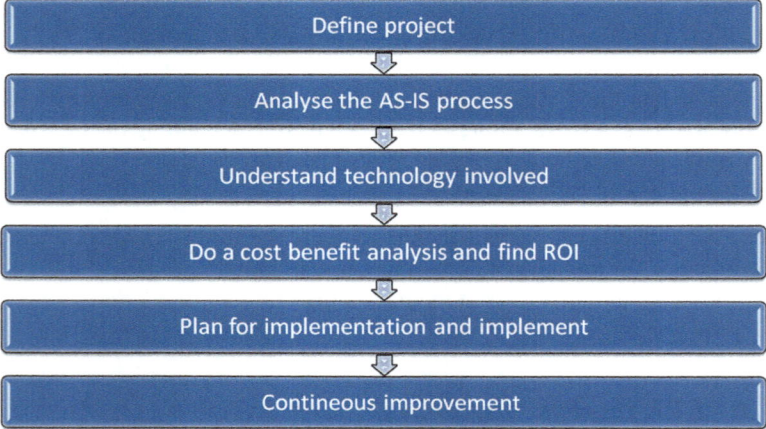

The advantage of this process over the previous one is the As-Is analysis which also includes the competitor study. The only problem in this method is that it is time consuming and expensive. Also, if the reengineering team belongs to the same organization, it may result in a tendency to think in a stereotyped fashion as per company culture. Thus outcome mayn't be as expected. However, once one has got a complete idea of the current process it might be relatively easy to understand what and how things are to be carried forward.

3.11.3   BPR Implementation Approach 3

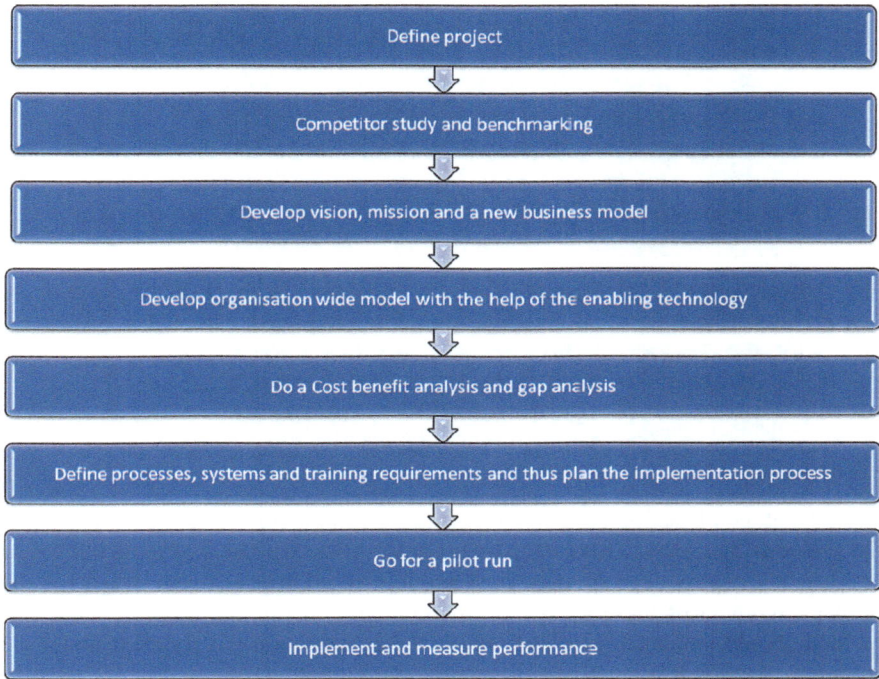

The advantage of this process is the extensive and well-established pre-implementation and implementation stage. However this is time consuming and will require more resources for continuous development which is lacking in this approach. Thus a continuous improvement process management system with an in-place key performance measures would lead to incremental improvements.

3.11.4   BPR Implementation Approach 4

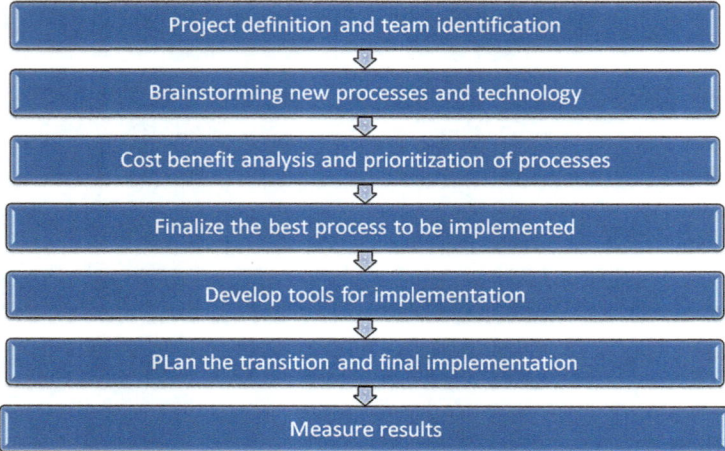

The advantage of this process is that it is faster in implementation as compared to the previous methods mentioned. The brainstorming step helps in generating new and bright ideas that can be used for reengineering. However what it lacks is the proper alignment of these ideas with the company vision and mission. Thus this method should be ideally implemented if the organization is very clear about the strategic direction it is heading to.

3.11.5   BPR Implementation Approach 5

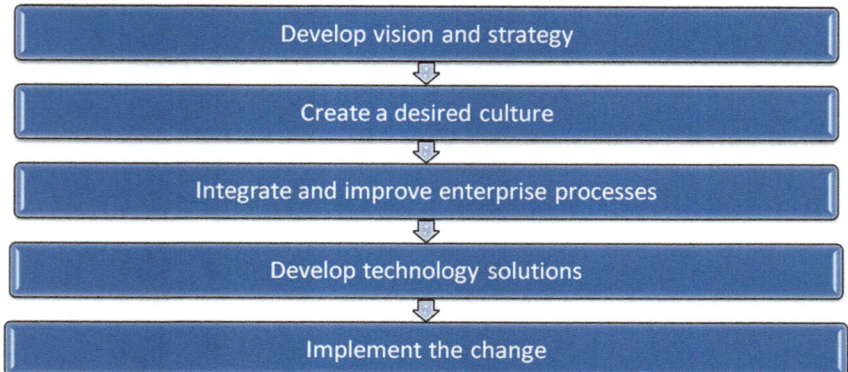

This method involves a very important step of building a culture for preparing the organization for the reengineering process, but it does not involve the study of the organization in the current situation. For example, for old organizations with legacy system, a culture change would be encountered and thus methods for dealing with the same should also be considered. Thus this process is advisable if the company already has well-defined processes and the main problem in implementation is resistance to change in the organization.

3.12   Best Approach

No approach can be called a best approach as they are situation specific. Like these approaches there are many other methods as well which can also be used for reengineering. But an organization should employ that method which best suits its requirements. The results are better when the decision taken is of the team as a whole and is based on an in-depth understanding of the advantages and the trade-offs existing. For deciding on the methodology, the organization needs to understand whether to change the existing vision and go for a new one, whether to go for As-Is analysis depending on existing resources and time, what period of time needs to be allocated for learning process, etc.

3.13   Case of Ford Motor Company

A good example of internal BPR is the Ford Motor Company. Their accounts payable was very bureaucratic and inefficient. More than 500 people manned the accounts department. The existing system used to operate as follows:

- Purchasing department generated a purchase order. A copy was sent to account department.
- Materials management received goods and sent a copy of the receiving document to accounts.
- Supplier sent an invoice to accounts.
- Accounts matched the purchase order against the receiving document and invoice.
- In case of a match, accounts department released payment.
- In case of a mismatch, accounts department held up payment and investigated.

In the redesign process, the purchase department started using online database for entering purchase order details when it was generated. The suppliers were told to stop sending invoices.

The redesigned process was as follows:

- Purchasing department generated a purchasing order and entered details in the online database.
- Material management received goods and entered the details of the receiving order in the database.

- The computer matched the receiving order information with the purchase order and generated a cheque which was then sent to the supplier by accounts.
- In case they couldn't find a database for the received goods, the order was returned.

Existing Process

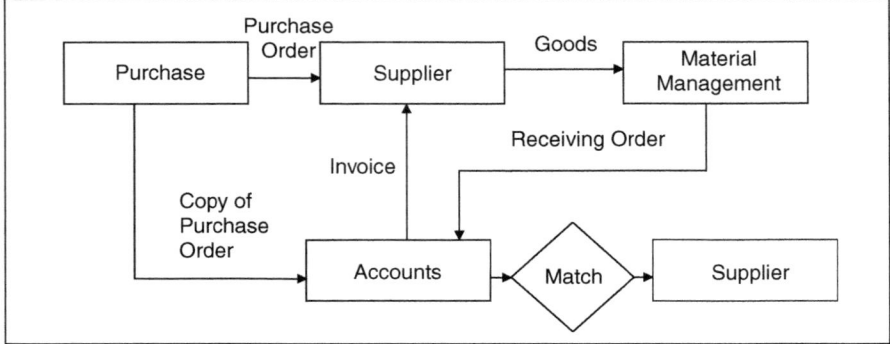

Redesigned Process

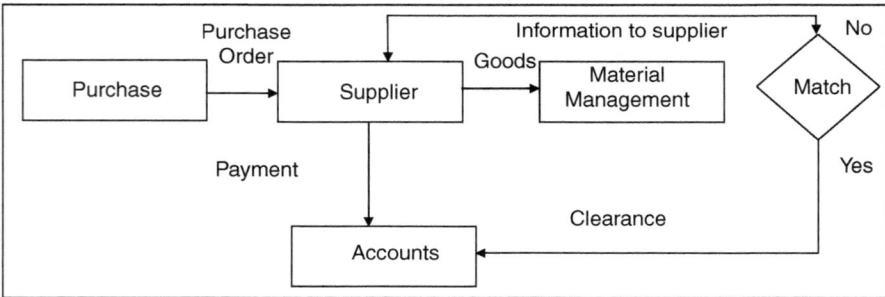

In the old process, accounts had to match 14 data items between the receiving document, purchase order, and the invoice before it could issue payment to the supplier. The new approach involved matching of only three items—part number, unit of measure, and supplier code—between the purchase order and receiving document record. Moreover, the matching was done automatically by the computer, which also prepared the cheque.

3.14 Conclusion

Business process reengineering changes the face of the organization completely. However since any change is usually resisted, change has to be managed properly. Thus it is very important that all the implementation steps are followed diligently and with utmost care. If needed, specific infrastructure should be created to help people cope with the change. For example, there can be new training programs, online learning systems, etc. Modifying the structure involves a major redefinition of job roles and accountabilities. So creating a temporary organization structure is helpful in such a situation. A temporary organization structure can empower people with the required power to bring about change.

If a "process-oriented" organization is not possible, the only way to ensure the success of BPR is to foster team spirit in the various organizational teams constituted for BPR. The HRD department has a key role to play in this. Careful thought has to be given to the design of structures for managing change to ensure that they serve the appropriate purpose. Enabling people to design their own way of managing change empowers and encourages them to invest commitment and energy in pursuing change goals.

Bibliography

http://www.enotes.com/management-encyclopedia/business-process-reengineering
http://webcache.googleusercontent.com/search?q=cache:SQ8nsLrElxYJ:www.scribd.com
http://en.wikipedia.org/wiki/Business_process_reengineering
http://www.prosci.com/bpr_method.htm
Kapur R (1995) Business process redesign. Global Business Press
Jayraman MS (1994) Business process reengineering

Chapter 4
Business Process Management
(Process Life Cycle, Process Maturity)

4.1 Objectives

By the end of the chapter, the reader is expected to have better clarity on the following outlined aspects:

- Evolution of business process management (BPM) and its several approaches with time
- [*Illustration* Japanese professional discipline, Toyota (TPS) tweaking these approaches (based on their cultural context) to build competitive advantage]
- Understanding business process management and its relevance
- Drivers and triggers for BPM and automated solutions
- Business process modeling—framework and steps—its utility in BPM
- Process life cycle synchronizing with organization life cycle; stages of process life cycle management (PLCM) in each organization stage
- Process maturity; various levels of process maturity and its organization impact as well as business impact
  (*Case Study* Siemens illustrating process maturity achievement/implementation)

4.2 Historical Background

As humanity continually strove for a better life (though Darwin proposed the evolution theory regarding adaptability of species on earth which was regarding survival and not betterment, which is the attempt of businesses), it is trade, transactions, and business which has maneuvered its way for an improved existence—thus businesses pursued for profits in a witch-hunt mode. Business was dissected, broken down, synthesized, and what not—all in this pursuit of maximizing profits. Various facets of this objective were sought—production efficiency, customer value, cost optimization, etc.—all modes finally leading to the same destination—profits! business process management is one of the many frameworks available for attaining this objective.

S. Mohapatra, *Business Process Reengineering*, Management for Professionals,
DOI 10.1007/978-1-4614-6067-1_4, © Springer Science+Business Media New York 2013

Now we discuss in brief how this concept of business process management gained momentum and how it has evolved till date. Further improvements have been founded upon the notion that work can be seen in hindsight as a process. This was the base idea towards the late nineteenth century. Frederick Taylor[1] pioneered this idea towards turn of century and before. He and his colleagues attempted to develop modern industrial engineering and process improvement—though the techniques were limited to manual labor and production processes. These processes though gained wide acceptance in early 1900s but gradually went obsolete by mid-century.

During the mid-century days, Taylorist process improvement approach was combined with statistical process control by Shewart, Deming, Juran, and other quality *gurus*. Their version of process management involved measuring and limiting process variation, continuous rather than phased improvement, and most importantly employee empowerment and authorization to improve their own process—thus introducing the concepts of workflow, process ownership, and accountability— which reflected in multiple functions of the business.

Illustration. This phase of methodology adopted is reflected in the production focus on the industries (post-Great Depression and World War II) especially in the context of Japanese firms. Japanese firms had the business need (which arose from recovering from World War II losses as well as the drive and capability in building global markets) and the discipline to put continuous improvement programs in place. Other firms in other contextual societies have adopted on similar lines of production focus as well as certain improvements based on statistical principles—but these required higher order of business discipline. Most notable among these firms was Toyota, which turned these approaches into a distinctive advantage in process management—the Toyota Production System (TPS).

Toyota Production System:

• Combined statistical process control with continuous learning through decentralized work teams
• A "pull" approach to manufacturing that minimized waste and inventory
• Treating every minor process improvement in processes as an experiment to be designed, measured, and learnt from

However successful implementation of TPS is limited to few firms; even Toyota has had more success in Japan than its elsewhere foreign plants (this reflects on the people, environment, and culture factor). Lesser stringent approach in "lean" techniques has been adopted in several American firms recently.

The next major phase in BPM history was towards the end of the twentieth century, especially during the 1990s, when many Western firms were staring at economic recession, in the face of strong competition, particularly the "optimized" Japanese firms. In this phase business process reengineering added several new approaches to the generic set of process management ideas:

---

[1] Frederick Taylor (March 20, 1856 to March 21, 1915), an American mechanical engineer who actively sought to improve industrial efficiency. He was regarded as the torchbearer of scientific management and one of the first management consultants. Taylor, also known for his "Efficiency Movement," was highly influential in the Progressive Era.

- Radical (rather than incremental) redesign and improvement of work
- Attacking broad, cross-functional business processes
- "Stretch" goals of order-of-magnitude improvement
- Use of information technology as an enabler of new ways of working

Reengineering was one of the first approaches that displayed considerable shift from production focus, and rather concentrated on business process primarily non-production, e.g., white-collar processes like order management and customer service. Radical redesign being its objective, it didn't emphasize on statistical process control or continuous improvement. Thus being overambitious and challenging implementation—reengineering gradually symbolized headcount reduction and largely disappeared (with signs of return are being observed now in the industry).

Most recent process management enthusiasm has revolved around "Six Sigma"[2] which typically deals with incremental rather than radical improvement. With the current postrecession phase posing its own challenges with respect to competition and business risks, a radical improvement is necessitated in business—thus reengineering has resurfaced on the business process management scene.

4.3 Defining Business Process Management

One aspect of business that clearly emerges out of all the production- and process-focus approaches followed to gain competitive advantage is the key to business' sustainability and profitability should be one among the three strategic options:

1. Customer intimacy—the best total solution for the customer
2. Operational excellence—the best total costs
3. Product leadership—the best product

All that we gain through our BPM approaches is gaining one of these strategic options. Now that so much has been said about BPM, its evolution, and its objective—the question naturally arises: What exactly is business process management? An underlying sense obviously is *management of business processes* with the organization being the primary focus; BPM is defined as

> The achievement of an organization's objectives through the improvement, management and control of essential business process.

There is a consensus among experts regarding this definition of BPM, which has been rephrased "as a management discipline focused on improving corporate performance by managing a company's business processes."

---

[2] Six Sigma was an approach created by Motorola in 1980s but gained popularity owing to General Electric in 1990s. "Six Sigma" essentially implies one output defect being within six standard deviations from the mean process output of a particular process, based either on customer-specified "mean" or industry standards. It typically focuses on relatively small work processes, thus presumes incremental improvement rather than radical change.

Thus, process management is an inherent and underlying theme of "normal" management. It is important for leadership and management to realize that improvement of business process must be continually maintained; there is no finish line for the same.

In essence, business process management is:

- More than just software
- More than just improving or reengineering processes—also deals with managerial issues
- Not just a hype or fad—it is an integral part of management
- More than just modeling—it is also about the implementation and execution of these processes, which requires analysis

Lastly but most importantly, as a management discipline, BPM requires an end-to-end organizational view and a great deal of common sense—either of which often in short supply.

4.4   Drivers and Triggers for BPM

Generic answer regarding the triggers for BPM is definitely "it depends"—on the organization's industrial context, macroeconomic context, its brand positioning context, and organization's process maturity—but it would vary from organization to organization and from situation to situation. However, a few categories of drivers and triggers have been identified and outlined as below.

Category	Drivers and triggers
Organization	• High growth—difficulty coping with high growth or proactively planning for high growth • Mergers and acquisition scenario—these cause the organization to "acquire" additional complexity or necessitate rationalization of processes. The need to retire acquired legacy systems could also contribute. BPM projects enable a process layer to be "placed" across these legacy systems, providing time to consider appropriate conversion strategies • Reorganization or restructuring—changing roles and responsibilities • Change in strategy—deciding to change direction or pace of operational excellence, product leadership, or customer intimacy • Organization objectives or goals are not being met—introduction of process management, linked to organizational strategy, performance measurement, and management of people • Compliance or regulation—for example, organizations currently have to comply with pollution, environment, and forest cover violation norms, hence process projects have been initiated—this process project has provided the platform to launch process improvement or BPM projects • The need for business agility to enable the organization to respond to opportunities as they arise • The need to provide the business with more control of its own destiny

(continued)

Category	Drivers and triggers
Management	• Lack of reliable or conflicting management information—process management and performance management and management will assist • The need to provide managers with more control over their processes • The need for the introduction of a sustainable performance environment • The need to create a culture of high performance • The need to gain the maximum return on investment (RoI) from the existing legacy systems • Budget cuts • The need for the ability to obtain more capacity from existing staff for expansion
Employees	• High turnover of employees, which could be attributed to mundane and repetitive work or the degree of pressure and expectations upon people without adequate support • Training issues with new employees • Low employee satisfaction • The expectation of a substantial increase in the number of employees • Wish to increase employee empowerment • Employees finding it difficult to keep up with continuous change and the growing complexity

Customers/suppliers/partners	• Low satisfaction with service, which could be due to:
	  – High churn rates of staff
	  – Staff unable to answer questions adequately within the required time frames (responsiveness)
	• An unexpected increase in number of customers, suppliers, or partners
	• Long lead times to meet requests
	• An organizational desire to focus upon customer intimacy
	• Customer segmentation or tiered service requirements
	• The introduction and strict enforcement of service levels
	• Major customers, suppliers, and/or partners requiring a unique (different) process
	• The need for a true end-to-end perspective to provide visibility or integration

Product and services	• An unacceptably long lead time to market (lack of business agility) • Poor stakeholder service levels • Each product or service has its own processes, with most of the processes being common or similar • New products or services comprise existing product/service elements • Products or services are complex
Processes	• The need for provision of visibility of processes from an end-to-end perspective • Too many hand-offs or gaps in a process, or no clear process at all • Unclear roles and responsibilities from a process perspective • Quality is poor and the volume of rework is substantial • Processes change too often or not at all • Lack of process standardization • Lack of clear process goals or objectives • Lack of communications and understanding of the end-to-end process by the parties performing parts of the process

(continued)

Category	Drivers and triggers
Information technology	• The introduction of new systems, for, e.g., CRM, ERP, and billing systems • The purchase of BPM automation tools (workflow, document management, business intelligence), and the organization does not know how to best utilize them in a synergistic manner • Phasing out of old application systems • Existing application system overlaps and is not well understood • Introduction of new IT architecture • A view that IT is not delivering according to business expectations • A view that IT costs are way out of control or too expensive • The introduction of Web services

Drivers and triggers for the organization to consider an automated solution may include:

- A high volume of similar and repetitive transactions
- Stability of processes
- A need to complete many calculations within the transaction—application integration
- A critical issue with processing time, i.e., time is of the essence—process integration
- A clear flow of high-volume transactions that need to be passed from one person to another with value addition at each individual
- A need for real-time monitoring of transactions (knowledge of transaction status)
- Transaction or "files" need to be accessible by many parties at the same time
- User-friendly technology
- Qualitative (that includes environment, macro-economy, and society) and quantitative RoI (based on NPV, IRR, and break-even analysis)

4.5 Business Process Modeling

Now that there has been ample deliberation on business process management per se, we would further discuss how to go about doing the same, i.e., prerequisites and methodology for business process management—precisely this activity starts with business process modeling activity. *Business process modeling* is the activity of elaborating an enterprise's processes so that the existing processes can be synthesized and improved. This synthesis and analysis of the process stem from benchmarking against the industry standards, best practices, or customer requirements. This activity is generally performed by business analysts who intend to improve process efficiency and quality. Role of IT isn't imperative in this modeling, though by creation of a process master, IT becomes the common driver for the business process modeling need. Various phases of business process modeling are

(1) *analyze*, (2) *design*, (3) *monitor and prototype pilot*, and (4) *implement*. It is an interesting aspect wherein this business process modeling aspect fit into Deming's PDCA (plan–do–check–act) framework.

Analyze. Analysis of a business process stems from the VMG (vision, mission, goal) framework of a company—where the project goals are detailed; accordingly department and function goals are also detailed down. Here it is to be noted that the project goals are derived from the business goals specified by the VMG framework. Thus the business goals and the benchmark objectives lead to the project goals whose processes are being analyzed in this phase. The benchmarking activity for the project can be internal as well as external. Internal benchmarking is carried out across the SBUs and departments of the firm over time as well as at a particular project instance. External benchmarking is done at industry level and with competitors (not necessarily from same sector, where similar processes in unrelated sector can also be analyzed for benchmarking purpose). Consent from partners is required for the external benchmarking exercise.

Breakdown of this analysis phase is as follows:

- Analyze the current process
- Define process objectives—this is typically derived from the project goals (though sometimes, it maybe distinct).
- Prioritize the processes (mere suggestions are made to the project owner by the business analyst, while former makes the due approval).
- Identification of stakeholders and their goals.
- Synthesize the As-Is process.
- Regulatory requirements compliance check.
- Determine business benefits—evaluate top management support for the project as well as process, and measure each individual's performance against the objectives.
- Analyze the business as well as technical feasibility of the project—this is a resultant of the domain characteristics as well as regulatory requirements and macroeconomic scenario.

Design. Various facets of this phase of business process modeling activity are listed as follows:

- Evaluation of the solutions and various alternatives—this evaluation is carried out through RoI calculation based on break-even analysis, NPV analysis, benchmarking against past executed projects, and qualitative benefits derived from the solution (the qualitative benefits may not be restrictive to the employees and organization and may also include environment, society, and economy in general).
- Prioritization of the To-Be solutions or detailed new processes—estimation of the processes that will be impacted, estimating their impact on business goals, and preparation of risk and impact index.
- Determination of key performance indicators (KPIs)—these are obtained from project goals as well as As-Is process analysis of first phase.

- Risk management plan
- Prototype design and pilot rollout

Monitor and Pilot Prototype. Activities involved in this phase of the modeling activity include the following:

- Identify the critical success factors (CSFs)—these are derived from the KPIs of the "design" phase as well through feedback from MIS reports
- Determine the project implementation structure—identification of the steering committee, detailing the roles and responsibilities, and outlining stakeholder interests in the project goals
- Outlining the roadmap for the rollout—milestones for CSF measurement through MIS reports for each milestone
- Prescribing the rewards and recognition scheme for the project team
- Defining the communication protocol with respect to the reporting structure and the escalation matrix and the procedures involved therein
- Specifying the Go-Live date and completion of the project—which is identified through the CSF attainment

Implementation. In this phase of business process modeling activities include the following:

- Redoing of certain process if required to attain the desired objectives—process improvement process (PIP) may be adopted
- Rolling out of the pilot/prototype to the entire organization
- Measurement of the results through MIS

4.6   Process Management Process

Processes transform inputs to outputs. This transformation is through a series of life cycle stages, each of which can be further broken down into a hierarchy of activities. Some important process attributes are inputs and outputs, participants, entry and exit criteria, activities to be performed, and measurements. Entry and exit criteria define when a process can be executed and exited and hence essentially define the process interfaces. A process may not be usable by a project in its entirety. Tailoring guidelines help projects fit the process to their project in an organized manner. If the process mandates specific tools and methods these must also be identified.

This process focuses on defining an entirely new process or documenting a process that is used but not written down. A new process may be defined:

- When the existing processes are not suitable for a class of projects that are executed regularly and there is extensive tailoring
- When there are major changes to an existing process
- To meet business strategy
- To meet organization-wide improvement goals

- On request from process users
- Based on proactive identification/environmental scanning of beneficial innovations
- To meet customer-specific needs

As stated, process definition proposals may be received from process users. These have to be evaluated and prioritized based on organizational quality and productivity goals and cost–benefits. Senior management authorization must be obtained before process definition is initiated. Process definition must be planned and the plan must address:

- Objectives
- Estimated benefits
- Resources requirements
- Analysis to be performed
- Assumptions
- Risks and mitigation plans
- Schedule

4.6.1 The Activities Involved in Process Management Definition

The following section describes steps involved in process management:

Identify processes to be defined.
Obtain proposals for process definition.
Evaluate process definition proposals for expected cost–benefits.
Prioritize process definition proposals.
Obtain senior management authorization (from MC).
Initiate process definition.
    Plan for process definition.
        Identify resources/working group.
        Define training requirements in processes and process improvements.
        Identify risks and mitigation plans.
        Identify appropriate methods and tools for process definition.
        Identify exit criteria, deliverables, and assumptions.
        Identify how process definition activities will be tracked and monitored by senior management (generally MC review).
        Prepare schedule.
        Group review plan and schedule.
        Baseline plan.
Create a draft sketch of the process.
    Define process.
        Identify lifecycle stages.
        Identify activities to a sufficient level of granularity.

Identify participants.
Identify inputs and outputs.
Identify entry and exit criteria.
Identify measurements and references.
Identify appropriate methods and tools for process execution.
Write overview.
Establish cross-reference to CMM and ISO, if necessary.
Define tailoring guidelines and special considerations.
Document process in process definition template.
Group review process, tailoring guidelines with users review process, and tailoring guidelines.
Review process definition with senior management as necessary.
Generate process definitions in the required format.
Review status with senior management.
   Update status to process users.

After defining the process, implementation needs to be planned and executed properly. An effective implementation can ensure success of a process. Hence, a systematic approach is required for process implementation. The following section describes the activities involved in process implementation.

4.6.2   Process Implementation Activities

Process implementation refers to activities, which must be carried out for piloting and implementing new processes or changes to existing process across the organization. Changes would be classified as either minor or major process changes. In the case of minor process changes, the process definition and proposed changes are reviewed, and the changed process is released with a notification to all the users. If required, orientation is imparted to the users. Implementation of major changes/new processes is more complex. It involves extensive planning, piloting, formal release, training, and organization-wide implementation. Planning is necessary for both piloting and implementation.
   Planning for piloting should address the following:

- Objectives
- Estimated benefits
- Selection criteria for pilot projects
- Identification of pilots
- Resources required for each of the pilots
- Training requirements
- Measurements and mechanism for capturing data
- Analysis to be performed
- Assumptions
- Risks and mitigation plans for pilots
- Schedule

Some of the criteria for selection of projects for pilots are:

- Appropriate project type
- Appropriate life cycle stage
- Project size, i.e., small, medium, and large where necessary
- Project constraints

During the pilot, data is collected to validate the objectives of the pilot. Senior management reviews the status of the pilots. At the end of the pilot, a post-pilot analysis is performed on pilot data to evaluate the benefits quantitatively and qualitatively. Cost–benefit analysis for organization-wide implementation is performed and recommendations presented to senior management for approval and authorization. Plans are drawn up for organization-wide implementation as appropriate.

Based on the pilots, it may be necessary to update the draft processes before organization-wide implementation. The updated processes are then released through a formal release mechanism.

Organization-wide implementation implies executing new projects with changed/new processes or transitioning existing projects to new or changed processes. Some of the existing projects may continue to use the old process.

Planning for implementation should address the following:

- Training requirements.
- Schedule for training (including senior management if necessary) and implementation.
- Pilot the process.
- Plan pilot.
- Identify pilot projects based on selection criteria, if necessary.

Pilot the process.
    Plan pilot.
        Identify pilot projects based on selection criteria, if necessary.
        Define objectives for pilot like quality, productivity, and cycle time improvements.
        Define data collection and analysis plan for the pilots to meet the objectives.
        Define training requirements.
        Identify risks and mitigation plans.
        Identify assumptions.
        Affected managers sign-off pilot plan and senior management authorization.
    Define objectives for pilot like quality, productivity, and cycle time improvements.
        Provide orientation and training to pilot project teams.
        Monitor pilot.
            Collect data.
            Record feedback.
            Record issues.
            Resolve showstopper issues.

Close pilot.
  Perform post-pilot analysis for actual benefits in quality, productivity, and cycle time.
  Perform overall cost–benefit analysis.
  Update draft process definition.
  Conduct group review if the changes are major.
  Baseline update process definitions and bring all QSD documents under configuration management.
Obtain senior management authorization for implementation.
Incorporate process definitions in quality system documentation (QSD).
Release formally.
  Conduct training.
Implement organization-wide
  Plan for implementation.
  Provide consultation support as required.
  Provide orientation to project teams.
  Implement process in projects, and monitor benefits.
Update status periodically or on an event-driven basis to senior management and process users.
Update actual benefits of the process improvement to senior management.

- Define data collection and analysis plan for the pilots to meet the objectives.
- Define training requirements.
- Identify risks and mitigation plans.
- Identify assumptions.
- Affected managers sign-off pilot plan and senior management authorization.
- Provide orientation and training to pilot project teams.
- Monitor pilot.
- Collect data.
- Record feedback.
- Record issues.
- Resolve showstopper issues.
- Close pilot.
- Perform post-pilot analysis for actual benefits in quality, productivity, and cycle time.
- Perform overall cost–benefit analysis.
- Update draft process definition.
- Conduct group review if the changes are major.
- Baseline update process definitions and bring all QSD documents under configuration management.
- Obtain senior management authorization for implementation.
- Incorporate process definitions in quality system documentation (QSD).
- Release formally.
- Conduct training.
- Implement organization-wide.
- Plan for implementation.

- Provide consultation support as required.
- Provide orientation to project teams.
- Implement process in projects and monitor benefits.
- Update status periodically or on an event-driven basis to senior management and process users.
- Update actual benefits of the process improvement to senior management.

Generally, work groups consisting of experienced project personnel with necessary expertise are formed for defining the processes. The work groups perform process definition activities. The status is reported to senior management and process users on a regular basis (through bulletin boards, meetings, Intranet, etc.).

The process management process comprises of all activities that are needed to define, implement, change, improve, and maintain the processes in an organization. The general life of a process is pictorially represented as

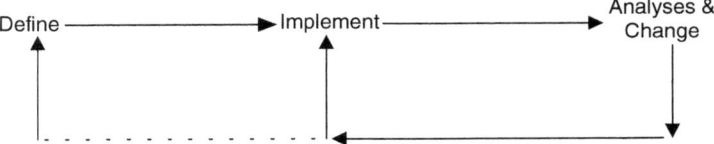

That is, a process is initially defined (standardized). Then, the process is implemented in the organization. In this phase the usage of the process is institutionalized. Once the process is implemented, it may be changed and the changed process may again need to be implemented. This cycle, which is based on the PDCA cycle of Deming, is a continuous process. Process management process describes how to process definition, process implementation, and process change.

4.6.3   Improving Processes Through Change Management

Process change management refers to activities which are carried out to identify need for changes to existing processes, and to process the change requests for further action.

Changes may be triggered by means of:

- Organizational business goals
- Inputs from organization-wide improvement initiatives like defect prevention, technology incorporation/changes
- Process improvement or change proposals from process users on QSD elements
- Introduction of new methods/technologies based on proactive identification/ environmental scanning of beneficial innovations
- Introduction of new tools
- Evaluation of processes/tools in limited use for organization-wide adoption

- Feedback from internal and external audits and assessments
- Lacunae in existing processes
- Feedback obtained from process users
- Analysis of process usage information obtained via the process assets
- Best practices and related seminars
- Analysis of Project performance data and process capability baselines (PCBs)
- Inputs from projects based on their defect prevention activities, tools introduction and process changes
- Implementation of models like ISO and CMM

All proposals/change requests are logged and classified as major or minor changes. Changes, which have minor or no effect on current project activities, constitute minor process changes. Some examples are closing of minor NCRs, structural reorganization of the process documentation, correction of cosmetic errors, elaborating for better clarity, updating missing information, and first-time documentation of current processes. Changes, which have a major effect on the current project activities, constitute major process changes. Major changes need planning, senior management review, and authorization. Changes, once authorized, can be incorporated by modifying existing processes. Minor changes can be baselined after review. Major changes however need to be piloted before finalization. In all cases, process users are kept informed of the status of the proposals.

Process change requests identified for incorporation into processes trigger the generation of modification requests by SEPG. All authorized major process change proposals are incorporated into the organization-wide process improvement plan maintained by SEPG. Minor changes are reviewed and authorized by SEPG manager.

Whenever new processes/major modifications to the existing processes are introduced, the projects that were using the process prior to the change may continue to use the previous version. In case of long running projects, the projects shall transition to the new/modified processes over a period of time (about 6 months).

Any business process, thus, will follow a framework of ETVXMF:

E—Entry
T—Tasks (activities)
V—Verification (review)
X—Exit
M—Measurement
F—Feedback

4.7 Process Life Cycle

Earlier we have detailed on why and how part of business process management, i.e., why it is required, when to do the same, and methodology for the same—business process modeling and its detailed phases. Now that so much is being said about analyzing, modeling, and reengineering the processes—we further delve into what all stages does the process goes through so that any analysis, transformation, redesign, and radical improvement can be attempted upon the same. Thus the objective of this phase of discussion would be to detail the phases through which a process attains maturity.

4.7.1   Process Life Cycle Stages

There are four life cycle stages for a process. They are:

Process definition
Process implementation
Process analysis and change/process consolidation
Process decay

It has been observed that a process evolves along with an organization or stated differently any organization can be said to be an aggregation of processes. An organization's life cycle follows a trajectory as outlined below.

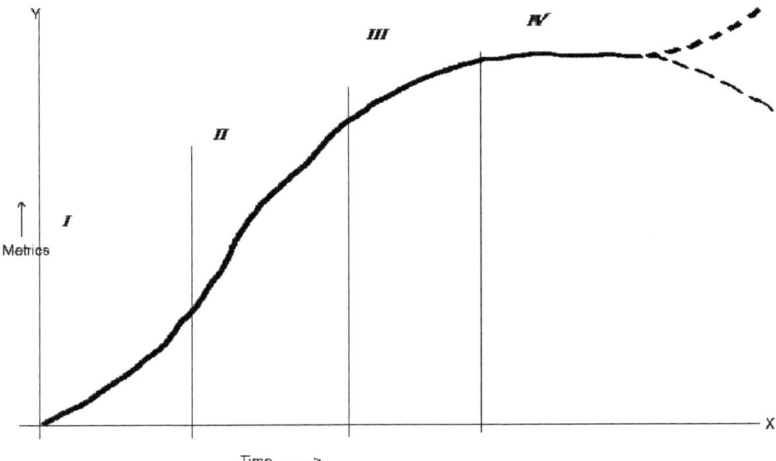

The figure shows an organization's evolution with time, the plot showing metrics for evaluating this growth. This metrics for evaluating an organization can be its process definition, its HR function stability, production process evolution, etc. An organization's metrics as shown in the four stages is typically reflected through similar stages of its process life cycle. In the following sections, we will dissect an organization's evolution which has been divided into four stages as shown along with the corresponding levels of process' evolution and maturity (in stage IV).

4.7.1.1   Stage I

In this stage an organization has kicked off its operation and in its formative stages. Hence, organization's focus areas for its business are:

- Turnover
- Customer acquiring and satisfaction of acquired customers
- Employee retention

Thus the process orientation, when an organization is in this stage, is chaotic, and all processes are characterized as ad hoc processes. There is almost no institutionalization or standardization of process. Even at individual level, processes cannot be predictive. Due to this speculative aspect associated with processes, this process evolution phase can be labeled as chaotic and ad hoc.

4.7.1.2   Stage II

An organization is characterized by its growth trajectory in this stage. Hence the metrics for evaluating the performance of its growth are different from that in stage I. The metrics for attainment of business goals are:

- Quality consistency (leading indicator)
- Turnover
- Customer satisfaction
- Repeat business (lagging indicator)

Corresponding to this phase of organization, process life cycle stage is associated with individualized processes. These individualized processes may range from being purely at individual level to either department or function level or at an activity level. Say, for example, a particular sales team follows weekly updating of sales data, while another may follow fortnightly schedule (thus specific to the department/function). This attribute of process maturity can be said as "go ask John" indicating about the subjective aspect of process maturity.

4.7.1.3   Stage III

An organization's productivity and other metrics are approaching a plateau. Hence the metrics for business goals in this stage are:

- Repeat business
- Productivity (leading indicator)
  - Process improvement process (PIP)
  - Automation tools
- Customer satisfaction
- Turnover
- Profits (lagging indicator)

Process maturity in this stage of an organization shows institutionalization through continuous improvement and standardization across organization. The institutionalized processes are now maintained in repository, adhere to the process capability baseline (PCB) and have been adapted through continuous improvement, hence include the best practices and corrective measures from earlier process stages. There are standardized processes, consistent and defined institutional processes, predictable process performance, cross-functional workflows, and processes defined; product quality and process quality thresholds are the metrics for measuring process performance in this stage.

4.7.1.4 Stage IV

In this stage an organization innovates and expands its offering. Hence typically there is focus on R&D. The metrics for attaining business goals in this stage are:

* R&D
    - No. of new products and services rolled out
    - No. of ideas converted to products
    - Percentage of turnover spent on R&D

* Turnover
* Repeat business
* Customer satisfaction
* Cost of production (often linked to quality of product)

Process maturity is optimal in this stage of process life cycle. Through continuous improvement processes have attained maturity, and hereon only radical changes in process definition and execution can help attain business success. Continual changes are introduced through process improvement process (PIP), or radical changes through process reengineering or Six Sigma implementation, in this phase of process life cycle.

Process life cycle management (PLCM) aptly fits into the Deming's PDCA framework. It is essentially the role of top management when an organization stages its transition from stage I to stage IV, wherein process maturity is stable, i.e., there is highest order of predictability, repeatability, and high confidence level in this maturity stage. Through continuous change management initiatives and constant support, this transition can be smoothly eased out across the organization. This change management apart from impacting business goals also factors in environment changes, macroeconomic changes, and the changes in business models. Business intelligence tools form an integral aid in this change management initiative.

4.8 Process Maturity

Maturity in any organization shows its ability to perform. Maturity assessments measure the degree to which an organization utilizes its processes, people, tools, products, and management. Assessments depict how the organization compares itself to its competitors or other organizations. It also helps to manage an organization and evolve it. It figures out opportunities to identify required standards, processes, and procedures improvement and facilitate improvements continuously.

Almost all maturity models define five levels an organization goes through as it becomes more competent. The competence increases at each maturity level organizational. The following figure shows the five stages.

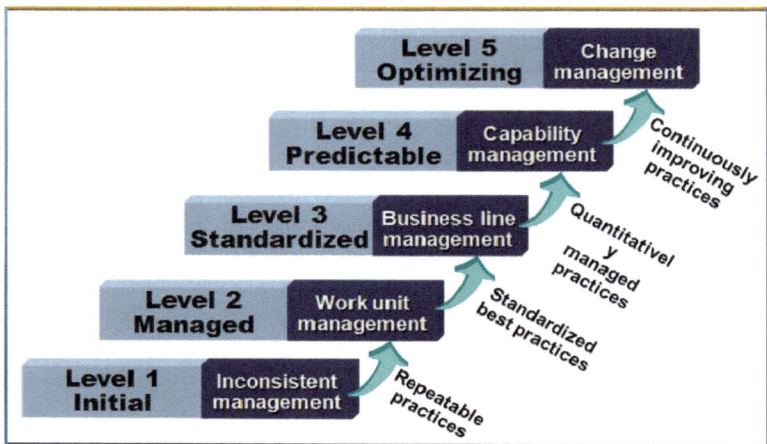

Once an organization determines on which stage it belongs, it decides the best method for implementation. These methods can broadly be divided into three types:

• Single-process approach
• Multi-process approach
• All processes approach

It is often prescribed that at low maturity level single-process approach should be adopted and it must change for organizations showing high level of maturity. The specific details can be shown in the following table for different organizations.

Approach	Technique	Comments
Single process	Problem management	Identify and solve most "adverse/painful" issues
	Incident management	Improve customer service and perception and set the stage for enhancements in future
	Change management	Focus on establishing control of changes and improve quality of service

(continued)

(continued)

Approach	Technique	Comments
Multi-process	CSIP	Improve more than one area affecting stakeholders and business requirements directly
	Customer satisfaction/ business impact	Using customer dissatisfaction and business impact analysis to identify starting point
	SWOT analysis	Identify starting point by strengths, weaknesses, opportunities, and threats (SWOT) analysis
	Benchmark	Assess organization and compare it to external and internal organizations
	Service target	Establish targets for improvement to services by involving customers; implement as needed to meet targets
All processes	Business/IT strategy	Incremental improvement driven by business
	CSI	Improvement driven from CSI
	Benchmark	Use benchmarking for incremental improvement

The benefits are plenty as shown below, but organizations need to learn how to do their assessment:

- Cost reduction
- Improved management ability
- Awareness of organizational capability
- Staff motivation
- Improved likelihood of success
- Better business/IT alignment
- Better decision making

The details of the process maturity model and the issues at each stage are being shown below for organizations:

4.8.1   Level 1: Initial Organizations

The following are the characteristics at level 1:

- Undisciplined: Few repeatable processes, often sacrificed under pressure.
- Individualistic: People rely on personal methods for accomplishing work.
- Inconsistent: Little preparation for managing a work unit.
- Inefficient: Few measures for analyzing effectiveness of practices.
- Stagnant: No foundation or commitment for improvement.

4.8.2   Level 2: Managed Organizations

- Committed: Executives commit organization to improving operations.
- Proactive: Managers take responsibility for work unit operations and performance.
- Managed: Commitments are balanced with resources.
- Repeatable: Work units use local procedures that have proven effective.
- Responsible: Work units are capable of meeting their commitments.

The following diagram shows the process areas in a level 2 organization.

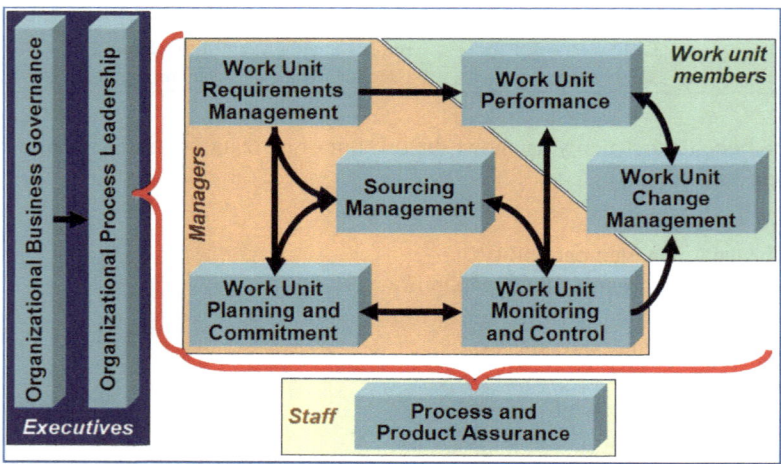

4.8.3   Level 3: Standardized Organizations

- Organizational: Integrate end-to-end business processes across functions; perform in silos.
- Established: Establish standard processes from best practices in work units.
- Adaptable: Standard processes tailored for best use in different circumstances.
- Leveraged: Common measures and processes promote organizational learning.
- Professional: Organizational culture emerges from common practices.

The following figure depicts the transition a firm faces while going from level 2 to level 3. As shown, the confederated work units gradually become standard processes which are further tailored to get absorbed as enterprise-wide end-to-end integrated business processes.

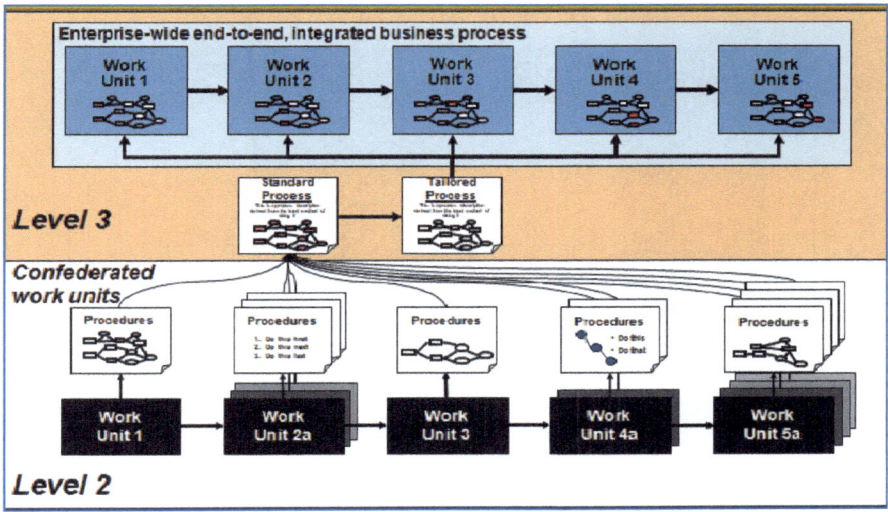

The level 3 process areas and the link between different work unit members and management are illustrated below.

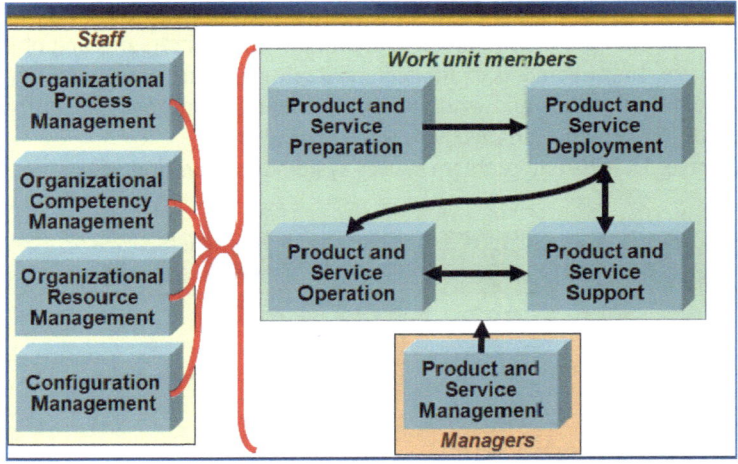

4.8.4   Level 4: Predictable Organizations

The following are the characteristics of the organization at level 4:

- Quantitative: Process variation, performance, and capability understood quantitatively.
- Stable: Variation reduced through reuse, mentoring, and statistical mgt.

- Empowered: Process data empowers staff to manage their own work.
- Multifunctional: Functional processes reengineered as roles in business processes.
- Predictable: Outcomes predictable from subprocess capability and performance.

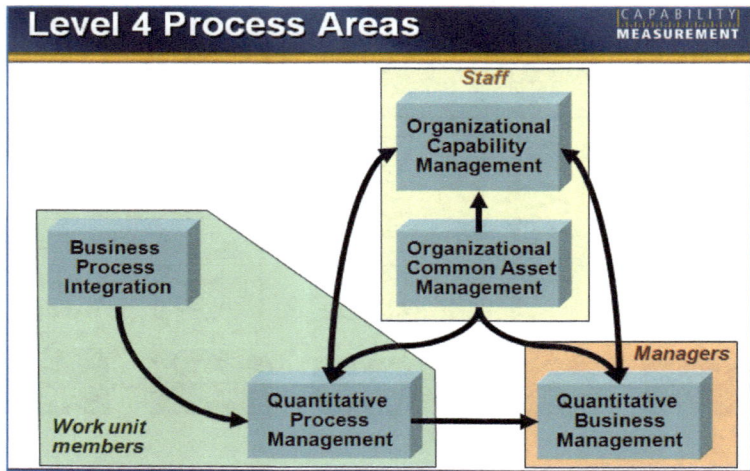

4.8.5   Level 5: Optimizing Organizations

The traits of an organization playing at level 5 are as follows:

- Proactive: Improvements planned to achieve business strategies and objectives.
- Systematic: Improvements evaluated and deployed using orderly methods.
- Continual: Individuals and workgroups continuously improve capability.
- Aligned: Performance aligned across the organization.
- Preventive: Defects and problem causes systematically eliminated.

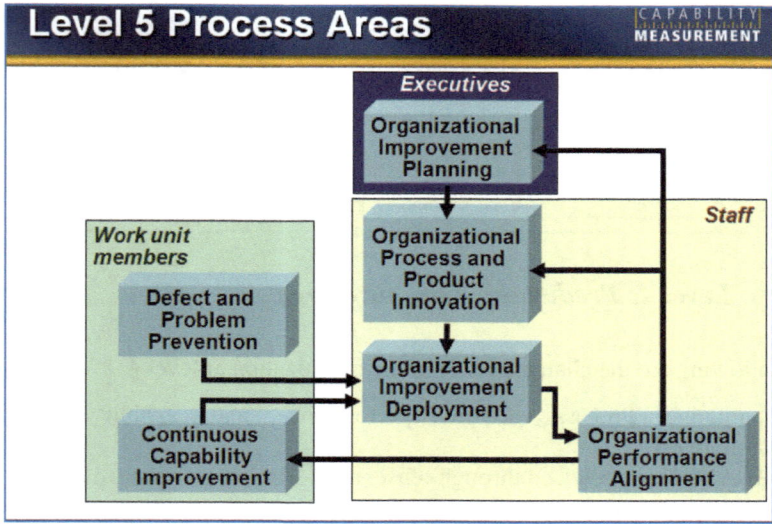

4.9 Case Study

4.9.1 Siemens: An example of Achieving/Implementing Process Maturity

The following example shows how Siemens was able to implement process maturity at each stage. The following were its issues and challenges faced:

- From maturity level 2 to 3, organization is more reactive to the past as compared to the future.
- Although organizations know when corrective actions must be taken, organization may not be able to predict the effectiveness of these corrective actions.
- Its focus was to share key steps in defining and implementing high maturity level 4 processes based on our experience and lessons learnt.

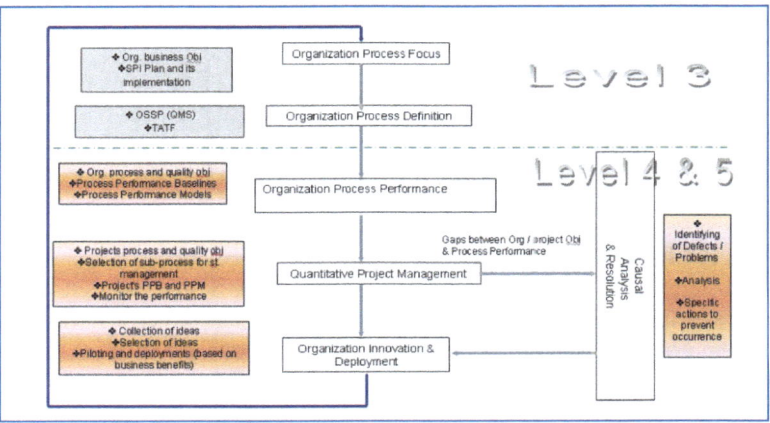

4.9.1.1 High Maturity Process Implementation Evaluation

In Siemens the higher management carried out an end-to-end evaluation for the high maturity process implementation. These were based on four aspects:

- Balance Score Card: Organization's strategy for its vision and its As-Is versus the To-Be model.
- Business Goal Matrix: It specifies selection of key indicators to measure the progress of strategy achieved.
- Process Baseline Report: It determines current capability to achieve vision/goal, and scope of improvement (short and long term).
- Process Prediction Model: It evaluates certainty to achieve goals based on current capability.

The following figure shows a quick view of a high maturity organization like Siemens both at project level and organizational level.

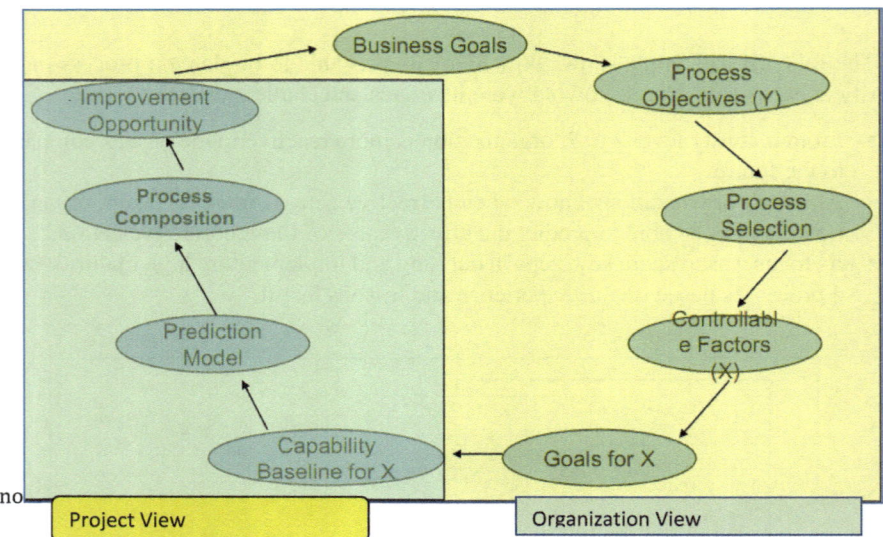

4.9.1.2   Business Goal Matrix

The next step for the senior management was to evaluate and select business goals critical to customer and business. The following diagram shows the business goal matrix.

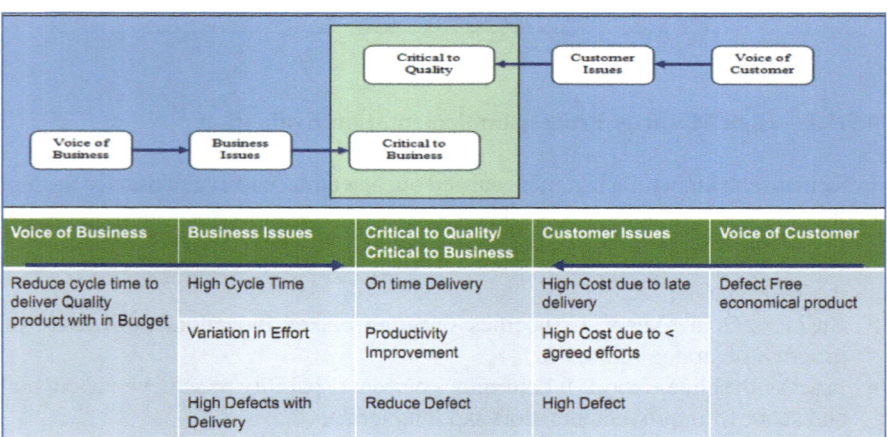

4.9.1.3   Organization Procedure for Process and Quality Performance

In this step the measures for common understanding to avoid ambiguity were defined for Siemens. Measurement procedures were established that helped in:

- Defining the process and measurement system to determine organization process performance
- Defining goal for process as well as individual controllable factor

Process objective	Processes	Definition	Scope of measurement	Controllable X factors
Schedule variance should not be greater than 5%	Schedule estimation and monitoring	Difference in between planned date of completion with actual date of completion	At each milestone	Actual efforts Skill level
Improve productivity by 5% every quarter	Engineering	Ratio of actual efforts and actual size	At each milestone	Actual efforts Skill level Review methods Review cycles
Delivered defect density <1 defect/per unit	Review, testing estimation, and monitoring	Less than 1 defects(review +testing defects) per actual unit size	At each milestone	Actual efforts Skill level Review methods Review cycles

4.9.1.4   High Maturity Process Evaluation

It is based on the fact that high maturity process is evolved and not revolutionized. The figure aptly shows that.

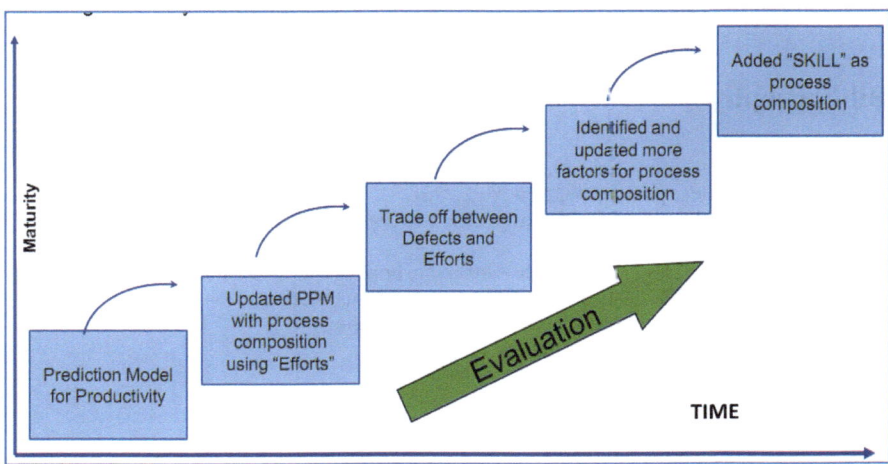

4.10 Summary

1. The immaturity of business processes strictly limits the value and success of IT systems.
2. The process maturity framework is a proven roadmap for improving process capability and unlocking the full value of IT systems.
3. The business process maturity model enables greater fidelity between the actual performance of business processes and their model-based representations.

4.10.1 The Golden Rules for High Maturity Process Implementation

- Business goal must be validated and prioritize with the help of business goal matrix plan.
- Involve practitioners, constitute various task forces such as:
  - Metric Task Force (MTF): Having members with good skills on statistics and business
  - Tailoring Approval Task Force (TATF): Good process knowledge
- Support from management and buying from project stakeholders is critical.
- Select and prioritize X factors based on co-relationship.
- Must have minimum 15 data points to determine the data distribution, stability, and capability.
- Implement mistake proofing in project quality reporting. Data quality is very critical else prediction will mislead.
- Encourage sharing the implementation high maturity practices and lessons learnt by each project on a periodic basis.
- Constitute process award to encourage of process implementation.
- Implement high maturity processes with evolutionary mode.
- Don't implement all controllable factors in "one go."

Bibliography

Jeston J, Nelis J (2007) Business process management—practical guidelines to successful implementations. Elsevier publication, New York, USA

Process Life Cycle Engineering http://www.usc.edu/dept/ATRIUM/Papers/Process_Life_Cycle.html

Process Life Cycle and Project Life Cycle Partnership http://www.bpminstitute.org/articles/article/article/the-process-life-cycle-and-project-life-cycle-partnership.html

http://www.itsmsolutions.com/newsletters/DITYvol2iss11.htm

http://www.comp.nus.edu.sg/~atreyi/papers/KMmat.pdf

Chapter 5
Organization Life Cycle and Its Relationship with Process Reengineering

5.1 Learning Objectives

The learning objectives of this chapter are

- To understand various models of organization life cycle and to suggest a generic model for the same
- To understand the characteristics and metrics of an organization during various stages of its life cycle
- To study and analyze various frameworks which can help in understanding organization evolution
- To understand the various reasons through which an organization can move from stage 3 of OLC to stage 2
- To understand the mapping of process life cycle with organization life cycle
- To study and analyze organization life cycle of nonprofit organizations
- To understand OLC through Computer Science Corporation case study

5.2 Introduction

Research on organizational development and structure has revealed that organizations like living organisms go through a development life cycle and they undergo very repetitive and predictable patterns of behavior throughout. At each stage of development, the organization has to face a new set of challenges, solving which it progresses through the next stage. The growth of the organization from one stage to another is characterized by solving the challenges faced at each stage which arises from the growth of the company and the external changes in the competitors, technology, markets, political, and the general external environment. Radical changes in leadership, management, and the way of thinking are required to balance control and flexibility to keep the pace of the progress. Failure to understand this might plunge the company into premature aging.

S. Mohapatra, *Business Process Reengineering*, Management for Professionals,   95
DOI 10.1007/978-1-4614-6067-1_5, © Springer Science+Business Media New York 2013

5.2.1   Organizational Life Cycle Model

Organizational life cycle (OLC) is a model that captures these patterns in the different stages of the life cycle. It is based on the biological metaphor (like living organisms) with a regular pattern of birth, growth, maturity, decline, and death. Similarly organizations go through several stages of growth, maturity, decline, etc. In order to understand the organizational development, several models have been proposed till now. Following are some of the important OLC models (http://faculty. fuqua.duke.edu/~willm/Classes/PhD/PhD_2008_2009_LongStrat/Readings/Class04_GrowthTheories/QuinnCameron1983.pdf).

5.2.2   Downs Model: Motivation Based

In the initial literature on OLCs, the focus was on government organizations. Downs gave a model for government bureaus with three main stages of development:

* In the initial stages, government bureaus have to struggle for autonomy and hence during this stage they focus on building legitimacy.
* The second stage is characterized by rapid expansion.
* The third stage of deceleration typically has formalization of rules and procedures. Predictability and coordination are most emphasized during this stage.

5.2.3   Lippitt and Schmidt Model: Management Concerns

Lippitt and Schmidt developed the earliest models on OLCs with a focus on the private sector. The model suggests that corporations' progress through three stages of development and the critical management concerns change as they move from one stage to another:

* *Birth*: The organization learns to become viable and creates an operating system.
* *Youth*: The corporation struggles to maintain stability in this stage. Reputation is also one of the major concerns.
* *Maturity*: The corporation works towards domain expansion at the same time focusing on agility (uniqueness and adaptability).

5.2.4   Scott Model: Strategy and Structure

Scott model based on the strategy and structure of the corporation is based on three distinct forms of corporate structures following a sequence:

* *Stage 1*: No formal structure, personal control, rewards are paternalistic, and mostly a single product.

- *Stage 2*: They are more characterized by functional systems, impersonal reward systems, etc.
- *Stage 3*: Their focus shifts towards R&D; they have multiple product lines and diverse markets.

5.2.5 Greiner's Model: Crisis Leading to Transition

According to Greiner, there are five organizational stages, each of which being followed by a Revolution. Only through solving the problems in the transitional phase an organization can move to the next phase.

- *Stage 1*: *Entrepreneurial and creativity stage.* There arises a need to rationalize organizational activities, overcoming the crisis of which organizations move to the next stage.
- *Stage 2*: *Growth through direction or rationalized leadership.* The main crisis that ought to happen here is that of autonomy from which arises the need of decentralizing decision making.
- *Stage 3*: *Growth through delegation.* The main crisis is the crisis of control because of nonintegrated goals in autonomous subunits which begin to emerge together post this phase.
- *Stage 4*: *Growth through coordination.* Project teams are formed and restructuring is done. This phase ends with red-tapism which leads to the next stage.
- *Stage 5*: *Growth through collaboration.* The organization is characterized by agility (organizational flexibility, spontaneity in management, etc.). The major crisis that can be expected is information overload and psychological saturation for which Greiner does not propose a solution.

5.2.6 Torbert's Model: Organizational Mind-Set

Torbert's model is based on the mentality of the members—i.e., the organization progresses with the changes in the mentality of the members. Organizational members become more aware of the causal factors and the organizational dynamics and they are able to work on the personal and interpersonal effectiveness. Although he does not specify how organizations move from one phase to another, he explains the change in organizational effectiveness in each stage. According to this model, the organization moves from stages of individuality, then to informality, and then there are problems with the group unity, and final stages are characterized by a sense of collectivity.

5.2.7 Lyden: Functional Focus

According to Lyden, organizations lay emphasis on functional problems that they face at each stage:

- *Innovation*: The organization adapts to and creates a niche in the external environment. (In highly stable environments, this stage may be characterized by goal attainment.)
- *Resource acquisition*: The main focus is on that and also on developing workflow procedures.
- *Goal attainment*: The next stages switch to goal attainment and optimization.
- *Pattern maintenance*: The final stage is characterized by pattern maintenance and structure institutionalization.

5.2.8 Katz and Kahn: Organizational Structure

This model is based on the organizational structural changes that occur as the organization develops:

- *Primitive system stage*: The production system is based on the cooperative organizational structure.
- *Stable organization structure*: It focuses on coordination and control. There are authority and maintenance systems to work towards this goal.
- *Elaboration of structure*: Adaptive systems are developed to deal with the changes in the external environment.

5.2.9 Adizes: Organizational Activities

This model focuses on organizational activities—as the organization develops, the focus of the organization shifts from one activity to another. In the initial stages, they would focus on entrepreneurial activity (E), then the focus towards efficiency in production results (P). Formalization of procedures and administration activities take importance in the next stage. Organizational decline occurs because of the overemphasis on administration and stability. This is the only model that emphasizes both on the developmental and declining phases.

5.2.10 Kimberly's Model

Kimberly studied the organizational development of a medical school and modeled the OLC based on it.

- *Stage 1*: Before the organization is actually formed, it involves formation of ideology and marshalling of the resources.
- *Stage 2*: Hiring staff which is the "prime-mover" of the business and other strategic activities.

- *Stage 3*: The organizational identity is formed; a sense of commitment is formed; and there is high physical, financial, and emotional investment from its members.
- *Stage 4*: Institutionalization where the rules and procedures are formed. The organization becomes more rigid, conservative, and predictable as it starts responding to external environment and pressures.

5.3 A Generic Organization Life Cycle Model

The generic model of organization life cycle consists of four stages (Fig. 5.1):

- Stage 1: Birth stage
- Stage 2: Growth stage
- Stage 3: Maturity stage
- Stage 4: Decline/revitalization stage

The four stages are explained in detail below:

5.3.1 Stage 1: Birth Stage

Birth stage is normally characterized by a potential technological change which can be exploited for business purposes. This opportunity could lead to a new start-up venture or an existing organization could form a new venture through a merger/joint venture. An entrepreneur who identifies the new market need or an improved product that could meet existing needs is the center of this stage. He gathers resources and produces and sells the product by himself. When the operational tasks exceed his capacity, it gives rise to actual organization.

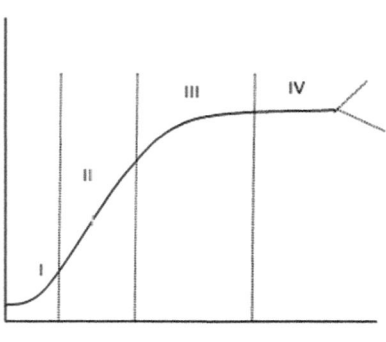

Fig. 5.1 OLC model

Three main forces at this stage are imperative to the successful development of the organization:

- Personality of the founding team (mission, vision, and the passion)
- Time and place of origin (the political, technological, and social climate—Does it welcome the product/offering of the company?)
- Human capital

5.3.2   Stage 2: Growth Stage

At this stage, the organization concentrates more on growth rather than profits. Hence it's characterized by rapid growth giving rise to the need for formal rules and procedures. Although not totally efficient, there are informal processes and procedures. Management concentrates towards goal achievement rather than efficiency and optimization. The marketing department is at the core driving the organization and setting targets.

5.3.3   Stage 3: Maturity Stage

At this stage, the organizational processes take shape and become mature. The organization works towards optimizing its efforts and increasing process effectiveness. The profits are stable and the organization works on the core competencies. Operations take the center stage at this point and the organization is completely process driven. Professional management team takes care of management and the organizational structure is well defined.

5.3.4   Stage 4: Decline/Revitalization Stage

The distinction between decline in the performance and absolute performance is subtle and hence evidence of a crisis becomes elusive. Absolute decline is when the firm outrightly loses market share; on the other hand stagnation (gradual performance decline) can be difficult to identify. Institutionalization of processes and the success achieved out of it lead to complacency. The organization starts to lose its agility. If unnoticed, it might lead to the irreversible loses. Hence at this stage, organizations go through radical rethinking and major restructuring of processes through BPR efforts.

5.4 Organization Characteristics and Metrics During OLC Stages

5.4.1 Organization Characteristics During OLC Stages

Characteristics of an organization vary according to its life stage in organization life cycle. The following table highlights the important characteristics of an organization during various stages of its life cycle (http://www.new.org/newsnotes/previousissues/issue12/LCycleStages.pdf; http://www.rmci.ase.ro/Logir./no8vol4/Vol8_No4_Article1.pdf; http://managementhelp.org/org_thry/org_cycl.htm):

Characteristic	Birth (stage 1)	Growth (stage 2)	Maturity (stage 3)	Decline/revitalize (stage 4)
Age and size	Young and small	Older and large	Older and largest	Once large
Bureaucracy	Non-bureaucratic	Pre-bureaucratic	Bureaucratic	Very bureaucratic
Goal	Survival	Growth	Internal stability, market expansion	Reputation, complete organization
Goal specificity	Operational and short run	Less operational, more general	Nonoperational, general, long run	Nonoperational, financial, strategic, focused
Orientation	Production	Production and marketing	Financial	Financial and R&D
Growth rate	Inconsistent but improving	Rapid	Slowing	Declining
Division of Labor	Overlapping tasks	Few departments	Many departments with well-defined job descriptions	Changing job description
Centralization	One-person rule	Department heads	Top management heavy	Top management heavy
Formalization	No written rules	Few written rules	Policy and procedure manuals	Change in policy and procedure manuals
Administration	No professional staff	Increasing professional and staff support	Large professional, support, clerical, and maintenance staff	Large professional, support, clerical, and maintenance staff. Focus on R&D staff
Internal systems	Nonexistent	Budget and information system	Control systems in place. Extensive planning, financial and support system	Well-designed internal systems. Changes in internal systems take place

(continued)

Characteristic	Birth (stage 1)	Growth (stage 2)	Maturity (stage 3)	Decline/revitalize (stage 4)
Communication and planning	Informal and face to face. Very little planning	Moderately formal. Budgets are there	Very formal. 5-year plan. Rules and regulations in place	Very formal. Change in planning
Decision making method	Individual judgment, entrepreneurial	Professional management, analytical tools used	Professional management	Professional management, bargaining
Lateral team and task force required for coordination	None	Top leaders and some use of integrator staff	High use of lateral teams at lower levels	Lateral teams at lower levels but new projects are in the hands of professional staff
Product/services	Single product/ service	Multiple product/ service with variations	Line of product/ service	Multiple lines of product/service
Reward and control systems	Personal, paternalistic	Personal, contribution to success	Impersonal and formalized systems	Extensive and tailored to product or department
Innovation	By owner-manager	By employees and manager	By separate innovation group	By institutionalized R&D group
Top management style	Individualistic, entrepreneurial *(generalists)*	Charismatic, direction-giving *(specialists)*	Delegation with control, team approach *(strategists)*	Team approach, attack with bureaucracy *(strategists, planners)*
Influence of environment	Great, organic, flexible, personalized, entire organization reacts	Somewhat predictable, knowable	Predictable and controllable	Predictability decreases

5.4.2 Organization Metrics and Tools/Techniques During OLC Stages

Depending on the goal of the organization, different metrics are used to measure the performance of the organization during various stages of its life cycle. The following table illustrates the various metrics and tools and techniques used during OLC stages:

	Birth (stage 1)	Growth (stage 2)	Maturity (stage 3)	Decline/revitalize (stage 4)
Metrics	• Turnover	• Turnover	• Cost of production	• Turnover
	• Customer acquisition	• Customer satisfaction	• Productivity	• Repeat business
	• Customer satisfaction	• Quality	• Customer satisfaction	• Customer satisfaction
	• Employee retention	• Repeat business	• Repeat business	• Cost of production
			• Turnover	• Productivity
			• Profit	• R&D
				• No. of new products
				• No. of new ideas converted to product
				• % of turnover as R&D budget
Tools and techniques	• Brainstorming	• Balance scorecard	• Benchmarking	• Brainstorming
	• SWOT	• Scenario analysis	• Scenario analysis	• Benchmarking
				• Scenario analysis

5.4.3   Action Steps to Be Taken During OLC Stages

The action steps to be taken during various stages of OLC are different. Following are the various action steps to be taken during various stages of OLC (http://tools. iscvt.org/_media/advocacy/wiki/organizational_life_cycle.doc?id=advocacy%3 Awiki%3Acraft_campaign_sidelinks&cache=cache):

1. *Stage 1 action steps.* The action steps of stage1 (birth) are

   • To develop an idea and a product
   • To develop preliminary systems of an organization
   • To develop the leadership skills of other people in the organization
   • To invite and accept investors and more experienced leaders for the organization

2. *Stage 2 action steps.* The action steps of stage 2 (growth) are

   • To take on more challenges
   • To accept the responsibility of your action or inaction
   • To experiment
   • To learn from each other and to be guided by experienced persons in the organization
   • To take appropriate risks

3. *Stage 3 action steps.* The action steps of stage 3 (maturity) are

- To share your wisdom and experiences with others
- To handover responsibility to others
- To set an example for the renewal of the organization

4. *Stage 4 action steps.* The action steps of stage 4 (decline/revitalization) are

- To experiment with new things
- To develop a new organizational leadership and a new strategic focus

5.4.4   Effect of Organization Life Cycle on Board of Directors

The role of board of directors (BoD) changes with the organization's phase of development. The following are the board-role implications of the four phases of OLC (http://tools.iscvt.org/_media/advocacy/wiki/organizational_life_cycle.doc?id= advocacy%3Awiki%3Acraft_campaign_sidelinks&cache=cache):

1. *Stage 1: Birth*—During infancy stage, board is composed of founders. Board members tend to be service providers. In this stage, there is very little planning as the needs is more obvious. Board carries out fund-raising activities as required and lays out policies. Evaluation focuses on present.
2. *Stage 2: Growth*—During growth stage, there is more staff to do the support work. But still the focus of the board is on operations. Board feels a need of more formal systems, but they are reluctant to make large changes in the organization. This reluctance is strong when the organization is experiencing program successes.
3. *Stage 3: Maturity*—During this stage, bulk of service and support is provided by the staff. Board struggles with the changing roles. Board is still providing services, but now the major attention area of board is addressing governance issues and finances.
4. *Stage 4: Decline/revitalize*—During this stage, the board have formally established roles and responsibilities. However, crisis situation may require a change in these roles and responsibilities. The focus of the board is to provide a new strategic direction to the organization. Board does whatever is necessary to meet the needs of the organization.

5.5   Framework to Determine Organization Evolution: S-Curve

5.5.1   S-Curve: A Framework to Determine
Stages of Organizational Evolution

S-Curve (http://dspace.mit.edu/bitstream/handle/1721.1/29889/47918846.pdf? sequence =1) is a framework which can help in identifying when is an organization going to exhaust its current way of operating. S-Curve illustrates two things:

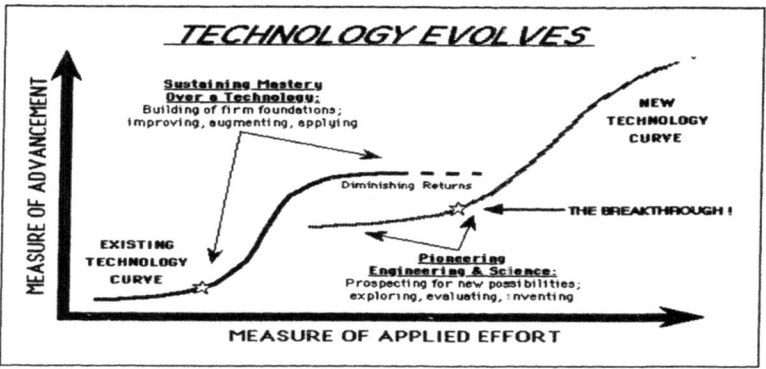

Fig. 5.2 The S-Curve

- Evolution of a given technology/process
- Breakthrough event when a new and superior approach becomes necessary and viable

For a given technology, the evolution process traces the following steps:

- Little advancement with initial efforts and subsequently, technology becomes successful.
- At this success point (lower knee of the curve), technology finally demonstrates its full utility.
- Once this point is reached and the technology becomes widely established, significant progress and improvements are made.
- Eventually, technology reaches its limits. Any additional and continued efforts result in little additional advancement only (Fig. 5.2).

These steps, *demonstrating efforts expended* versus *performance gains*, take place in the shape of an S-Curve.

If an organization wants to go beyond the limits presented by the top of predecessor's S-Curve, the organization must search for new alternatives. There will be another S-Curve associated with the new alternative. If the new alternative demonstrates a viability to surpass the limits of its predecessor, it is a breakthrough event.

S-Curve can be used as a metaphor to determine how stages of organizational evolution occur. If you pay too much attention to the current or continuing issues of the organization, its effort to work on new ideas will be severally hampered. Therefore, the organization may not be able to identify the next paradigm shift.

5.6 Mapping of OLC to Growth in Organisms: Principle of Homeokinesis

5.6.1 Homeokinesis: A Framework to Map Growth in Organization to Growth in Organisms

The process of growth in a business organization is very similar to that of growth in an organism (http://epress.anu.edu.au/info_systems/mobile_devices/ch11s04.html). An analogy can be drawn between the two. The process of growth in a business organization follows the following steps: An increase in profit of a business organization results in an improvement in return on investment (ROI). With improved ROI, the organization attracts more funds from investors. These funds can be used to reinvest for expansion, and to gain more market control. This will further increase the profit of the organization. However, there are limiting factors like increase in competition, etc. which will stop this *positive feedback loop*.

Similarly, an organism cannot perpetually maintain growth and it cannot ensure its survival and viability forever. After the growth stage, the organism matures, declines, and then ends. The growth cycle of an organism can be explained using the principle of homeokinesis. Any living system has to be in a homeostatic or dynamic equilibrium state in order to remain viable. But a living system deteriorates over time and then expires ultimately. Thus, there is a limit to a living system. Thus, a living system is really in a state of disequilibrium, known as "homeokinesis." *Homeostasis* is the climax state which the living system is trying to achieve, but is never achievable. Homeostasis can be described as a "homeokinetic plateau"—the region within which negative feedback dominates in the organism. After 25 years of age, human body starts to deteriorate but it can still function. After achieving maturity, a living system requires more energy and effort to keep itself under control. Beyond the "upper threshold," the living system is again operating in a positive feedback region, and at the same time, it is deteriorating. Gradually, the living system loses its integration and functioning, and thus, results in the expiry of the system.

Organizations are much more complex systems which comprise a group of people, processes, and technology as compared to a living system. Therefore, it is very difficult to make a direct analogy between organizational changes and organism changes. Proper amount of control must be present for both organizations and organisms, to be in the region of homeokinetic plateau. Poor integration and chaos will be produced by too little control and too much control will produce poor adaptation and inflexibility (Fig. 5.3).

In general, organizations may experience decline and death. However, this process is less definite and more complicated in organizations as compared to organisms. The reason is the difference in their abilities to extract and utilize energy.

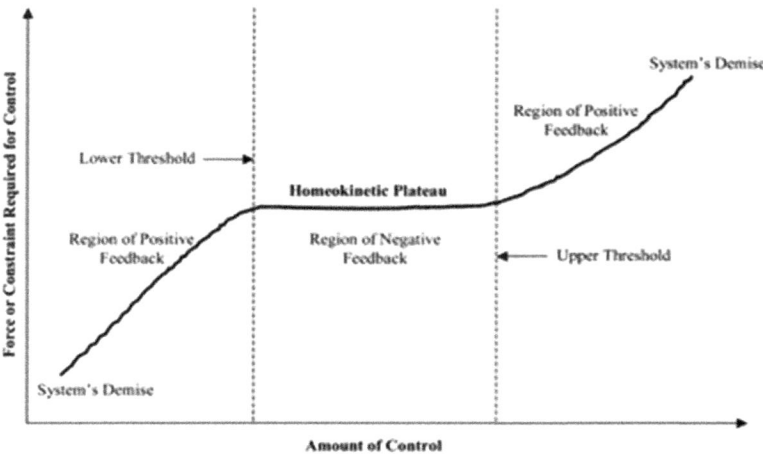

Fig. 5.3 Homeokinetic plateau (system should be maintained in this region)

They have different capacity to reorganize themselves upon encounter with unexpected and chaotic factors. An organization is more resilient and capable than organisms with respect to natural decline. This is supported by the difference in the timing and duration of their life cycle phases as well. *Whereas for a particular type of organism, the duration of each phase in the life cycle is relatively definite, it is very difficult to specify such duration for organizations.*

5.7   Transition from Stage 3 to Stage 2 of Organization Life Cycle

5.7.1   Reasons for the Transition of an Organization from Stage 3 to Stage 2

An organization which is currently in stage 3 of organization life cycle can very well move to stage 2 of organization life cycle. There are four main reasons for this movement:

1. *Merger and acquisition*: When an external entity comes into an organization, it needs to integrate the processes, system, products, and culture of that entity. The processes, systems, and culture of the two organizations may vary a lot. Therefore, under such a situation the organization does not have well-defined processes and systems in place. And thus, it can move to stage 2 of OLC.

2. *Process decay*: It may so happen that the organization redefines its processes. Under such situation, with the redefining of the processes, the organization may move to stage 2 of OLC.
3. *Change in macro environment*: Change in macro environment of the organization can take place because of three reasons:

    (a) *Policy change*
    (b) *Business model change*
    (c) *Environment change*: Environment is defined by a 1×3 matrix:

Environment	Employees and family
	Society at large
	Government/policy/macro economy

4. *Inability to meet benchmark values*: If the organization is unable to meet the benchmark values it has set for itself, it may move from stage 3 to stage 2.

5.8 Mapping of Process Life Cycle with Organization Life Cycle

5.8.1 Process Life Cycle

A process life cycle contains four stages:

1. *Stage 1*: In stage 1, processes are *chaotic and ad hoc*. The phrase "Go ask George" best describes stage 1 of process life cycle. The predictability, reliability, and confidence limit of the processes are at the lowest level.
2. *Stage 2*: In stage 2, the processes are *individual processes*. Processes are related to individuals and individual projects. The predictability, reliability, and confidence limit of the processes are better than stage 1.
3. *Stage 3*: In stage 3, *processes are institutionalized* via an organization-wide repository. *Process capability baseline (PCB)* is defined and lessons/best practices are learned. The predictability and reliability of the processes are high and the confidence limit is highest. A *benchmarking* exercise needs to be conducted in stage 3. Continuous improvement happens. *Process Improvement Process (PIP)* is conducted at this stage.
4. *Stage 4*: In stage 4, *processes are optimized*. And *continual improvement* happens at this stage. *Business process reengineering (BPR)* comes at this stage.

Fig. 5.4 Process life cycle (PLC)

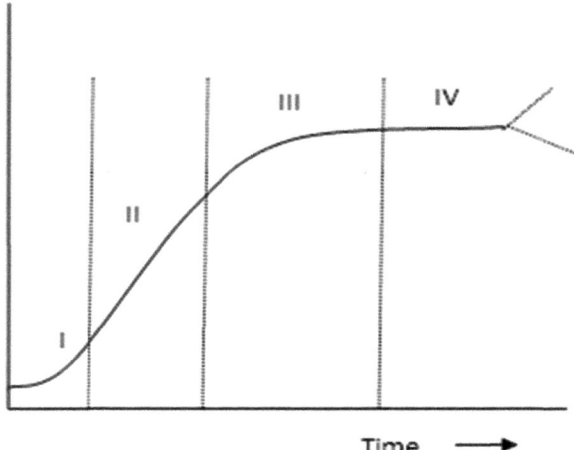

Fig. 5.5 Organization life cycle (OLC)

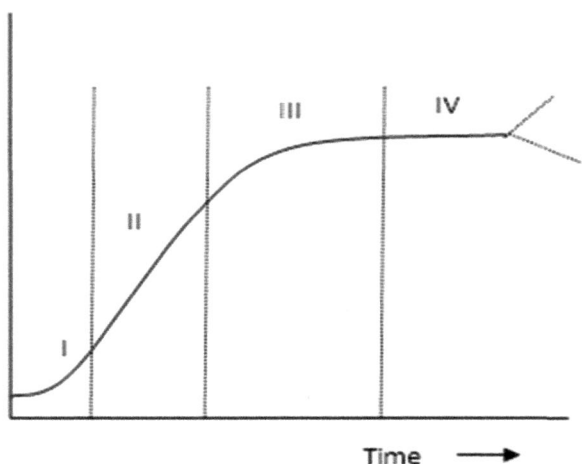

5.8.2   Mapping of Process Life Cycle with Organization Life Cycle

An organization may have many processes running for it. Whereas the organization moves through its own life cycle, these various processes of the organization move through their own life cycles. It may happen that during one stage of organization, a process may have completed its life cycle. Thus, *one organization life cycle may have many process life cycles within it* (Figs. 5.4 and 5.5).

5.9   Organization Life Cycle for Nonprofit Organizations

5.9.1   Overview of Nonprofit Organization Life Cycle

A nonprofit organization life cycle comprises of six stages. The key question, duration, obstacles, and opportunities vary across these stages. The following table provides an overview of the life cycle of nonprofit organizations (http://www.speakmanconsulting.com/pdf_files/NonProfitLifeCyclesMatrix.pdf):

Stage	Driving question	Duration (years)	Opportunities	Obstacles
Grass roots— invention	Is this dream feasible?	0–5 years	Creativity, excitement to start	Initial resistance, lack of funding and support
Start-up— incubation	How to start this dream organization?	1–2 years	Leadership, excitement of investors, excitement of people belonging to the organization	Resistance to formalize systems, investors may pull out
Adolescent— growing	How can this be built into a viable model?	2–5 years	Sense of accomplishment, diversification	Absence of systems, too many changes and lack of change management, no accountability
Mature— sustainability	How to ensure the sustainability of the model?	7–30 years	Adequate resources, new staff, new ideas	Lack of risk-taking ability, focus on operations only
Stagnation and renewal	Can it be renewed? How?	2–5 years	Wisdom and best practices, ability to exploit strategic partnerships	Resistance to change, unable to address key issues, wearing off of enthusiasm
Decline	Should it be closed?	1–2 years	Merger or complete turnaround	Absence of leadership, financial crisis, lack of passion, resistance from staff

5.9.2   Characteristics of Nonprofit Organization Life Cycle

	Grass roots	Start-up	Adolescent	Mature	Stagnation and renewal	Decline
Program and services	Extremely informal	Simple programs, strong commitment to deliver services	Establishment of programs, focus and consistency in program delivery	Long-term program planning, addition of new programs	Inconsistent program quality and delivery, loss of market sight	Loss of credibility, reduction in referrals
Staff leadership/ management	Visionary leader	Single-minded founder	Strategic division of labor	Need for well-rounded executive and delegation of authority	Need for a change agent, founder is most likely to leave	Major conflict between executive director and board
Staffing	Volunteer driven, no paid staff	Sense of family, volunteer driven	Increase in staff size, no job description	Diversified and specialized staff. Hiring of professionals	Low staff morale, volunteers leave	High conflict among staff, key staff leaves
Administrative systems	No real office	Few formal systems	Unsophisticated systems	Programs and systems in place	Well-developed systems, red-tapism, poor planning	Poor internal control, too much red-tapism
Finances and fund raising	Resources are in-kind	Limited financial resources, focus area	Relationships built with funders, volunteers	Diverse funding schemes, significant cash reserves	Insufficient cash reserves, no new funding sources	Unable to meet payroll, crisis situation
Marketing/ community awareness	Not yet a concern	Word of mouth, no formal communication, poor external communication	First promotional material, word of mouth	Marketing plan developed	Reactive, not proactive, cut down in marketing budget	No marketing, negative rumors about the organization

5.10   Case Study: Computer Sciences Corporation

Computer Sciences Corporation (CSC) is an IT and business services company with its headquarters in Virginia, USA. It employs around 90,000 people in 90 countries and is one of the largest player in outsourcing. Its services include advising clients on the acquisition and utilization of IT, business strategy, modeling, simulation, engineering, operations, change management, and business process reengineering. The following case traces 50 years of the organization across the four stages of OLC (http://www.slideshare.net/rajinani/organization-life-cycle-csc; http://www.csc.com/about_us/ds/40546-our_history; http://www.csc.com/about_us/ds/40546/40550-five_decades_of_success).

5.10.1   Stage 1: Birth

Challenges faced: In 1958, there were only 4,000 computers in this world. It was a very small market, where all the needs were fulfilled by IBM.

Growth strategy: In order to grow, CSC targeted those hardware vendors who were not supplying software. It provided system software (program in assembler) of the hardware supplied.

5.10.2   Stage 2: Growth

Organization structure: As the organization grew big, CSC attracted some of the brightest scientists and engineers to work with it. The marketing function of the organization was handled by Fletcher Jones, who served as the President of the organization as well. Roy Nutt, Vice President, handled technology.

Problems faced: During this time, the business of the organization was running at a steady pace. However, it was more dependent on the system software business of hardware vendors. In order to boost growth independent of them, there was a serious need to decouple with the system software business.

Change in the organization focus: The US Federal Government was the largest computer user during that period. CSC recognized that and it anticipated the convergence of computers and communications. Therefore, CSC bought two ITT divisions which were engaged in Systems Management and Communications Systems Engineering for the US Defense Communications Agency. With this acquisition, CSC acquired unmatched capabilities in the design and development of communications-based computer systems.

5.10.3   Stage 3: Maturity

Organization structure: In 1965, CSC became the largest IT services company in the USA. In order to increase operational efficiency and to develop effective strategy for company, William R. Hoover joined as the CEO of the company. However, the founders of the company continued to serve as president and vice president of the company. The daily affairs of the company were being handled by the new management.

Problems faced: With the US markets getting saturated and entry of new players in the market, there was a dire need to expand internationally in 1970s.

Global expansion: At this juncture, CSC started making its presence felt in Europe and Middle East. UK was its first destination abroad. Later on, in 1994, it acquired Ploenzke AG, a German IT company. Further, it acquired CSA Holdings in Singapore and thus stepped in Asian region as well.

Other ventures: By partnering with existing clients, CSC tried to enter into outsourcing arena. It took up consulting assignments for some of its customers.

5.10.4   Stage 4: Decline/Revitalization

Organizational structure: Towards the end of 1990s, CSC had a huge and strong presence outside USA. Handling such huge and global workforce became a problem for CSC. Because of acquisition and local needs, business segment heads were being replaced by regional or country heads. Therefore, CSC was facing a number of operational problems in managing the workforce globally.

Problems faced: Competitors were becoming strong, and there was intense competition from the USA as well as European competitors. Operational costs of CSC were high compared to its competitors. The entire workforce of CSC was posted in cost intensive labor countries. This increased the labor cost of CSC. CSC was over-dependent on Fed's work. At the same time, there was a rapid change in Web-based technology. All these factors made CSC inflexible to the changes in the environment. CSC used to get 40 % of its income from Fed's work and this work demanded very little technological research.

Decline: Both EDS and IBM overtook CSC. CSC was now at the third position in IT services companies. For the first time in 1998, there was a sequential decline in its revenues. In 1998, a hostile takeover by Computer Associates was thwarted.

India story: IT services companies of the whole world were looking at India as IT hub. CSC was a little late in entering India. It came to India in 2001 with acquisition of PMSI. After that, there was a rapid growth in CSC India. Its head count increased from 500 in 2002 to 17,000 in 2008. It acquired Covansys during this growth phase. It opened its offshore operations in China in 1998. This increased the offshoring capabilities of CSC and helped in cost reduction measures. India became the last resort for the revival of CSC.

Organizational changes for revival: In 1997, CSC formed its operations into business verticals: life sciences, insurance and banking, infrastructure support, and information systems. Organization reporting hierarchy was defined. Division heads will directly report to business heads. With the changes and acquisitions, CSC made a strong case of revival.

5.11 Summary

This chapter deals with the study of organizational life cycle and its characteristics and metrics. There are several models of organizational life cycle in the literature. The report makes a summary study of nine most important organizational life cycle models. Different models, though highlight similar stages of organizational life cycle, differ in their presentation. For example, Down's model is based on motivation, Lippit and Schmidt model is based on management concerns, Scott model is based on strategy and structure, etc., Greiner's model is based on the crises which lead to transition, Torbert's model is based on organizational mind-set, Lyden's model focuses on functions, Katz and Kahn focuses on organizational structure, Adizes on organizational activities, and Kimberly's model studies the organizational development of a medical school.

A generic organizational life cycle model is presented which consists of four stages—birth, growth, maturity, and decline/revitalization. The characteristics and metrics of an organization are different during different stages of life cycle. The board of directors is also affected by the life stage of the organization.

In order to identify the stages of organizational evolution, S-Curve can be employed. An analogy between organizations and organisms is drawn. Though there are many similarities between organizations and organisms, there are significant differences also. An organization is more resilient and capable than organisms with respect to natural decline. Also, the duration of each life stage of an organism is almost definite, whereas it is not definite for an organization.

An organization can move from stage 3 to stage 2 of OLC owing to several reasons like merger and acquisition, process decay, change in macro environment, and inability of the organization to meet its benchmark values. Mapping of process life cycle to organizational life cycle results in the fact that one OLC can contain many PLCs.

The life cycle of nonprofit organizations is different from life cycle of for-profit organizations. They vary both in the stages as well as the characteristics of various stages of the life cycle. A case study on Computer Science Corporation (CSC) demonstrates how an organization moves to various stages of OLC during its 50 years of existence.

It is observed that the various models of organization life cycle essentially hovers around four stages—birth, growth, maturity, and decline/revitalization. The characteristics of an organization vary depending on the stage of the organization life cycle it is in. Further, for different stages of OLC, there are different metrics and tools/techniques to set organizational goals and to gauge organizational performance. OLC differs for different organizations depending on their industry and business type. The OLC of nonprofit organizations is different from OLC of for-profit organizations.

An organization can very well move from stage 3 to stage 2 of OLC. Thus, an organization is not static; it is a dynamic entity. The life cycle of an organization can be compared with the life cycle of organisms. However, significant differences exist between these two.

Process life cycle can be mapped with organization life cycle. One OLC can contain many PLCs. Further study may include the variation in organization life cycle depending upon the industry characteristics.

Chapter 6
Business Process Modelling

6.1 Learning Objective

Processes form the heart of every organization regardless of its size, type, or age. These processes may be formal and documented or informal existing in people's heads. Regardless of their type processes are generally complex, require deep understanding, and need to be communicated well. Needless to say business process modelling (BPM) has evolved as a top priority for companies in the recent years. A survey of CIOs has found that a top business priority for their company was business process improvement. There are a number of options for improving business processes—like business process reengineering; adopting new process management techniques, such as Six Sigma; or enhancing old systems through adding new capabilities.

This chapter attempts to give an overview of business process modelling. It also discusses where and how it fits into organization. BPM is not restricted to IT systems alone. It is all about how a business runs its processes in the best possible manner. This chapter covers the following topics in a comprehensive manner:

- The need for business processes; their benefits and limitations
- What is business process modelling (BPM)
- How BPM has evolved over the years
- The requirements for process modelling
- How to carry a step-by-step procedure for BPM
- Process modelling standards and the BPM techniques
- ROI calculation for a business process model
- Common pitfalls of ROI
- Case study: Qwest telecommunications
- Difference between business model and framework

S. Mohapatra, *Business Process Reengineering*, Management for Professionals,   117
DOI 10.1007/978-1-4614-6067-1_6, © Springer Science+Business Media New York 2013

6.2   Why Do We Need Business Processes?

Every firm has a purpose. For example for Maruti it is making and selling cars, for Apollo Hospital chain providing healthcare services; for HUL selling FMCG products and commodities and so on and so forth. For the firm to achieve what it intends to do the work is broken down into a number of different functions, viz, marketing, operations, finance, human resource, etc. These functions must be perfectly synchronized with each other for the firm to be able to achieve its goals. Each function has its own objectives and roles and responsibilities assigned so that they achieve the organizational goal. For example HR handles recruitment issues and deals with the trade unions. Each function therefore defines a number of process or "standard methods," which are carried out in "repeated manner."

By having *repeatable business processes* the firm achieves the following objectives:

- Processes which are consistent tend to give consistent results.
- It gets easier to train people when you have standard processes defined.
- There are lesser chances of errors.
- Experience gained with processes over time may be used to refine and fine-tune them so that they perform even better.

But business processes have their own *limitations*. These limitations might be *internal* such as some situations may not quite fit the standard processes and need to be addressed individually. There might be *external limitations* like business processes of one function might need to interface with the processes of another function, like design team and production team using the same design templates. If one department changes the template to suit their processes it might be business processes in the production team as well.

6.3   Business Process Modelling

So what is business process modelling (BPM) all about? It is an activity undertaken by business analysts or managers to represent the processes of a firm in its current state so that it may be analyzed and steps might be taken for further improvement. *Information technology (IT)* usually accompanies BPM and is one of the major driving forces and reason for successful implementation of BPM. *Change management* is also commonly used to get the new processes in place. It is generally carried out in *stage III of the organization life cycle* (OLC).

6.3.1   BPM Background

The term "business process modelling" was coined by S. Williams in 1967 when he came up with his article "Business Process Modelling Improves Administrative

Control" in the field of system engineering. His idea as that the techniques used to understand physical control systems could also be used to understand business processes. Since then a number of techniques have evolved over the years such as

- Gantt Chart (1900)
- Flowcharts (1920)
- Functional Flow Block Diagrams and PERT (1950)
- Data Flow Diagrams and IDEFs (1970s)

By the 1990s the firms had started viewing their business in terms of processes instead of functions and procedures. The process oriented view looks at the chain of events in the firm at a cross-functional level whereas traditional modelling techniques were mostly used to estimate time and cost. This cross-functional view has become all the more important in today's world due to increased business volume, complexities, and interdependencies.

6.3.2 Process Modelling Requirements

Complete information—One of the most important requirements for BPM is to have the complete information about processes. With incomplete information the process model may be too simplified. On the other hand with too much information the process model might become riddled with complexity. Having the right level of abstraction is very important. The information on existing processes may be gathered through any of the following methods:

- Questionnaire
- Interview
- Checklist

Realistic processes—It is also important to ensure processes in BPM are actually practical enough to be implemented in real life. This problem mostly occurs because initially the BPM processes are theoretically planned out before being implemented. Hence it becomes to think for their practical feasibility when being implemented.

Process partitioning—When there are too many processes in a process model it becomes important to partition them in some way. Partitioning may be done in international standard or best practices basis or depending on functionality or roles and responsibilities.

Process iteration—Sometimes the processes in real life can be complex involving a number of decision points. Based on the decision at each such point different process flow paths may be chosen which might cause high degree of iteration. It is important to identify these iterations and the conditions under which they occur. The more the number of iteration, the more complex becomes the process.

Complexity and interactions—A process might have number of elements. The relationship and the interaction between these elements lead to complexity. It is important to understand at what level of abstraction the BPM is being carried out.

Traceability—Also one of the important features of BPM is traceability, that is, at any point in the process life cycle, the artifacts must be traceable to the original process which generated it. For example a booking process which requires invoice to be produced and sent to the customer has to be linked to the invoicing process associated; else the whole thing will fall apart.

6.3.3   Step-by-Step Procedure for BPM

1. *Identify the process trigger*

   Every process has a start point. When one is doing BPM one needs to identify this trigger which initiates the process. It might be one of the following:

   • External event
   • Invoked as a Web service
   • Human intervention
   • Scanned document

   The invoking trigger may or may not be in the BPM environment.

2. *Identify the steps/tasks*

   Once the process trigger has been identified, the set of tasks under each process need to be identified as to how they in the process map. There might be some human-facing and system-facing steps of the combination of the two. In a traditional workflow there might be more of human-facing steps. While modelling a process one needs to identify what the steps are and what kind of participation is required from the people or the system at each step.

   For human-facing steps one might need to know what the person is supposed to do for it will determine the number of participants, the tools (shared whiteboards, discussion forums) and interfaces required, etc. For system-facing steps integration can be achieved from Web services.

3. *Other considerations*

   External interfaces—For BPM one also needs to identify the external participants, when they will be involved in the process, how to alert them (via mail or any other alert system), the external user interface that might be required, etc.

   Monitor—One needs to identify what sort of data needs to be captured in the process to best monitor the state of the process itself. Only the data captured in the process can be monitored or used in the analytics for that matter. Hence it is very important to identify what data needs to be captured for reporting and analytics purpose.

   Stability—In BPM one also needs to check how frequently the processes change or the process environment changes. For example do the business rules need to be changed frequently? Is there a high staff turnover so that there are staffs with varying skill level at any point of time? If such is the case BPM needs to be able to handle the situation.

6.4   Service-Oriented Architecture

Service-oriented architecture (SOA) is helpful in exposing the functionality of infrastructure applications as reusable services. BPM can use these services as steps in the business process. Thus SOA insulates BPM being involved in the details of the system. While doing BPM one needs to find out what kinds of services are already available inside the organization. It is important lest one recreates the service already existing. Also some services are available in the external environment in the public domain at a cost or also free sometimes. One can make use of them also. Identifying such services both inside and outside the organization is important. For example one might need to call functions in the legacy application at a particular point in the process. It might be called through a service layer without writing the code again. This is how SOA is helpful in BPM.

6.5   Simulation and Optimization

After having the process initiated, steps defined, kinds of services required identified one needs to go for simulation/optimization. Simulation helps to identify the bottlenecks that hamper the process and from where the ROI from the process is going to come. The simulation environment helps to identify the *key performance indicators* (*KPIs*). These generally involve the time saved and the cost reduced as compared to the old process. Also various scenarios may be tried to see how the time and cost may be reduced, etc.

6.5.1   Process Modelling Standards

6.5.1.1   Graphical Notation Standard

Business process modelling notation (BPMN) is a standard diagrammatic representation used for drawing business processes. Though it is like flowchart it has some process attributes also embedded in it. It is easy to understand and the standardized representations ensure there are no communication issues and collaborations become much easier.

6.5.1.2   BPMN Flow Objects

There are three types of BPMN Flow objects, namely,

Event—Event is basically a trigger or something that happens that might impact the process flow. It could be the start or end of a process. It could be an incoming message or alert, etc.

Activity—Activity is simply a work step which could be automated or human facing. It is represented by a rectangle with rounded edges.

Gateway—Gateway is a point to convergence or divergence indicating whether a sequence of steps merges or branches out.

The pictorial representation is as follows:

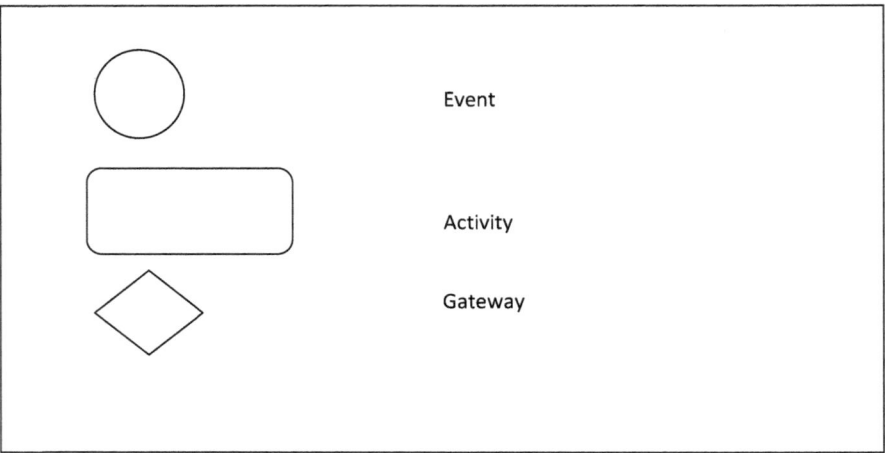

6.5.1.3 BPMN Connecting Objects

There are three types of connecting objects in BPMN, namely,

Sequence flow—This flow is used to indicate in which order the activities will be performed. It is used to show the basic flow in process map.

Message flow—Sometimes the flow of process might not be sequential such as requiring interaction between two organizations or departments. In such cases information flow happens through messages.

Association—These are used to provide additional information or documentation. They connect non-flow objects in the flowchart.

The pictorial representation is as follows:

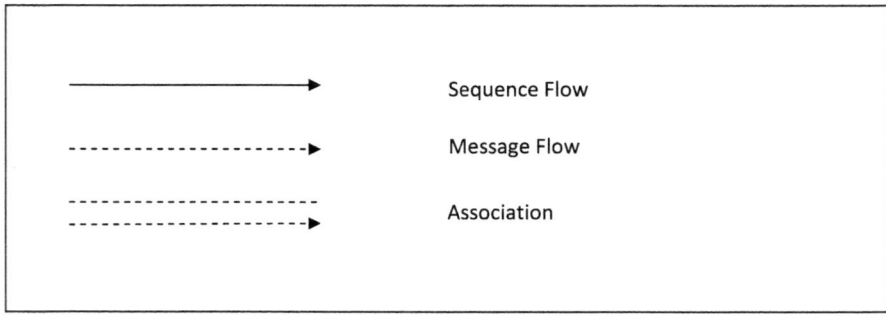

6.5.1.4   BPMN Swimlanes

Pool—It acts as a graphical container for a set of activities. It usually has several lanes in it.

Lanes—These are used to separate a set of steps from each other usually to indicate that they belong to different departments or business roles.
   The pictorial representation is as follows:

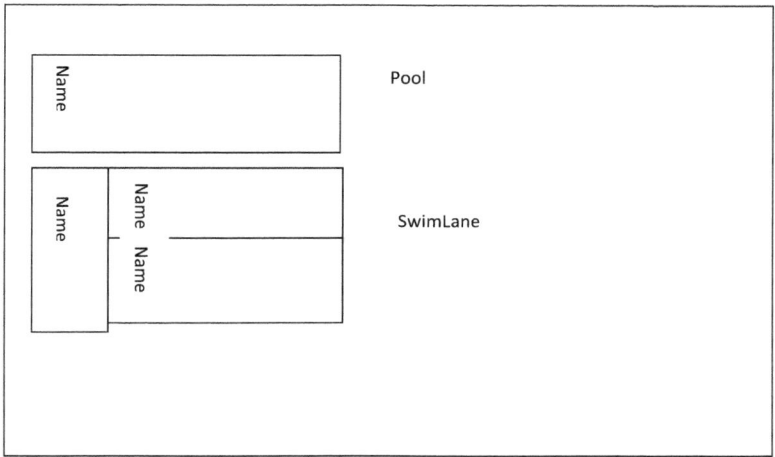

6.5.1.5   BPMN Artifacts

Also there are three more objects which are not classified under any of the above. There are as follows:

Data object—It usually represents some additional information that moves alongside the process like some document or record. It does impact the flow of process as such.

Group—It is used to graphically arrange a set of activities for documentation or analysis purpose.

Annotation—They are used to provide some descriptive information like what is happening in the process.

The pictorial representation is as follows:

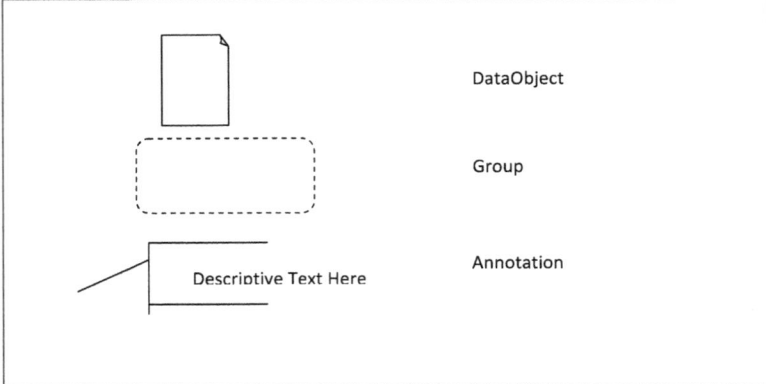

6.6   Business Process Modelling Steps

A business process

1. Has a goal.
2. Has specific inputs.
3. Has specific outputs.
4. Uses resources.
5. Has a number of activities that are performed in some order.
6. May affect more than one organizational unit. Horizontal organizational impact.
7. Creates value of some kind for the customer. The customer may be internal or external.

6.7   Business Process

A business process is a collection of activities designed to produce a specific output for a particular customer or market. It implies a strong emphasis on how the work is done within an organization in contrast to a product's focus on what. A process is thus a specific ordering of work activities across time and place, with a beginning, an end, and clearly defined inputs and outputs: a structure for action.

6.7.1   Connections

• *Supply link from object information.* A supply link indicates that the information or object linked to the process is not used up in the processing phase. For example, order templates may be used over and over to provide new orders of a certain style — the templates are not altered or exhausted as part of this activity.

- *Supply link from object resource.* An input link indicates that the attached object or resource is consumed in the processing procedure. As an example, as customer orders are processed they are completed and signed off and typically are used only once per unique resource (order).
- *Goal link to object goal.* A goal link indicates the attached object to the business process describes the goal of the process. A goal is the business justification for performing the activity.
- *Stateflow link to object output*
- *Stateflow link from event.* A stateflow link indicates some object is passed into a business process. It captures the passing of control to another entity or process, with the implied passing of state or information from activity to activity.

6.7.1.1 Goal Object

A business process has some well-defined goal. This is the reason the organization does this work and should be defined in terms of the benefits this process has for the organization as a whole and in satisfying the business needs.

6.7.1.2 Connections

Goal link from activity business process: A goal link indicates the attached object to the business process describes the goal of the process. A goal is the business justification for performing the activity.

6.7.1.3 Information Object

Business processes use information to tailor or complete their activities. Information, unlike resources, is not consumed in the process—rather it is used as part of the transformation process. Information may come from external sources, from customers, and from internal organizational units and may even be the product of other processes.

6.7.1.4 Connections

Supply link to activity business process. A supply link indicates that the information or object linked to the process is not used up in the processing phase. For example, order templates may be used over and over to provide new orders of a certain style— the templates are not altered or exhausted as part of this activity.

6.7.1.5 Output Object

A business process will typically produce one or more outputs of value to the business, either for internal use or to satisfy external requirements. An output may be a physical object (such as a report or invoice), a transformation of raw resources into a new arrangement (a daily schedule or roster), or an overall business result such as completing a customer order.

An output of one business process may feed into another process, either as a requested item or a trigger to initiate new activities.

6.7.1.6   Connections

Stateflow link from activity *business process.*

6.7.1.7   Resource Object

A resource is an input to a business process and, unlike information, is typically consumed during the processing. For example, as each daily train service is run and actuals recorded, the service resource is "used up" as far as the process of recording actual train times is concerned.

6.7.1.8   Connections

Supply link to activity business process. An input link indicates that the attached object or resource is consumed in the processing procedure. As an example, as customer orders are processed they are completed and signed off, and typically are used only once per unique resource (order).

6.7.2   Assessing Reengineering

6.7.2.1   Business Process Reengineering

It is the analysis and redesign of workflows and processes within an organization to achieve certain business goals. It is often a stage in a BPM project which is meant at aligning each and every process to have a focused movement towards the greater strategic vision and mission. Let us look at the various stages in the BPR cycle.

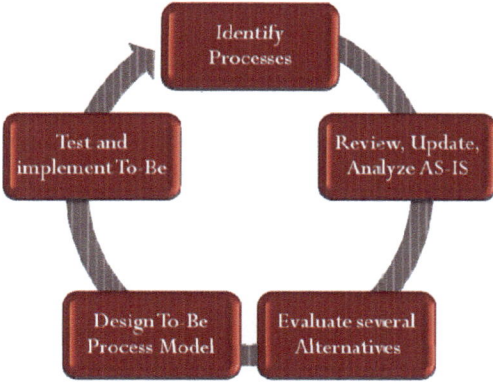

Well, the above cycle clearly defines the various stages of business process reengineering. Here, we have tried to implement a new stage in between analyzing As-Is and designing To-Be process model. This stage would be called "*evaluating several alternatives*."

The alternatives emerge out of the analysis of As-Is process model. It is at this stage that the organizations along with *the consultants have performance-based and risk-adjusted cost–benefit analysis of each alternative process*. These alternatives would differ on the following aspects:

1. *Strategic direction*

    (a) The organization top management sponsors the BPM project to be able to move ahead in a specific direction that will lead them to specific goals in a specific time frame. This focus gives rise to several tactical plans. The various process states have to be changed so as to facilitate the new tactical plans.
    (b) The several alternatives will have different tactical strategies to achieve the business goals.
    (c) Thus, for each of them the To-Be model will differ in model and implementation.

2. *Impact*

    (a) Since each To-Be model will differ in model and implementation they will thus definitely have different business impact.
    (b) Impact parameters:

        • Qualitative impact:

            – HR policies
            – Change management issues
            – Organization structure
            – Decision making, SOA (schedule of authorization)
            – Workforce motivation and issues
            – Leadership style

- Quantitative impact:

  - Key performance indicators (KPIs)
  - Metrics

  (c) The selection of a particular alternative will be based on whether that alternative does promise the required returns in terms of the qualitative and quantitative impact.
  (d) The prioritization of processes is also done based on the impact.

3. *Risk involved*

   (a) Risk involved can be measured by various risk assessment index measures.
   (b) This will clearly identify the various possible risks (controllable and uncontrollable).
   (c) Risk management steps should be identified and if risk management or prevention is costly than risk occurrence loss, then that model should be rejected. But, again it is subjected to top management perception.
   (d) Moreover, if certain risky opportunities are indispensable for achieving the target business goals, the To-Be models should be tweaked so as to absorb most of the risks.

4. *Implementation plan*

   (a) The methodology

   - The implementation methodology for the various alternatives will differ because they emerge from different tactical plans. By methodology, here we mean the way of going about the implementation of the reengineering process.
   - Sometimes, it's a pilot model first. In some cases, it is implemented in different phases. In some other cases, it is implemented all in one go.
   - Feasibility is a major concern in this case.

   (b) Cost of implementation

   - This is no doubt one of the most important factors in deciding. No project can proceed without top management and sponsor support.
   - The varying costs could be due to the different process models, the people cost involved, change management costs, opportunity costs due to stalled business, and other miscellaneous costs.

   (c) Time required

   - Time is generally a big concern since all strategies are played across a time horizon and lack of faith for time can result in the competitors gaining ground.
   - Time for different alternatives will vary due to the flow, methodology of implementation, and also issues that need to be tackled or hurdles that need to be overcome.

(d) Change management involved

- This includes the change in employee attitude involved, management of various workforce issues, training, etc.

6.8 Assessment Issues (Fig. 6.1)

6.8.1 Has the Organization Changed Its VMG (Vision, Mission, Goals)?

Frequently, organizations undergo a change in their VMG maybe because of a change in the leadership or business objectives or some other market forces. The important thing to realize here is that if such changes occur, the process modelling that was done some time back (*maybe a few years!*) will not hold effective henceforth. Thus, either there has to be a change such that the impact on the focus and strategic direction is not negative or the changes in the entire process model are negligible.

Yes, in a sense, for a large organization, such macro level structural changes are cumbersome and costly to handle, not to mention time taking. And time is one of the axis variables for any kind of strategic decision making. So, how do organizations handle such issues.

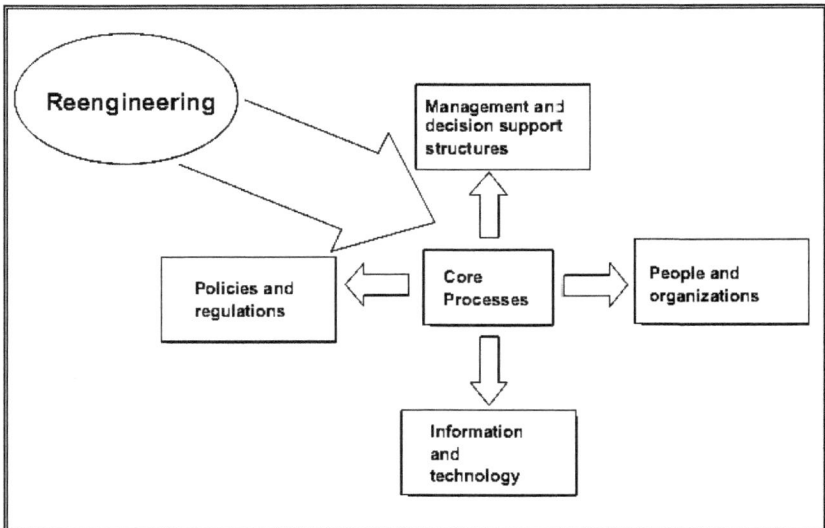

Fig. 6.1 BPR drives many business changes

6.8.1.1   Important Assessment Questions

1. Has the organization identified the changes because it will result in a serious redefinition of R&R of the organization?
2. Is the strategic level planning focused on the most important stakeholders and critical priority customers?
3. Are they in sync with the organization's current products/services?
4. How does the BPR modelling support such change? This is the most important deciding factor and constraint!

And since it affects almost all of their customer groups directly, the organization should also check whether the interests of the various stakeholders and customer groups are not harmed.

6.8.1.2   Important Assessment Questions

1. Has the organization identified its main customer groups for its various products and services, the impact on these groups if there is a strategic level change?
2. Has the organization also identified all the stakeholders, big and small, and check the impact on the strategic level change on the interests of these stakeholders? And how does the organization plan to tackle it?
3. The change in the dynamics of the industry and the affect of it on the customers and the stakeholders?
4. Has the organization thus identified key areas of consent and veto for these customer groups and stakeholders? What could be done to address those?
5. What would be thus the impact of the various new process structures on these?

6.8.1.3   Similarly, the Other Issues that Need to Be Tackled Are

1. Has the organization identified performance problems and set improvement goals and CSFs?
2. Should the organization engage in BPR?
3. Is the reengineering project effectively and correctly managed?
4. Has the project team analyzed the target process and developed feasible alternatives?
5. Has the project team completed a sound business case for implementing the new process?
6. Is the agency following a comprehensive implementation plan?
7. Are agency executives addressing change management issues?
8. Is the new process achieving the desired results?

6.8.2 Is the New Process Delivering Desired Results?

Here the important questions will be

1. Measurement

   (a) Does the organization have a process metrics system in place at all?
   (b) Does the organization consistently perform on the set KPI targets?
   (c) How is the change management done? Is the transition that has been made possible actually sustainable?

2. Continual improvement

   (a) Is there a PIP (process improvement process) continuously in place for dynamic improvements in the process model?
   (b) Are the performance reports and data used effectively to bring about improvements in the shortcomings identified?

6.9 Workflow Modelling

A workflow is basically characterized by

1. A sequence of activities.
2. It is an abstraction of real work.
3. It is a pattern of activities with roles assigned to each process, responsibilities defined, information flows.

6.9.1 My Definition of Workflow

Workflow is the process of automation of procedures according to a set of business rules and constraints to achieve certain business goals out of an activity set along with mapping tasks with resources and roles.

6.9.2 The Key Benefits of Workflow (Fig. 6.2)

So we can say that while processes have defined inputs and outputs, system, and flow, the workflow basically comprising of many subprocess flows is a pattern of activity within a function or cross-functional.

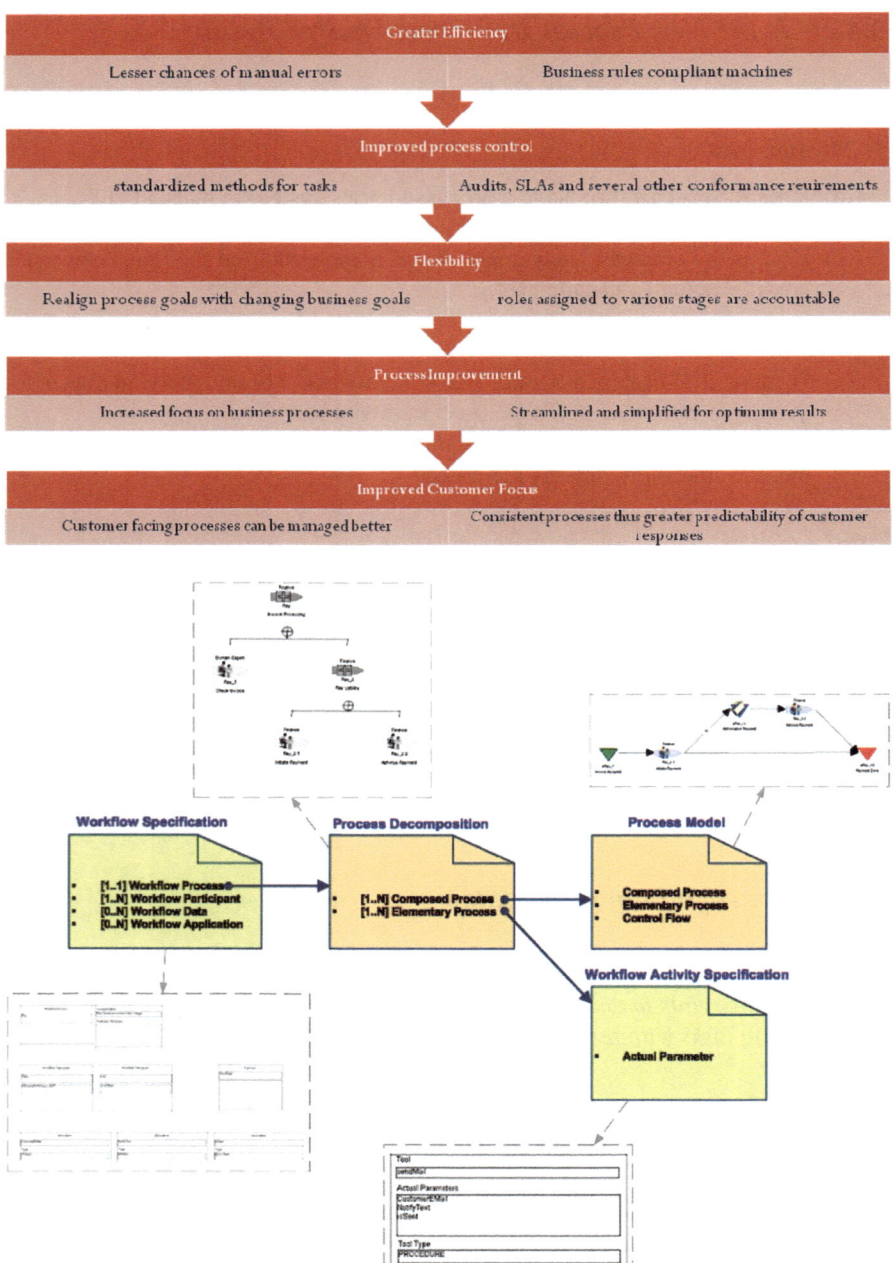

Fig. 6.2 Workflow and process flow

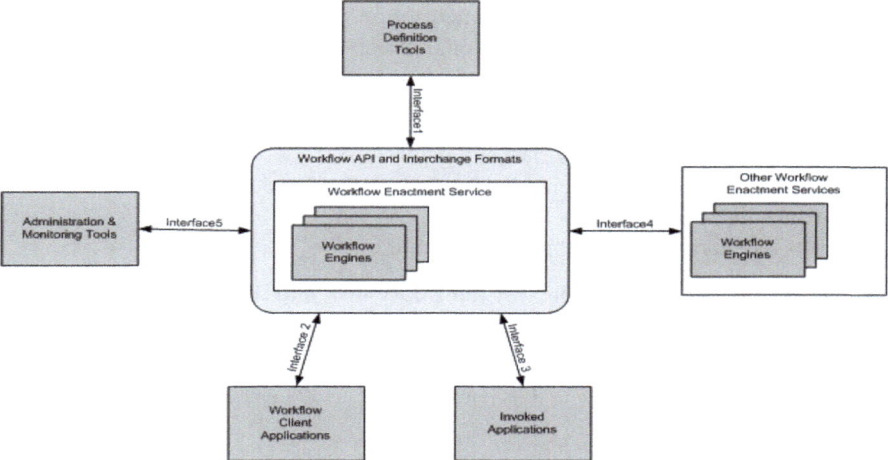

Fig. 6.3 Workflow management reference model

Workflow engines and management techniques are much more complex and beyond the scope of this chapter. Workflow Management Coalition (WfMC), founded in 1993, has established common terminology and standard interfaces for workflow management (Fig. 6.3).

Workflow definitions generally fed in XPDL consist of activities, transitions, applications, participants, and workflow-relevant data.

The most important part of the modelling process is the model selected for the business process. A business process is a collection of various activities designed to produce a specific output for a particular customer or market.

A business process can be represented in the following format:

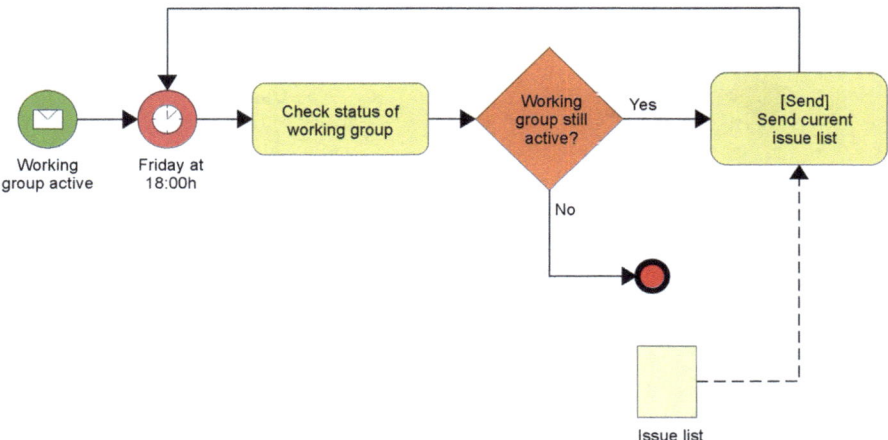

The scope for such notation is limited to the business processes involved. For instance, elements such as organizational structures, functional breakdowns, and data models will not be a part of the above notation. The various elements which will be a part of this notation are as follows:

Flow objects like events, activities, and gateways
Connecting objects like sequence flow, message flow, and association
Swimlanes like pool and lane
Artifacts like data object, group, and annotation

The following diagram represents the above flow and connecting objects:

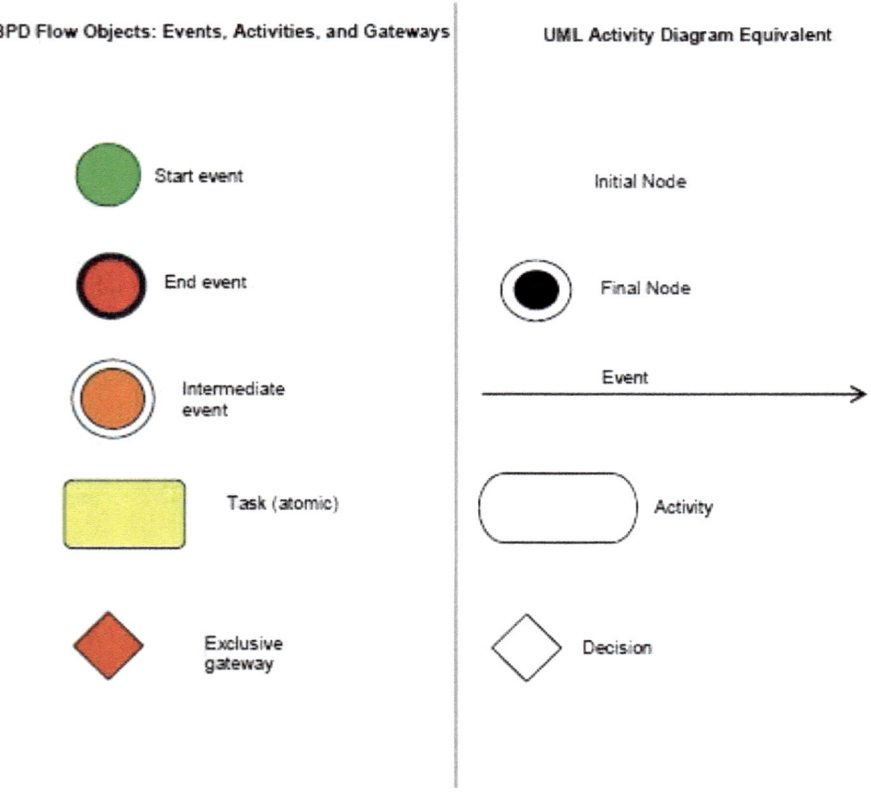

The following diagram represents the swimlanes and artifacts:

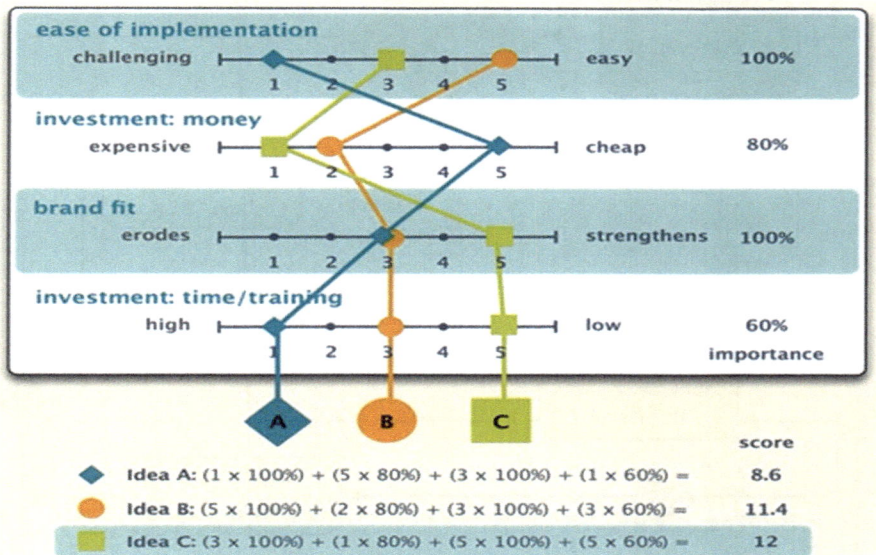

The following are some of the examples of business process diagrams:

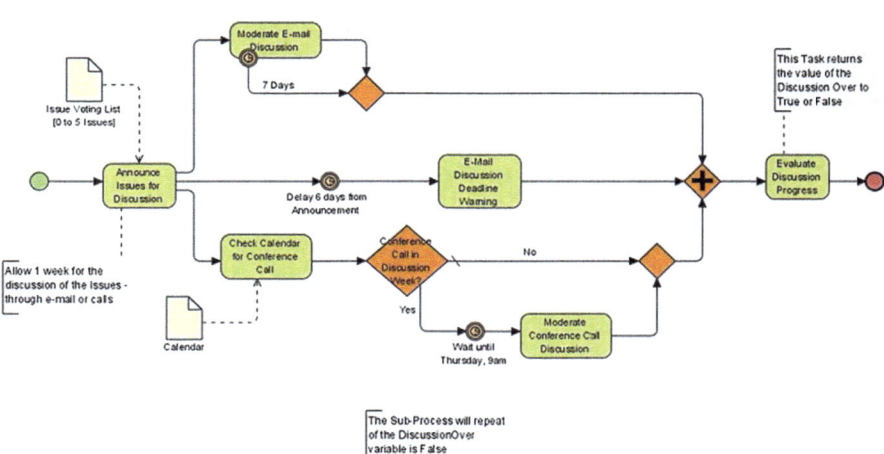

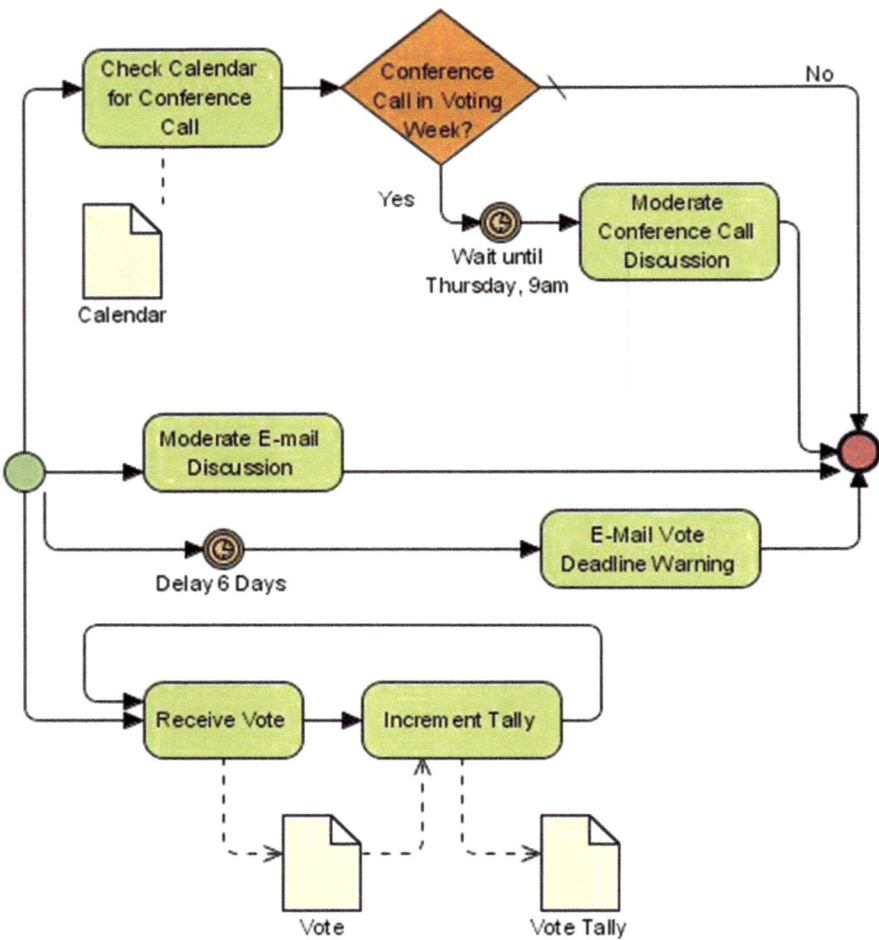

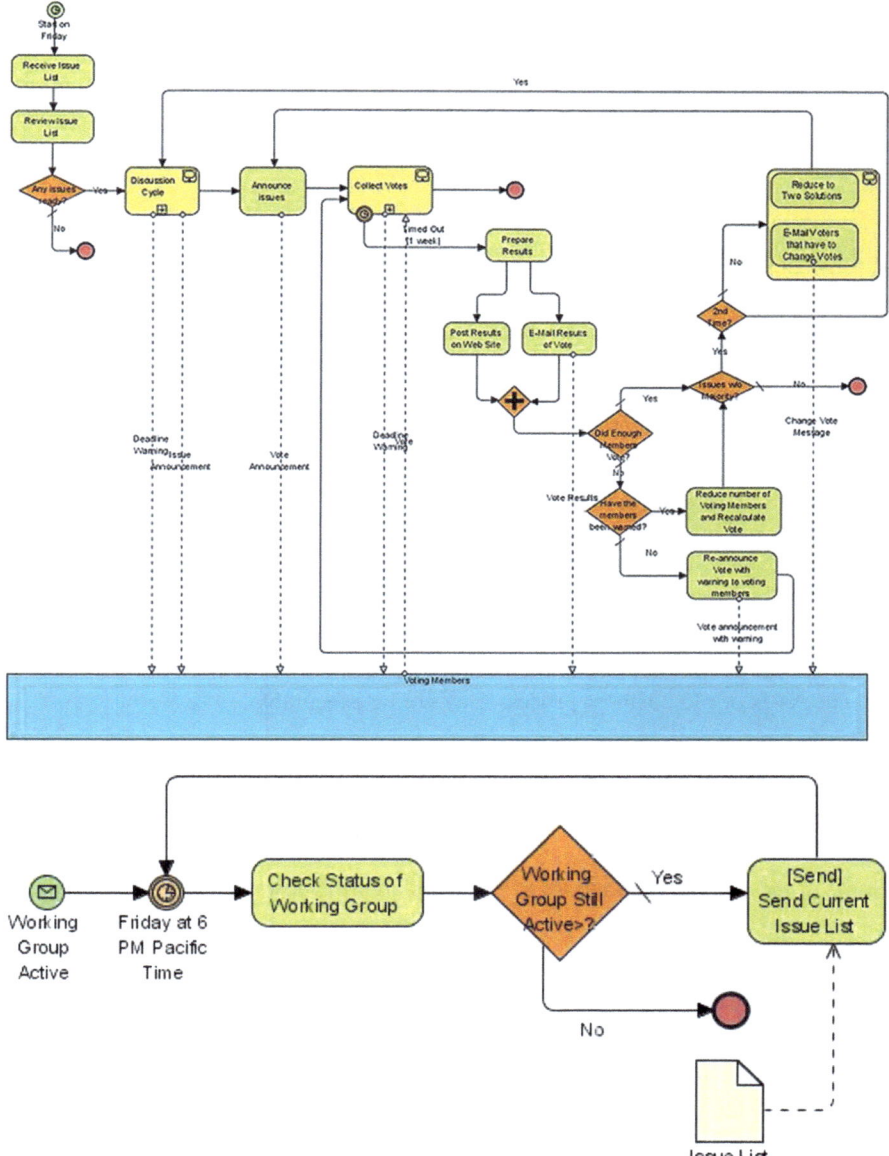

6.10   Types of Business Process Submodel

6.10.1   Private (Internal) Business Processes

These are specific to the internal processes of the company or organization and are generally called workflow or BPM processes.

6.10.2   Abstract (Public) Processes

This represents the interactions between a private business process and another process or participant. Only those activities that communicate outside the private business process are included in the abstract process.

6.10.3   Collaboration (Global) Processes

A collaboration process depicts the interactions between two or more business entities. These interactions are defined as a sequence of activities that represent the message exchange patterns between the entities involved.

Some of the processes which can be included in the above framework are as follows:

- Detailed private business process
- As-Is or old business process
- To-Be or new business process
- Detailed private business process with interactions to one or more external entities (or "black box" processes)
- Two or more detailed private business processes interacting

The As-Is or old business process may not be executable.

6.10.4   Weaknesses of the Business Process Models

Some of the notable weaknesses of the BPM are as follows:

- Ambiguity and confusion in sharing BPMN models
- Support for routine work
- Support for knowledge work
- Converting BPMN models to executable environments

There are various software which are available to make things easier and more organized. The main features which are noteworthy of such software are as follows:

- Written operational procedure
- BPMN conversation diagram
- Identifying business process elements using textual analysis
- Process map diagram
- Event-driven process chain diagram
- Data flow diagram
- Organizational chart

6.11   Case

This is a case for the receiving and awarding of grants to a list of recipients on basis of their cases submitted.

Let us look at this example of a simple online proposal system for grant-giving process (Fig. 6.4).

6.11.1   Steps

1. Set up

   (a) One coordinator + 1 backup coordinator to compose call for proposals (CfPs).
   (b) Reviewer list.
   (c) There can be a unique appraisal criteria for each CfP.
   (d) Formatting for drafting CfPs decided by coordinator.
   (e) Coordinator also discusses and declines proposals.
   (f) Also, at this stage, visitors to the Web site can view all details for CfPs and how to give grants procedure.

2. Receive and review of proposals

   (a) Coordinator initiates → selects reviewers from the list.
   (b) Automatically mails to reviewers containing proposals and a link to the appraisal page.

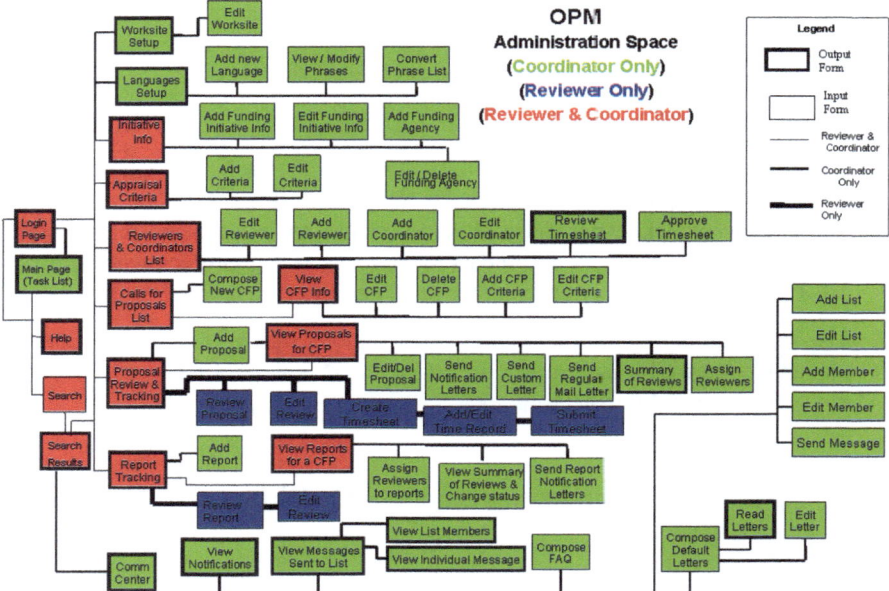

Fig. 6.4 Workflow—grant management

(c) He has access only to those proposals which he has been assigned to when logged in to the site.
(d) Each reviewer is also given a set of criteria, ranking scale for each criteria, and finally the forms get submitted online.
(e) Proposal tracking and review page monitored by coordinator.
(f) Facility for reminder mails.

3. Summarize proposal reviews → decision of the committee

(a) Review summary → generated by coordinator when reviewers are done with their reviews.
(b) The average weighted score is calculated for each form submitted by the reviewer (rank × weight).
(c) Automatically scores and generates reports.
(d) Coordinator can set a proposal call to "awarded" status.
(e) The system also assesses budget required versus total grants collected.
(f) 1-page summary for the viable proposal portfolio → program committee members; final decision for selection and decision of award amounts.

4. Update proposals, track budgeting, and notification of results

(a) After the selection is finalized by the program committee, the "awarded" or "decline" status is given to each CfP by the coordinator.
(b) A notification letter is also generated from formats already decided in stage 1 by the coordinator.
(c) This letter can be tweaked by the coordinator based on the context to suit the needs.
(d) The public Web site makes the awarded proposals available to the public.
(e) Public can discuss the awarding of a particular proposal on discussion threads on the site.

5. Accept and review reports

(a) Interim/final report is required to be submitted by each recipient of grant.
(b) Each report passes on from coordinators to the reviewers.
(c) Reviewers make comments online; a summarized message is sent by coordinator containing these comments to the respective grant recipient.
(d) Cycle continues until coordinator finally accepts the reports.

Users for the above are prestigious organizations like WHO, British Council, Canadian Centre for Philanthropy, HRD (Canada), Ministry of Economy (Turkey), Ministry of Foreign Affairs (Denmark).

6.12 Workflow Management and BPM: Difference (Fig. 6.5)

As we can see, the workflow management software generates work lists and these work lists have the process definitions XML in them. Workflow engine(s) are the center of this arrangement here where they use workflow data that might change

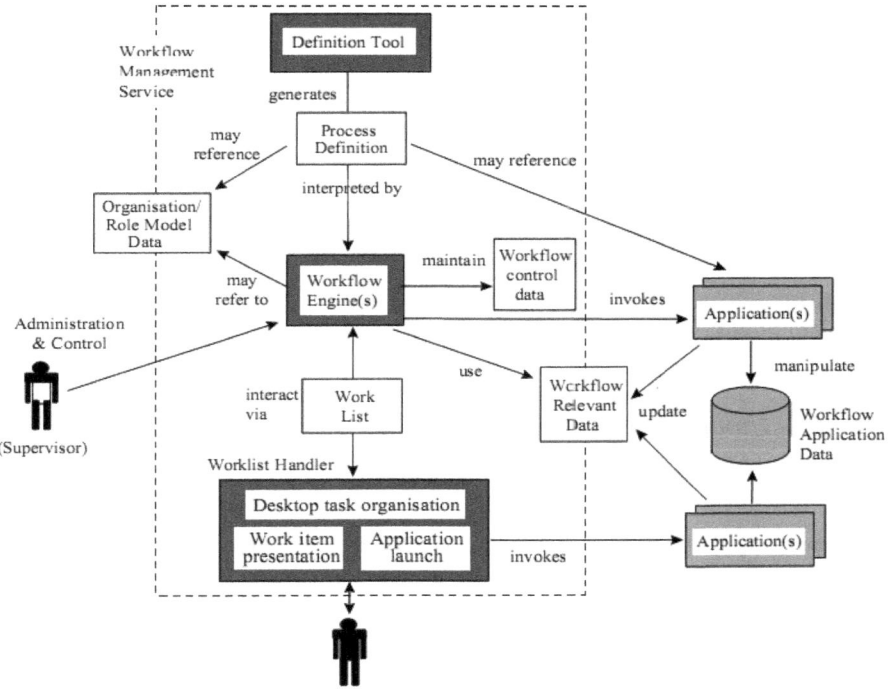

Fig. 6.5 Applications, workflow engine, and process

dynamically, interpret process definitions, and continuously interact with the work list. This is beyond the scope of this chapter, so we will keep that to it and focus more on the application part.

The big question here is—What is the difference between workflow and BPM?

Workflow deals with sequence of activities generated by application data while BPM deals with everything from definition to execution of business processes and not on specific work lists. Certain BPM are implemented on SOA where services are the most granular. In any case, BPM is the superset of workflow.

Integration with externalities: Limited in workflow systems while total integration with documents and external files on BPM

6.13   ROI

To assess the models and to find the best ones that meet the business goals, we need to measure the return on investment. In case of business process models, the ROI is calculated from the standpoint of attaining competitive advantage and reducing the costs.

6.13.1 *Reducing Costs*

There are a number of areas where we can achieve cost reduction. Lot of time can be saved, and the error rates can also be reduced drastically by implementing the right model:

- Data can be automatically exchanged between systems and cannot have someone manually feed the data to two systems. This saves time and brings down the number of errors caused due to human intervention.
- Self-service option can be provided to the customers and thus we can save on the salary of customer service representatives.

6.13.2 *Competitive Advantage*

It is a little difficult to justify this from an ROI point of view:

- Here the best results that can be achieved are in terms of reducing time to market. If you can make your processes very efficient internally, you can accomplish a much lower end-to-end cycle time. So if you are involved in product development stage then if you launch a new product a few months earlier than your competitor, then you can reap huge profits and gain a huge competitive advantage. The new revenue that will be generated is difficult to quantify but it is definitely one of the areas that should implement business process modelling.
- You can also make your customers happier. The issues that they are facing can be handled faster using automation, etc. The service can be made much better by providing the customer access to a variety of channels (self-service/Web). This can bring in lot of future revenues. Satisfied customers will generate more profit and also bring in more customers.
- Capacity can also be increased by efficient business process models. The number of employees will not be affected but the number of products produced per unit time can rise. This will create a platform providing a growing environment where the output will be increasing with the same workforce. This will be a big help in a competitive environment where it is essential to keep the pricing down.
- The decision-making process of the executives can also be enhanced. They can access the required information much faster. They can get to know quite easily about the working of the business processes and how they are affecting the vision and goals of the organization.

6.13.3 *Calculating ROI*

To calculate the ROI the following needs to be taken care of:

- The current processes need to set baselines. We should be able to find out how long it takes us to do our activities after the new model is adopted. For this identification of baselines is very crucial.

- After the model has been designed, some kind of simulation in the processes is required.
- We also should identify the metrics using which we will be calculating the ROI.
- The difference between the As-Is and the To-Be should be clearly understood.

There are a number of metrics. But they should be chosen wisely depending on the industry you are in and what your vision, mission, and goals are.

For example, in a transaction-processing environment, it can be the waiting time for each step, i.e., the end-to-end process. It can be the waiting time per caller or call-back rate if it is a call center.

After the metrics have been selected, the ROI calculation model is decided on. It can be the internal rate of return, NPV, break even period etc. The finance department are the best people to decide on that. Then a best case/worst case analysis is to be done. It is better to use a worst case scenario to calculate the ROI if it is the first BPM project taken by the organization because the implementation will be justifiable even if all objectives are not met.

6.13.4   Common ROI Pitfalls

The following will give an idea about how ROI may not give the results that was expected:

- The business process models may quadruple the capacity but that does not ensure that there will be definite increase in revenue. There might not be so much demand for the product.
- Even if you provide easy access to information to that customers or make self-service option available to them, it does not mean that they are going to utilize it.
- Even it was discussed above that application of business process models will not diminish the workforce but only increase the capacity, we might actually have to go for head count reduction to stay in the competition. If the industry is not growing it will be unprofitable to hold on to all the employees.

6.14   Case Study

Qwest is a telecommunications company operating in North America. This company provides data, voice, and video services to enterprises and residential customers. The company started missing opportunities and missed man service level agreements with the customers. To tackle these issues, Qwest developed a center for process excellence. The objective was to increase customer satisfaction through faster servicing of the customers and documentation of the processes to reduce ambiguity and automating the processes. In collaboration with existing business process teams, the center for process excellence put into action business process management suite (BPMS) that streamlined the processes that were disjoint, deviated from established process standards. The center also brought in change management processes that stressed on faster and effective implementation of defined processes. As a result, Qwest is now a well-known in-demand service provider and is able to effectively measure the improvements in its business processes.

Situation: Qwest had lost a process-centric approach to its provisioning operations. This process includes order collection and management, work distribution, requirements capture, price and offer management, and other interdepartmental processes and activities. Agility and flexibility was missing in their operational support system (OSS). This gave rise to gaps in standardization and automation. It looked like small islands of automation. These were bridged by manual process as the OSS lacked the ability to do that. The held order rates and the cycle time had almost become unacceptable. The work was getting delayed because of incomplete or insufficient information, and the total time to complete a process was also quite high. The manual work that was being carried out was unmeasured, untracked, and thus resulted in efficiencies. The lack of process standardization was showing.

So Qwest took the help of business process management to work its way around these inefficiencies and build a business process center of excellence. With the help of the teams from all the departments, this new team decided to set and document standards, manage process repositories, and facilitate change control. Qwest chose TIBCO's business process management suite. These tools helped to standardize, improve, and optimize the business processes. It started by applying the BPMS to two processes that demanded immediate attention. The first one was price and offer management. This was essential because to deal with an interdepartmental business process, the organizational dynamics need to be smooth. The second process that was taken into consideration was order data collection. This process affected the work distribution.

Best practices: Qwest implanted Forrester's identified best practices. They made careful planning and designed a full-proof structure for the project:

- *Holding open roundtable planning discussions*: Face-to-face hands-on discussions among all the stakeholders of the company including the end users. This would lead to the success of the project. One director suggested that there be two projectors, one showing the business model and the other screening the actual application. This will give a more clear idea to all.
- *Building a prototype first*: Vendors for BPMS assure that their tools are capable of handling any project and project can be from of any degree of complexity, may belong to any domain or require any scale of integration. But it is not so. The company going for BPMS should test the vendors and make them prove their wares. In our case, Qwest asked TIBCO to "prove it" in the form of a prototype and thus gained a lot of insight into the problem and its solution. The prototype helped the company in establishing a new strategy for building user interfaces. These interfaces were basically for the business process-driven applications.

- *Optimizing as processes were implemented*: In many cases the metrics are not identified properly in the past. So it becomes difficult to optimize the business process entirely in the very beginning of automation. But Qwest did not make the mistake of applying an "As-Is" process. Qwest was continuously planning for improvement throughout its process analysis phase. The changes that it made resulted in huge efficiency gains.

The initial implantation was a success. There was positive effect on the data quality, on the cycle time. The results were dramatic. But Qwest did not settle for this. It continued its success stories step by step by encouraging the people in the organization to take part in "the business process process." As the baseline, it selected its existing data for simulation. Then the tools (business process modelling and simulation) were distributed. This way all will be able to identify the changes that were being made and also be able to predict the results.

The baseline, i.e., the existing data, was used to show the change that had occurred and how the project was progressing. It was easier to demonstrate change management and show the agility with which the company was moving and how small changes can produce huge impacts on the bottom line. Qwest was one of the few companies that actually took advantage of this type of data-driven simulation capability.

Best practice results: Improvements were seen in both order data collection and price and offer management. These were measurable tco. At the outset, held orders dropped by 10%. Cycle times were reduced by 20% because of the insights provided by automation. Since these successes were quantifiable, this encouraged people to adopt a different approach in handling processes. Since the results were measurable, it was captured and was communicated to all. The vision of the project could be justified bringing in a positive attitude towards this change for good. The response from the employees was excellent and they showed eagerness to participate in all the phases of the implementation.

6.15   Business Framework Versus Model

A framework is a set of principles, standards, and rules which provides the support system. It might not be the whole picture but it provides a strong base to build upon. A framework has a variety of components that are used to construct models.

An example: The CMMI framework is process improvement approach that provides organizations with the essential elements of effective processes. Using the CMMI framework different models can be generated based on the needs of the organization using it. Hence, the phrase "CMMI models" refers to all possible models that can be generated from the CMMI framework. There are five maturity levels in this framework numbered one to five. Each maturity level comprises a predefined set of process areas. Each maturity level stabilizes an important part of the organization's processes.

A business process model illustrates how the diverse managerial activities like marketing, selling, human resources, manufacturing, strategizing, financial arrangements, etc. work together in an interconnected consistent manner to generate the bottom-line profits from a business initiative:

- A model for each business process enhances the understanding of the owners and the managers regarding the operations of the company and hence aids in the decision-making process.
- A model captures the business processes very well and helps in getting idea regarding the best tools and methodologies.
- In order to create a process model, a few steps need to be followed. In step the knowledge of the process gets better and better. The importance of that process to the functioning of the business is understood.
- A detailed, accurate business process model will be able to explain the strengths, the weaknesses, and the bottlenecks in the existing operations.

An example: The following is an example of a business process model. Here the goal is to take the customer orders. Then these orders are shipped out. The process begins with an inquiry. Later the shopping cart, book catalogue, warehouse inventory, and online pages get involved. In this stage the customer order is of significance. In the second half the process is required to respond to the order and then ship it. This calls for the involvement of the shipping company. The process ends when the customer receives what he had ordered for.

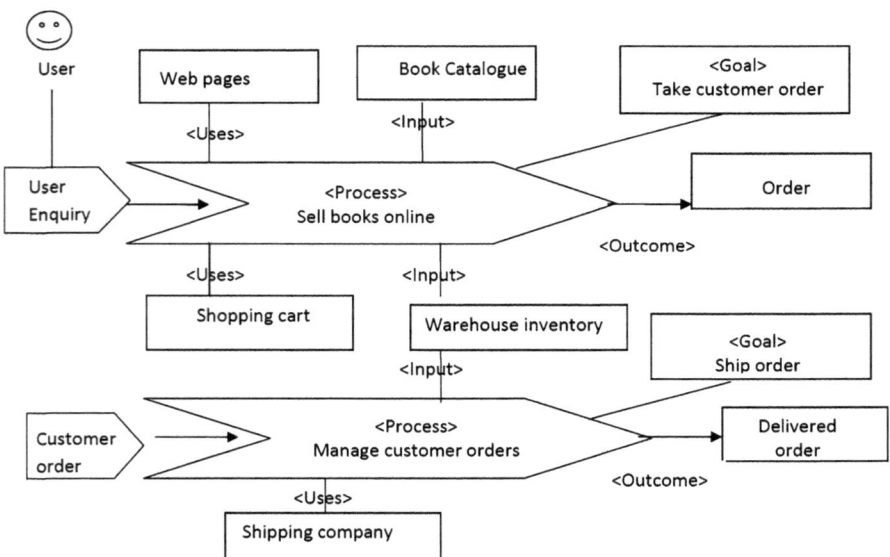

6.16 Summary

We discussed about how we can represent knowledge about businesses and their processes in form of models. This is the best methodology that facilitates the understanding of business analysts who build detailed specifications of the processes starting from the top management objectives in an organization. This methodology is useful when there is plan to fabricate new processes or document the current processes, etc. Process modelling not just gives a clear understanding of the workings of the existing practices but also helps in forming an idea regarding what should be done in the future. It puts into test all that is being done now and gives a perspective of how things need to be done. In a transaction-based system, this should be the very first step. Organizations adopting business process modelling have a tough job to tackle but also a plethora of opportunities to keep making continuous improvements in their functioning.

Bibliography

Turbit N. Business process modelling overview. http://www.projectperfect.com.au/.../info_business_process_modelling_overview.pdf

Kemsley S. Business process modelling. http://www.tibco.com/.../business-process-modelling_tcm8-2404.pdf

Kesner RM. IT service delivery: models and frameworks. http://www.auerbach-publications.com/dynamic.../2467_1359_42-40-30.pdf

Maturity models—a framework for organizational improvement. http://pmi-ittelecom.org/pmtopics/maturity-models-a-framework-for-organizational-improvement/

What is capability maturity model integration? (CMMI) http://www.selectbs.com/process-maturity/what-is-capability-maturity-model-integration

Rudden J. Making the case for BPM: a benefits checklist. http://www.bptrends.com/.../01-07-ART-MakingtheCaseforBPM-BenefitsChecklist-Rudden.pdf

Bider I. Choosing approach to business process modelling—practical perspective. http://www.ibissoft.se/publications/Howto.pdf

Teubner C, McNabb K, Levitt D. Case study: qwest uses process simulation to move at the speed of business change. http://www.tibco.com/multimedia/ss-qwest_tcm8-2367.pdf

Sparks G. An introduction to UML tutorial business process. http://www.sparxsystems.com.au

http://www.wisegeek.com/what-is-a-business-process-framework.htm

Chapter 7
People Issues with BPR and Change Management

7.1 Objectives

The major objectives of this chapter revolve around highlighting change management and people issues during a typical business process reengineering exercise.

The following aspects have been covered:

- Importance of change management during a BPR exercise
- Intricacies of a typical change management process
- Major people-related issues that emerge in a typical BPR exercise
- Common frameworks used across the industry for change management during BPR
- Best practices of change management during BPR
- Case study of Toyota Australia on successful handling of change management during a BPR exercise

7.2 Introduction

It's common knowledge that at the base of every process are people. Hence unless people are convinced with certain processes, those processes can never succeed. Same is the case with business process reengineering. Given the fact that BPR leads to massive changes within the organization, the importance of softer aspects like managing change becomes paramount.

As per statistics, 84 % of BPR projects fail owing to some people-related issue. According to Gartner, although consultants and companies take all possible measures to make sure that a certain BPR exercise is flawlessly executed, they invariably end up undermining the importance of managing change and people which eventually leads to the failure of the project.

Far too many projects have failed in the recent past for the simple reason that some aspect of managing change was underplayed. With this as the context we now

S. Mohapatra, *Business Process Reengineering*, Management for Professionals,   149
DOI 10.1007/978-1-4614-6067-1_7, © Springer Science+Business Media New York 2013

get into details of what change management is and how it plays an important role during a BPR exercise.

7.3   What Is Change Management?

According to Wikipedia, "Change management is a structured approach to shifting/transitioning individuals, teams, and organizations from a current state to a desired future state." It is a set of processes which are employed to ensure that significant changes are implemented in a systematic, orderly, and controlled manner. It is essential to overcome the human aspect of resistance to change in order to achieve organization goals of effective transformation in an orderly manner.

Organizational change can be missionary, strategic, operational, technological, etc. Smooth transition from one state of behavior to other is essential to bring an organization-wide change. Most of the organizations want change to happen without any resistance from its employees and partners. This is possible if a well-structured approach is used for managing change. Organization change management includes both processes and management tools used to make changes at an organizational level.

Management's role is very important in change management. It is their duty to facilitate and enable change. It has to first identify processes that are obsolete and come up with new processes which are more effective for organization. The managers have to then identify and estimate the impact which this change will bring on the organization and individual employees. The impact study should be detailed and cover the impact which will occur at various levels including technical and behavioral and work processes, etc. Managers should not impose change on employees but make them embrace the change.

The management should try and access the reactions of its individual employees on the change. Some changes bring lots of resistance while others are beneficial as it brings least resistance from employees. Changes are very beneficial for organization but employees find it difficult to understand that because of their preconceived notions and fear regarding change. It is the duty of a manager to use a proper framework which anticipates all changes with risks and has methodologies to overcome these changes.

There are many academicians who have written about importance of behavioral change for change management. One such great academician Davenport who always emphasized on technology and innovation still believed that "organizational and human resource issues are more central than technology issues to the behavior changes that must occur within a process." He believed process change creates cultural changes by changing people's behavior. According to Davenport, "Change incurred by process innovation is not only broad, but deep, extending from the visions of managers to the attitudes and behaviors of the lowest level workers. Its significant behavioral component makes process innovation based change qualitatively different from other forms of large scale restructuring." Thus if the

employees understand the benefits of the change for both individual and organization then the change management process becomes successful.

People are generally resistant to change because of inertia. A force which is
greater than this inertia is required in order to make people adopt change. Managing
change is therefore very important for every manager.

7.4 Importance of Change Management and People in BPR

An organization going for business process reengineering (BPR brings about radical changes in the business processes) has to deal with change management.
According to a survey conducted by Charles Tennat and Yi-Chieh Wu of *Warwick
Manufacturing Group, University of Warwick, Coventry, UK,* to understand the key
factors for the success of BPR.

BPR brings in change of business processes of a wide variety like business planning,
advertising, and technology management. However the graph above shows the

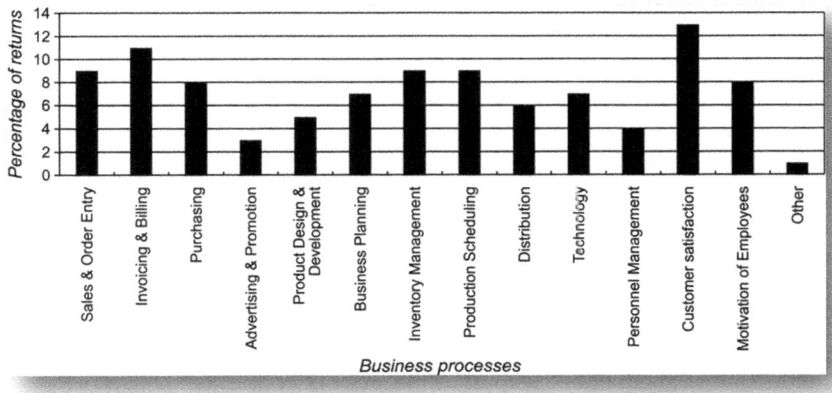

Expectation of change in business processes

priority is generally given to the front-ended processes like customer satisfaction,
sales order entry, invoicing, and inventory management. Such business processes
directly contribute to the top line of the organization. These processes are carried
out by many people from across the functions, e.g., an order fulfillment process
involves operations, finance, and sales departments. For the processes to be changed
it becomes evident that the people handling them should be ready to embrace the
change. Also according to the survey, 78 % of the respondents felt that people issues
should be tackled along with BPR project concurrently. This highlights the importance of people for a successful BPR.

BPR is about bringing radical change in the way business processes are carried
out in an organization. This not only changes the business process alone but entire

business is affected. As BPR involves cross-functional changes, it is not possible without the support from people involved in the business processes. People have to become agents of change. Communication at all levels is very important for change to happen in a planned manner.

7.5 Major People-Related Issues in BPR

The employees of the organization have lots of preconceived notions and issues about BPR, some of which are:

- *BPR is a downsizing exercise*
  The employees think that BPR is carried out by the top management just to lay off people. Such types of assumptions make the behavior of the employees to be rigid and thus resisting any change.
- *Reduction of power and authority*
  Employees fear that the power they enjoy currently will be lost once BPR is done. They feel the authority.
- *Difficulty in dealing with day to day job activities specially during BPR implementation*
  When the organization starts implementing BPR the daily activities become complex as the employees have to deal with new and old activities simultaneously and they are not convinced completely.
- *Organizational restructuring*
  Employees fear that organization restructuring might result in new superior under whom he/she may not be able to work efficiently.
- *Fear of the unknown*
  If the employees are not properly convinced about the expectations and changes from the new processes they are bound to be fearful of the new processes. They start doubting about their capabilities to carry out new tasks.
- *Uncertainty regarding the new roles and responsibilities*
  Employees fear that the new processes will require new skills to be learned; otherwise there can be performance issues. So a lot of hard work will be required to acquire new skills.
- *Increase in transparency of processes*
  Employees also fear increasing in transparency will bring better monitoring and thus work has to be done in a more efficient manner.
- *Cost cutting disguised as BPR*
  Many times employees feel that BPR is used only for cost cutting and thus they will lose jobs and have to work more.

Due to the above-mentioned people issues it becomes difficult for the team to implement BPR. As mentioned before research shows that majority of the BPR projects fail because of people issues.

7.6   Change Management Frameworks

The very fact that change management is an extremely diverse concept means that there isn't a full-proof framework for successfully implementing the same during BPR exercises. However, by virtue of the numerous BPR projects that have been implemented over the years, some of the norms have come to the fore-front. These norms have been molded into industry-accepted frameworks. However, before we get into the details of frameworks it's important to under-stand the impact that the various components of a BPR exercise have on the employees within the organization.

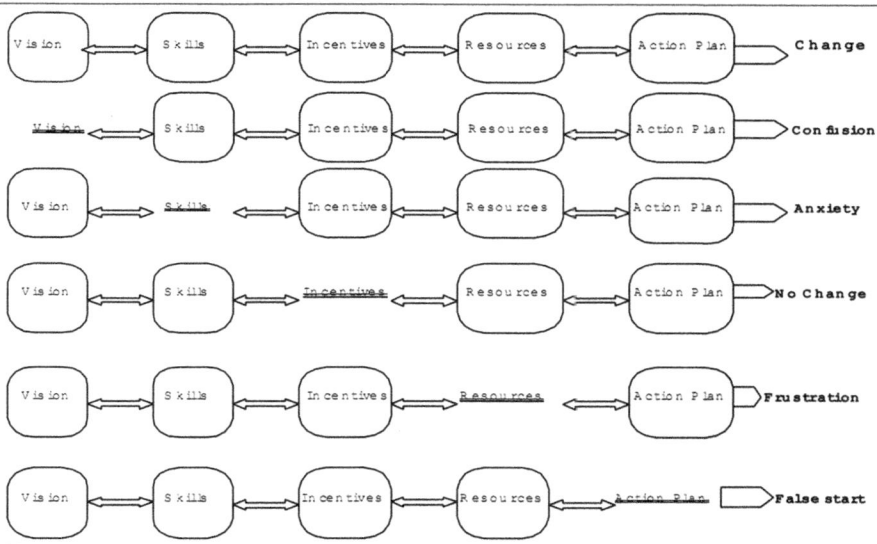

The diagram above shows the five basic elements required for a BPR exercise, namely, vision, skills, incentives, resources, and action plan. It depicts the impact that the absence of each of these elements has on the mind-set of the employees.

- In order to bring about change, all the five elements need to be present.
- In case "vision" is absent, it leads to confusion amongst the employees as to why a certain BPR exercise is being implemented.
- The absence of skills leads to anxiety as employees are unable to find confidence in the reengineered process and are unable to understand the accountabilities.
- The absence of "incentives" leads to employees not being motivated enough to support the BPR exercise and being involved in the reengineered exercise. Thus every BPR exercise needs to have incentives for the workforce.
- Lack of resources leads to frustration amongst the employees as they are unable to understand how to make use of the reengineered processes.
- Finally, lack of a post-BPR action plan gives the process a false start which soon tapers off to expose the blinding realities of the employees being unable to under-stand the utility of the reengineered processes.

This is how each of the BPR elements is equally important to ensure a successful change management in a BPR exercise. With this as the base we now look at some of the industry-established frameworks deployed by companies to bring about change management during BPR exercises. At this stage it's important to remember that each of these frameworks simply assists change management at certain stages of the BPR and is not exhaustive in their own rights.

7.7 McKinsey's 7S Framework: Analysis Phase

McKinsey's 7S framework is one of the widely used frameworks for change management in a typical BPR exercise. Interestingly the framework is used for analytical purposes rather than implementation reasons during the process. It's used to understand the basic structure of an organization from a change management perspective and then subsequently draft a change management strategy.

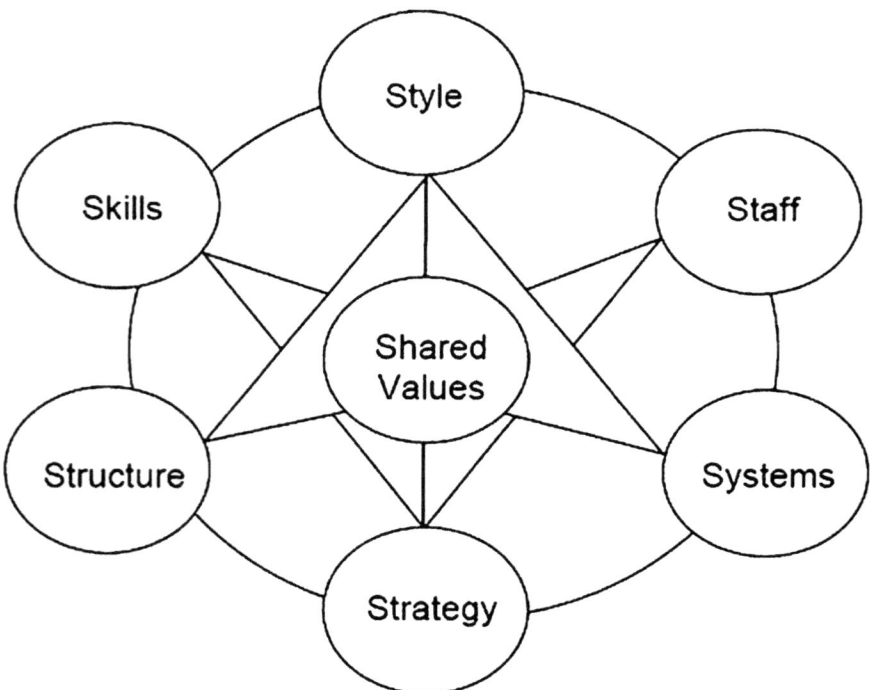

The diagram above highlights the components of the 7S model. As evident from the diagram, all the elements revolve around "shared values" of the organizations. Each of the outer elements is known as trigger. Change in any one of them results in change in the rest of the elements as evident from the interconnection. Ideally in case of BPR it is the "systems" element which happens to be the trigger. Thus for BPR with systems as the trigger, the impact on the remaining elements is predicted and forecasted. Once the impact has been forecasted, the elements with maximum impact are drilled further to analyze the crucial areas and this leads to development of strategies vis-a-vis change management. Thus with the help of the 7S model, all aspects of an organization are analyzed with respect to change management during BPR.

7.8   Change Management Heat Map

Yet another important tool used during the change management process of a BPR cycle is the change management heat map. Shown below, the heat map is used to narrow down on employees who are likely to create maximum hurdles during the change management process.

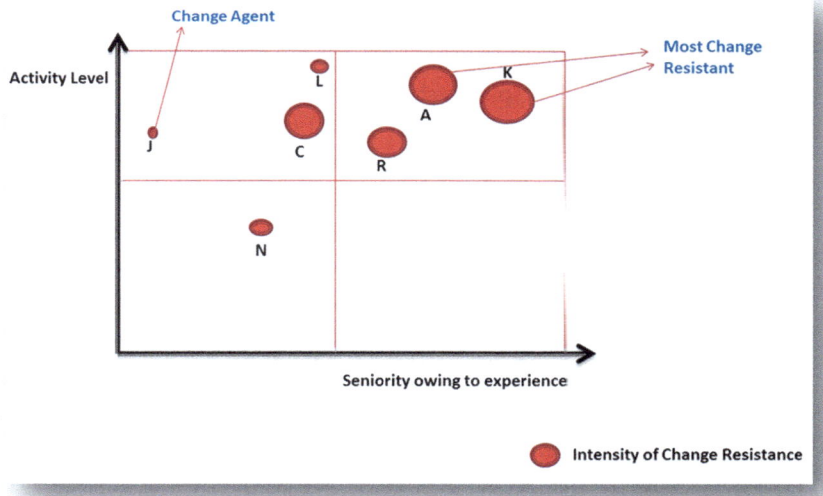

The heat map basically consists of the classification of all the key employees who are likely to be affected by the BPR process in one of the quadrants. As seen the heat map is a 2×2 matrix with the parameters being "seniority" and the "activity" level of the employees. The heat map also depicts the intensity of change resistance that can be expected for each of the employees.

Through the heat map it's determined as to where the power center within the organization lies and how does one deal with those expected to provide maximum resistance to change.

7.9   End-to-End Change Management Framework

Having had a look at some of the most common frameworks used at various stages of the change management process during a BPR implementation, we now look at an end-to-end exhaustive framework for change management. The framework has been designed by Prosci's research after having analyzed over 900 change management implementations over the past 7 years.

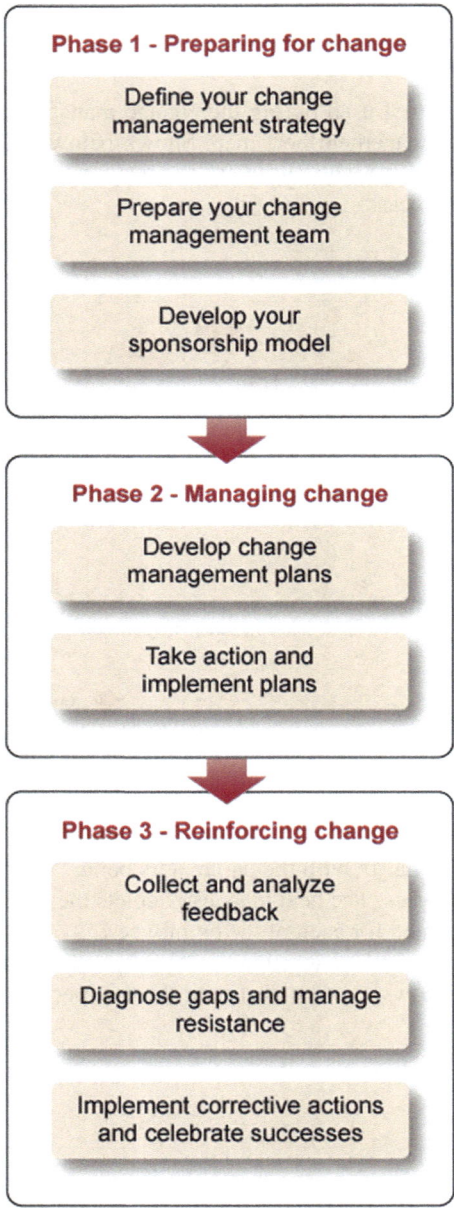

The framework consists of three distinct phases. In the first phase the organization is prepared for change by defining the change management strategy, preparing the change management team, and narrowing down on the sponsor who would head the change management process. In the second phase, strategies are designed to manage change by developing change management plans and implementing them. Finally in the last phase, the suggested changes are reinforced in order to strengthen the new processes. This is done by collecting and analyzing feedback, diagnosing the gaps and managing resistance, and implementing the corrective actions. As a result of this framework, change management is deployed right across the organization in an extensive manner.

7.10   Best Practices in Managing Change During a BPR Exercise

The following are the set of best practices recommended during a change management exercise as a part of an extensive BPR exercise:

- *Performing Readiness Assessment*
  Even before the change management process begins, it's important to determine whether the organization is ready for the expected extent of change. Far too often companies miss this step only to realize midway that the organization might not be able to handle such extensive change. As a part of this exercise, assessments tools are used to check the readiness of employees based on the history and organizational structure.
- *Communication and Communication Planning*
  It is very important for any change management program to have communication at every stage of the reengineering process. Right from the idea to implementation every stage of the process should be communicated very well with the employees in order to maintain transparency and get their involvement. Use of face-to-face communication helps in handling sensitive aspects of organizational change management.
- *Use of Innovative Medium of Communications*
  It has been observed that e-mail and written notices are very weak in conveying the message to employees. Employees generally don't like to attend seminars also. Nowadays companies need to try some innovative ways to convey the importance of BPR to their employees. One of such way is to have a role play or a skit which shows the current status of the company, its problems, and then how BPR can solve these issues in long run and short run. The benefits of BPR to employees and organization as a whole should be communicated clearly. It should be depicted in a humorous way so that people are not bored and yet get the message clear. Such tactics have great benefits in bringing the employees together and making them ready to accept change.
- *Manager Training and Coaching*
  Even before the change management is implemented, it's important to train the supervisors and leads who would be leading the change management exercise. This is done on the basis of the initial readiness assessment and is crucial

in ensuring that the right set of change management processes is implemented during the exercise.

- *Extensive Employee Training*
  Training of the employees in order to get them acquainted with the new processes is by far the most crucial aspect of a change management exercise. Project team members are normally designated to come up with the training requirements on the basis of skillset and behavioral aspect of the existing employees. Lack of this appropriate training is bound to lead to a disaster.
- *Regular Feedback Mechanism*
  While the change management process is under process, it's important to collect regular feedback from all the stakeholders who are being impacted owing to the BPR exercise. This helps in refining the change management exercise as per the existing environment within the organization.
- *Regular Resistance Management*
  At every step of the BPR exercise, it's important to determine the intensity of resistance being faced within the organization against the altered processes. This needs to be done on an extremely regular basis as managing resistance on a continuous basis is much simpler than managing it all at once at the end of the BPR exercise. In this process, the change management heat map is used to determine the reaction of power centers to the various changes and accordingly strategies are developed to manage them.
- *Top Management Support*
  This is one of the most important aspects of the change management exercise during BPR. Presence of an appropriate sponsor who along with the top management is completely in favor of the BPR exercise is a must. The organization will adapt to the changes only if it sees the confidence of the senior management in the changed processes. Lack of this could severely dent the effectiveness of the BPR deployment.
- *Celebration and Apt Recognition of Success*
  Along with the importance of the core strategies in implementing change management, what's also important is celebrating the success of the changed processes with the employees and the stakeholders on the whole. This conveys a clear message of the changes working in the desired manner and further motivates the stakeholders to work towards improvements in the processes.

7.11 Case Study: SAP HR/Payroll Implementation at Toyota Australia

In the early part of the year 2004, Toyota Australia realized that it was badly struggling with the internal processes encompassing employees and workplace issues. Most of the processes were operating in silos with hardly any interdepartmental communication. The existing payroll platform was extremely outdated and was proving to be an expensive as well as complicated affair to handle. Moreover, the platform was incapable of handling even subtle changes in compensation-based issues thereby forcing immense manual handling of the processes.

With the processes getting uncontrollable with every passing day, Toyota Australia hired consultants to sort out the issue who in turn suggested a business process reengineering exercise to completely revamp the HR and payroll processes within the organization. Thus after a lot of due diligence and analysis, the team finally narrowed down on the implementation of SAP HR/payroll implementation for the entire organization. However, since the implementation was bound to affect even the smallest of payroll processes, challenges were immense and most of them required change management.

7.11.1   Challenges

Precisely, the major challenges were

- *Pay*: Employees were concerned as to how their pay would be affected owing to the BPR exercise. It's an obvious fact that when the wages and personal details of employees are involved in a certain reengineering process, concerns are bound to be high, and this is exactly what the case was at Toyota Australia.
- *Diversity*: Toyota Australia had the distinction of encompassing diverse groups of people with completely different ethnic backgrounds and a wide range of skillset. Thus it was quite clear that each of these groups owing to their diversity would react in different manners which meant varying change management strategies had to be put into place to handle this diversity.
- *Acceptance*: With the expected change in work requirements and skills, the biggest challenge was to ensure that both the employees and the business accept the changes as net positive.

7.11.2   Change Management Process

- An exclusive change management team was created whose only job was to ensure that the various stakeholders were in sync with the ongoing process changes.
- An exhaustive readiness assessment was done to ensure to analyze the extent to which the organization was ready for the change management process.
- From time to time, impact assessments were done which would then result in fine-tuning the way the BPR was being done.
- The entire exercise was presented as an employee-driven initiative so as to take the employees into confidence and make them feel that it was all for their good and welfare.
- Extensive change communications were developed with each of them being tailored to different end-user groups which as mentioned before were extremely diverse in nature.

- A separate training and support strategy was designed for each of the departments, further drilling down to the different user groups. This ensured individual attention for the comfort of all the employees.
- A detailed training needs analysis was done from time to time.
- Road show presentations were conducted from time to time to make the employees aware of the extent of change that was taking place and to ensure that all the pent-up anxiety within them was released.
- Extreme involvement of the senior management was ensured to take the employees in confidence and make them realize the importance and benefits of the BPR exercise.

7.11.3 Outcomes

As a result of this exhaustive change management strategy, the BPR exercise was a roaring success. The organization achieved an extremely successful outcome with acceptance across all the different and diverse groups. The process ensured that the business ownership was seamlessly transitioned. This helped in overcoming the geographical barriers and ethnic diversities across the organization.

Extensive training ensured that managers were comfortable with their new roles from day 1 and made the seamless transition with utmost ease. In addition to this with the increased confidence in the changed processes, productivity increased manifold. All in all, over 4,500 employees of Toyota Australia were now being paid the right amount at the right time and were privy to the right amount of information.

Thus with these extensive set of change management strategies, the BPR exercise at Toyota Australia was a runaway success.

7.12 Summary

As seen right throughout this chapter including the case study, if handled in a methodical manner, successful change management during BPR isn't all that difficult. However, as mentioned previously, the biggest issue with change management is that it varies extensively as per situations and organizations. However, after innumerable BPR projects, we now have designated frameworks for handling all these situations, some of which have been mentioned in this chapter.

Thus with the active support of the top management and by deploying a structured and methodical change management approach, any BPR exercise can be successfully executed with the desired results.

Bibliography

http://www.managingchange.com/bpr/bprcult/content.htm
http://en.wikipedia.org/wiki/Change_management
http://www.emeraldinsight.com/journals.htm?articleid=1524121&show=html&
http://www.managingchange.com/bpr/bprcult/4bprcult.htm
http://www.scribd.com/doc/7249477/Toyota-Bpr
http://www.change-management.com/tutorial-change-process-detailed.htm
http://www.emeraldinsight.com/journals.htm?issn=1463-7154&volume=7&issue=2&articleid=8
    43469&show=pdf

Chapter 8
Change Management Approach in Implementing BPR

8.1 Objective

The title of this chapter is *BPR Implementation Steps and People View*. The first section of this chapter would deal primarily with the nitty-gritty of business process reengineering implementation in any organization. We intend to explore the implementation steps to a great level of detail. In other words, the objective here is to understand the implementation of BPR at a granular level.

The second section of this chapter would cover the *people* aspect of any change initiative within an organization. The focus would be primarily on BPR-related change initiatives. We would like to identify the issues that crop up due to the resistance shown by employee and the ways of dealing with them.

The final section of this chapter would be a case study of an Indian organization where one of the major BPR initiatives stumbled upon a roadblock created by the resistance and noncooperation displayed by its employees. This case would illustrate the importance of *people* for the successful completion of any project.

8.2 Background

The term *business process*, in its truest sense, was first used by Adam Smith in 1776. Since then, it has become a global standard. All the activities carried out within an organization are logically grouped together (based on their business outcome) and documented. Each such group of activities is termed as a *business process*.

As an organization advances in its life cycle its business processes no longer remain adequate. This happens due to the following reasons:

- As time progresses, the business requirements change. This makes the old processes either inefficient or obsolete.

- Some of the processes become redundant with time, hence leading to nonproductive utilization of resources.
- If the organization expands, organically or inorganically, its business processes require a drastic change.

An organization can handle such situation in two different ways as follows:

- *Process improvement process*
  Process Improvement Process or PIP leads to an *incremental improvement* in the process outcome. It is generally carried out when any stable process needs modifications to suit the changing business or organizational requirements.
- *Business process reengineering*
  In contrast to PIP, process reengineering aims at a *transformational improvement* in the process outcome. It involves going back to square one and reinventing the wheel. Business process reengineering attempts to bring about dramatic results in terms of cost, quality, or speed. BPR usually takes place in the later stages of the organization's life cycle when the processes become mature and start to decay.

The origin of the term *BPR* dates back to 1993, when Michael Hammer and James A Champy defined it as "*Reengineering is the fundamental rethinking and radical redesign of business processes to achieve dramatic improvements in critical, contemporary measures of performance, such as cost, quality, service, and speed.*" [1]
Since then, business process reengineering has become a popular topic in the business circle. With the advancements in information technology, BPR has reached a new pedestal altogether. BPR, when combined with technology-enabled automation, has the potential to provide drastic improvement in the process performance.
However, in the early years of BPR, the entire focus was on the technology aspect of it. The *people* aspect was, more often than not, being ignored. This led to the failure of BPR initiatives in a large number of organizations where the employees presented hostility and resistance to such initiatives. As a result, in the later years, change management became an integral part of the BPR. In this chapter we would be dealing with the people aspect in considerable detail.
Several methodologies have been prescribed by different academicians and practitioners for the successful implementation of BPR in an organization. In this chapter, we have tried to provide an implementation approach by taking clues for all of them and pulling together the best features from each one of them.

8.3 BPR Implementation

From contemporary literature, there are several methodologies available for implementing BPR in an organization. However, we have tried to consolidate them and develop a framework that contains the best features from each one of them. The framework is as below.

---

[1] http://www.easy-strategy.com/michaelhammer-and-Jameschampy.html.

8.3.1 *Initiate Strategic Change*

As said by many "*if you fail to plan, you plan to fail*," planning is an integral part of any reengineering initiative. This step prepares an organization for BPR by asking questions like

- Is BPR needed? If yes, what are the objectives?
- Who would be impacted by the reengineering activity?
- How much effort would be required to carry out BPR? Who will be involved?
- How would the success of the initiative be measured?

Each of the sub-steps is described in detail below:

8.3.1.1 Define Project Organization Structure

A project organization structure (pos) is a composition of people (or positions) who would be directly involved in any project effort. A POS is similar to an organization chart, except that it deals with only one project. It defines the *reporting* as well the *escalation* structure for a project. A typical POS would look like

Defining a POS before the project starts offers several advantages:

- The POS facilitates smooth implementation and coordination of the project efforts.
- It reduces the possibility of any ambiguity, disruptions, or conflict.
- It encourages communication amongst team members by laying down proper chain of command.

8.3.1.2 Identify Stakeholders and Their Objectives

Before initiating any reengineering activity, it is crucial to identify all the stakeholders involved in that process. Typically, the stakeholders for any process are the process-owner, other employees, and the customer(s) who derives value from that process. It is important to understand the expectations of each of these parties and identify the areas where the process is falling short of those expectations. Only after doing this gap analysis, the objectives of the BPR exercise should be set.

8.3.1.3 Align the Goals to the Vision and Mission

In order to obtain significant results, it is imperative that the goals of the reengineering activity are in perfect alignment with the vision and mission of the organization. In other words, the project goals should be in sync with the strategic goals.

Such alignment would help in attaining outcomes that are of strategic importance to the company as well as to the customer. Apart from that, it would be easier to garner the support of the top management on BPR activities if the project goals fit perfectly into the bigger picture.

8.3.1.4 Define Critical Success Factors

The elements that would determine the ultimate success or failure of any project are called the critical success factors or the CSFs. CFSs are the areas that must be given continued attention and special by the BPR team.

The identification of the CSFs for any BPR activity should be done in the first stage itself. This would ensure that none of these crucial elements is ignored or overlooked at the later stages of implementation.

8.3.1.5 Solicit Consulting and Technology Partners

The organization, undergoing BPR, may lack the domain or technical expertise required to carry out the change. If so, they must solicit external partners for the project. Such solicitation is a time-taking process as it involves several steps like sending request for proposal (RFP), evaluating proposals, and awarding the contract. Hence, it should be carried out in the planning stage of the project. The company must exercise due diligence in choosing a partner. The partners should be selected based on their expertise and cultural fit with the organization.

8.3.2 Current Process Diagnosis

Not all practitioners agree to this, but it is critical to understand the current state of the processes before making any attempt to reengineer them. Unless the current processes are well documented and understood, the reengineering team might overlook some of the process details. Such fallacy can lead to disastrous results. Hence the process owner (along with his/her team) should be involved in this step to ascertain that none of the details are left out.

8.3.2.1 Map Current Processes

There are several tools available for the purpose of mapping processes. Most powerful of them are *process maps* and *activity charts*. A process map has a detailed description of what the process does, who is responsible for what, and how the success of the process is measured. An activity chart is a diagram that shows all the operations or tasks involved in a process. The employees who are accountable for the process should be involved in the BPR at this stage.

8.3.2.2 Perform Cost Analysis

This step deals with an in-depth analysis of each activity within a process. Firstly, the time taken by each activity for completion should be assessed. Secondly, the cost of each activity in terms of resources should be measured at this stage. There are tools and simulation methodologies available to carry out this assessment.

8.3.2.3   Perform Gap Analysis

Once the above step is completed, the BPR team would be able to weigh the current performance displayed by the processes against the desired performance. This step is crucial in the sense that, when the reengineering team designs the To-Be processes they would make sure that the gaps and disconnects identified here are bridged.

8.3.2.4   Identify Value-Adding Processes

The organization evolves with time, so do processes. With the change in the business requirements and other external factors, the value delivered by a process changes. As a result, not all processes within an organization are value adding. Some of them are either obsolete or redundant. This step of BPR implementation aims at classifying the process as either value adding or non-value adding (NVA). NVAs are dropped in subsequent stages.

8.3.3   Process Redesign

The objective of this step is to establish a desired end-state for the process undergoing the reengineering initiative. This step involves a few critical decisions that the BPR team has to make in terms of choosing a To-Be process from the available alternatives and developing metrics for measuring the success of the reengineered process.

8.3.3.1   Study Best-in-Class Processes

The first step in redesigning a process is to benchmark it against other similar processes carried out elsewhere. Benchmarking can be done either internally (other departments or business units within the same organizations) or externally (not necessarily against competitors or within the same industry). The outcome of the benchmarking exercise is a set of best practices being followed by the benchmarking partner(s).

8.3.3.2   Design New Processes

In this stage, the reengineering team evaluates the various alternatives generated by the benchmarking exercise. Based on the compatibility with the organization's strategic goals, one of the alternatives is selected. The chosen process is then adapted to the norms of the organization undergoing BPR. Fresh process maps and activity charts are prepared at this stage.

8.3.3.3 Validate New Process Against the CSF

As mentioned earlier, CSFs are critical to the overall success of the project. Hence, at this stage the new process is evaluated for its adequacy on all the critical success factors. If not, the process is modified in order to accommodate all the CSFs.

8.3.3.4 Conduct Cost–Benefit Analysis of Reengineered Processes

The order of implementation of the reengineered processes is decided based on the benefits accrued and the costs involved in each of them. The processes that provide the maximum benefits in a short run are the first ones to get implemented.

8.3.3.5 Develop KPI Metrics

The degree of success of any process is determined by certain metrics known as the key performance indicators or the KPIs. At this stage of BPR, the KPI metrics are developed for the reengineered processes. The KPIs, developed here, would play a very crucial role in the final stage of the BPR where the process-performance would be monitored.

8.3.3.6 Assign New R&R

The reengineered process might require a deviation from the current team structure and existing chain of command. The BPR team, at this stage, would define new roles and responsibilities in order to execute the reengineered processes.

8.3.4 Plan the Implementation and Go Live

This is the phase where the reengineering efforts face the maximum resistance, from hostile antagonists to passive adversaries, all determined to kill the effort. This is the reason why the change management programs to create a culture of acceptance have to be started in parallel with the BPR implementation. In this stage we focus on developing a project plan to implement the new redesigned processes in form of a work breakdown structure. Here, we need to focus on developing the relationship with the implementation partners so as to ensure a smooth transition from old to new processes in order to minimize the change resistance and deliver as promised.

8.3.4.1 Evaluate Automation Areas

With the advancement in technology, it can be safely said that no BPR initiative these days is complete without evaluating where technology can play a key role in providing a key strategic advantage. The redesigned processes should be evaluated to ascertain where technology can be used to provide an automated solution. This may involve anything from developing small in-house applications to using an off-the-shelf ERP system. Choosing the technology, the subsequent vendor and the implementation partner will play a key role in how the project unfolds.

8.3.4.2 Develop Project Plan

The project plan must take into consideration the project organization structure, information systems, business procedures, organization policies, and people along with the newly designed processes. The requirements for the construction of the new processes should be organized in the form of a work breakdown structure (WBS). The WBS should account for all the roles and responsibilities for every task.

8.3.4.3 Synchronize Plan with Partners

This is a crucial stage in the implementation wherein all the stakeholders sign and agree upon the WBS. The statement of work (SOW) agreement is signed between the organization and the implementation partner. The SOW clearly states the different roles of the design and technical support teams, and their responsibilities along with the different service-level agreements between both parties. This signifies the beginning of the actual implementation.

8.3.4.4 Create Prototypes and Simulate Plans

This phase practically prepares you to go live. Here, we prepare for the transition from the old processes to the new ones. Based on the WBS, the prototypes of the new systems/processes are created and tested against the CSFs. This phase is kept in place so as to simulate or test the transition from old process. During the process we check for problems that may arise during actual transition, check how people react to the new prototypes, try to mitigate risks associated with the transition, and build the system as working parts. This phase is also used to perform one-time activities like data migration. This ensures that the employees are slowly and steadily exposed to the new processes, roles, and responsibilities and do not face a sudden shock when the entire set of new processes go live.

8.3.4.5   Initiate Training

Training of the employees on the actual new processes begins along with the development of the prototypes. Employees are already exposed to the new system through theory sessions on the new designs and expected roles before these sessions. Here, they get a practical exposure to the new processes and work hands-on on these new prototypes. This ensures that once the system goes live the employees are completely ready to perform their expected roles right from inception of the processes.

8.3.4.6   Prioritize Plan and Go Live

It is very essential to phase out the implementation based on the importance of the processes. The processes can be prioritized based on vision and mission, business benefits, importance to stakeholders, cost of implementation, number of employees affected, etc. These factors may vary based on the organization's needs and policies. The processes are implemented according to the priority. It is important to conduct an organization-wide feedback to understand where the implementation process could be improved.

8.3.5   Monitor Process and Feedback

This phase begins after the implementation is complete. This phase however does not have a fixed time limit in the WBS/project plan like the other phases. This phase is rather a continuous process indicating that never stop trying to improve our processes. Here, we firstly measure how successful the implementation has been and check whether the CSFs as defined before the start have been achieved. We check this on a periodic basis and keep track of the ROI gained. Apart from this we also evaluate all the employees as per the KPI's definition for their roles. This helps us keep a track of the usage of the new process. Constant feedback is solicited from the employees, industry best practices research is conducted, and changing market demands are considered in order to constantly gauge the need of improving the processes.

8.3.5.1   Measure Success and Track KPI Progress

Here, we focus on measuring the success of the BPR implementation. The KPIs defined in the earlier stages are reviewed on a periodic basis to track how we have performed. Apart from this, we also solicit feedback from all the affected employees to understand how well we have delivered on our promise. The employees give feedback not only on the BPR implementation cycle but also on the *culture change management program* that had been running in parallel. This is a stage in evaluating our performance as implementers and would go a long way in improving the future BPR implementation cycle.

8.3.5.2   Review Performance Against CSF

The objective here is to evaluate whether the whole BPR initiative has made business sense and to evaluate if we have achieved what we had set out to achieve. We periodically cross-check the outcome with the critical success factors as decided before the project began. The ROI is measured on a periodic basis and the business benefits accrued are presented to all the stakeholders.

8.3.5.3   Conduct Usage Reviews and Evaluate R&R

The objective here is to evaluate the *culture change management program*. The progress is measured by evaluating how many people feel more informed, how well the top management is satisfied with the change, and how well the new teams have adapted to the new processes. A way to achieve this is to carry out attitude surveys and discrete chats with employees in key roles. It is important to involve all the stakeholders in the surveys even if it means involving customers or suppliers if they are directly affected by the change. An important aspect is to tie up the evaluation of the employees as per their new system usage with the appraisal process to ensure we track this aspect at an individual level.

8.3.5.4   Conduct Compliance Audits

Compliance audits must be planned on a periodic level to gauge the usage levels of the system on a periodic basis. Compliance audits check at a granular level whether the process is being correctly followed. Following each and every step in the process is of at most importance in order to ensure quality and efficiency. Compliance audits score each team on their compliance with the newly defined processes. Awards for leaders and penalties for the defaulters can be associated with these audits in order to ensure that the processes are being followed to the tee. The compliance audits can also evaluate whether individuals are performing their assigned responsibility.

8.3.5.5   Conduct Process R&D

Business nowadays is constantly changing due to ever-changing demands of customers. It is therefore imperative that an organization always has one hand on the pulse of the market and is quick to react to market changes. Technology is another important dimension that is evolving constantly, enabling organizations to better serve their customers. It is hence important that an organization continuously studies the best-in-class processes, industry standard practices, and benchmarks its own processes against these. This continuous research and development, market pulse, and feedback from employees would help organizations to constantly think about improving the existing processes.

8.3.6 The Iron Triangle

Traditionally, to be successful any organization has focussed on three important dimensions—the people, process, and technology. These dimensions form the foundation pillars for managing change, risk management, or even managing entire projects. Referred to as the *Iron Triangle*, an organization must integrate these three aspects seamlessly in order to be successful.

The organization must focus on each of these aspects in the following order of importance:

People: Understanding the needs of the people and driving them to be committed to your strategy is of prime importance. It is also important to have well-defined roles and responsibilities.

Process: The process details the steps through which the people perform daily tasks in order to achieve the larger objectives of the organization. The organization must develop its capabilities and processes to deliver maximum value to the customers. The organization also needs to develop internal processes to ensure smooth coordination and functioning of all its employees.

Technology: With the people aligned and the process developed, technology can be applied to ensure consistency in the application of the process and provide guidelines to keep the process on track. Technology should make it easier to follow the process.

These three dimensions must be aligned strategically to the business objectives of the organization. When any organization undergoes BPR, the two dimensions of the *Iron Triangle* that are changed are mainly the *process* and possibly the *technology*. It is thus imperative that the *people* dimension should also be of focus in order to maintain the balance in the organization. The employees in the organization are bound to be affected by the shift in status quo and it is important that this shift sets in gradually so that the people are made ready to accept change rather than reject it. The following sections explain ways and means to gradually bring in the change and work towards aligning the mind-set of people to maintain the equilibrium in the golden triangle of the organization.

8.3.7 *Managing Change*

Managing organizational change in a large BPR initiative is not just a scientific process, but it is also an art that requires constant subjective judgments. That does not discount the fact that the change effort must be scientifically modularized into well-defined sets of activities for key stakeholders in the organization.

Our change management framework (Fig. 8.1) demonstrates the human aspects of change and its impact on operational output of the firm while also suggesting key

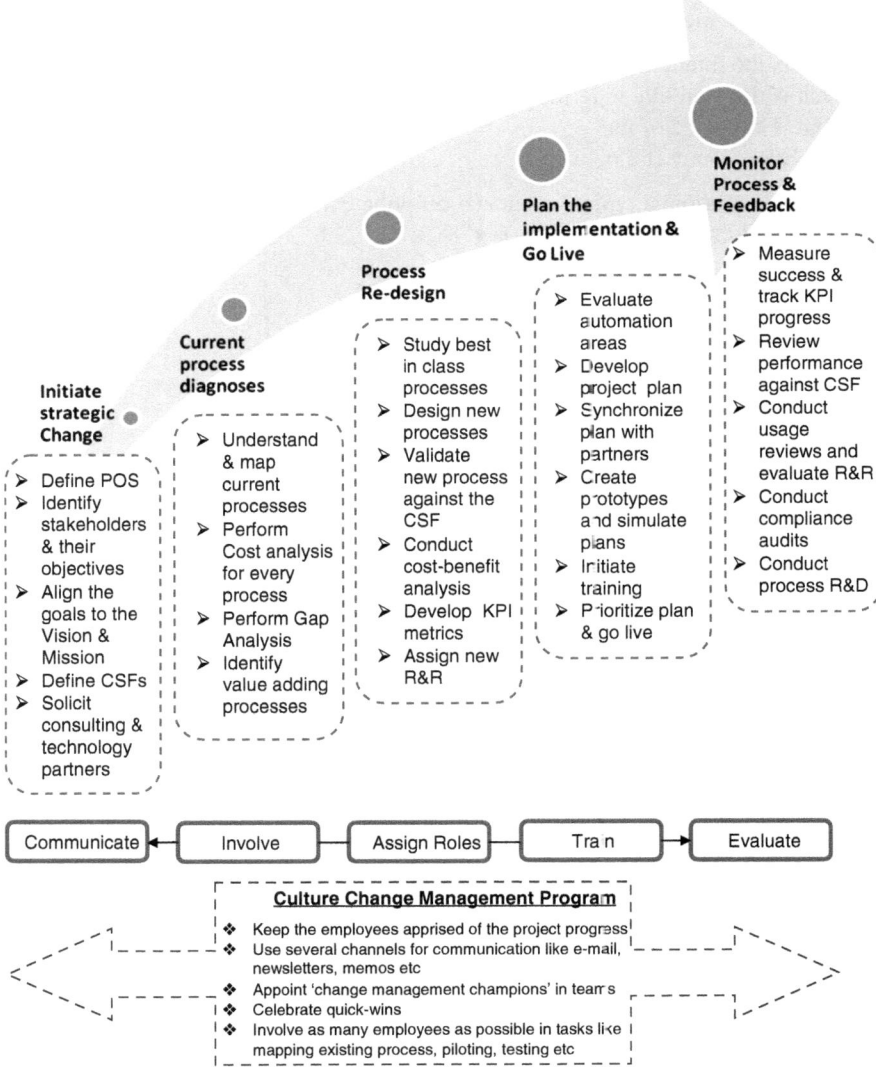

Fig. 8.1 Change management framework

steps that must be taken to increase the probability of success and reduce the pain associated with change.

Each of these steps needs to be detailed out based on the specifics of the organization and the business processes being reengineered. As an illustration, the first-level breakup is provided below. Further breakup will be contingent upon the characteristics of the BPR target and the actual tasks being executed.

8.3.7.1 Initiate Communication for Change

Clarify key questions to impacted stakeholders:

- What is the intent of the exercise?
- What is the plan like in terms of people and timelines?
- What is expected of me?
- How does it impact me?

As an illustration, a typical organization-wide communication sent at the initiation of a BPR exercise is sampled (Fig. 8.2).

8.3.7.2 Assess Change Areas

- Create a cross-functional team of *change evangelists*.
- Understand targets and impact from key employees.
- Collaboratively create a change plan that is mutually agreed upon.
- Clearly define a target To-Be state.

Fig. 8.2 A typical Project Organization Structure

A number of tools are templates are used by various organizations to provide a structure to the assessment process. Depending on the kind of business processes being reengineered, it could be a combination of financial assessment, motion and time study, quality process assessment, operations review, audits, etc.

The outcome of this phase must include a To-Be process map and a To-Be financial model that elaborates the impact of this initiative on the business unit's earnings.

8.3.7.3 Communicate Change Execution Plan

• Communicate change execution plan in nontechnical readable format to staff.
• Solicit potential issues and pitfalls from impacted groups.
• Address identified issues.
• Finalize plan and the desired To-Be operating model.

8.3.7.4 Execute Change

• Create a strong program management office (PMO).
• Clearly define roles and responsibilities of key stakeholders (ref. Fig. 8.3)
• Measure progress against predefined success criteria.
• Logically conclude and announce success.

8.3.7.5 Stabilize Operations

• Measure, analyze, improve, and control.
• Define continuous improvement targets.
• Remove any auxiliary support utilized during transformation.
• Validate operational effectiveness through end-user surveys/feedback.

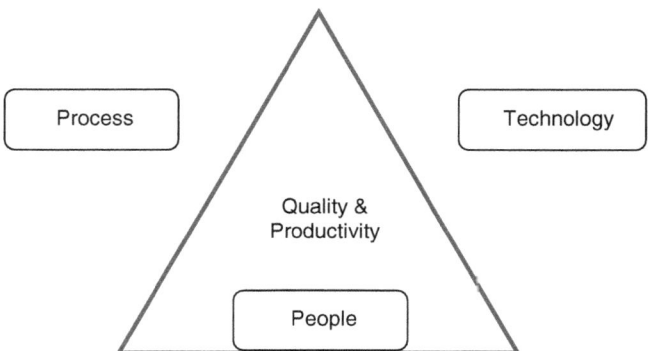

Fig. 8.3 An Iron Triangle

```
Message from the CEO

As part of our ongoing initiative to improve our effectiveness and
streamline operations, I have asked Sanjiv Kumar, who heads our global
operations to lead an effort to conduct a Business Process Redesign
Project.  This effort is scheduled to begin in the first week of the new
year and will continue until the second quarter of FY'12.  The
objectives of this effort are to:
     o  Identify opportunities to streamline our factory operations and
        supply chain processes from supplier to consumer.
     o  Create standard processes, where possible, across factory
        locations, SKUs and across markets.
     o  Develop the ideal operating model that defines the organizational
        structure, process, roles and technology to support a world-class
        factory model.

We have engaged Black Consulting Group to augment our team and put
structure and industry best practices around the execution of this
project.

The project team will primarily be working from our Detroit site
offices,and will visit our other locations and interview selected
suppliers on a need basis so please make yourselves available should
your time be requested by the project team. I expect that many of you
will be participating from both an information sharing and a solution
design perspective.

I am very excited about the opportunities that we have ahead of us, and
I encourage each of you to think creatively on how to improve our
business and better serve our customer and share the same with the
project team.  Please join me in making this project successful.

Please let me know if you have any questions and thanks in advance for
your support.

Sincerely,
Bob Williams
CEO and MD
Detroit Machine Tools
```

Stabilizing operations is about minimizing the instances of the process breaching control limits. Thus well-defined control limits for the To-Be processes are prerequisite for this exercise. It involves substantial amount of data collection and analysis in this step. As an illustration, Fig. 8.4 shows the data collected from clients during the stabilization phase to measure completion of the reengineering exercise.

R = **Responsible** (the role responsible for performing the task)

A = **Accountable** (the role with overall responsibility for the task)

C = **Consulted** (the roles that provide input to help perform the task)

I = **Informed** (the roles with vested interest who should be kept informed)

Tasks / Activities	Program Director	Relationship Manager	Project Managers	Consultant / Advisor	Contracts Manager	Metrics Controller	Financial Controller	Legal Advisor	Human Resources	Compliance	External Supplier
Finalize governance framework	A,R	C							I		A,R
Identify key roles and responsibilities at organizational, functional, and operational level	A,R	C,I	I	I	I	I	I	I	C,I	I	I
Establish meeting frequency for Steering Committee (SC)	A,R	C	I	I	I	I	I	I	I	I	C
Establish meeting frequency of Program Management Office (PMO)	A	A,R	C	I	I	I	I	I	I	I	C
Establish status report template for SC and PMO	A,R	C	I	I	I	I	I	I	I	I	C
Understand contractual elements having impact on the BPR viability	R	A,R	R		R	R	R	R			C
<<Add additional activities here>>											

Fig. 8.4 Raci matrix illustrated

8.3.7.6 Share Rewards of Success

- Create excitement, celebrate success, and let employees know of the outcome.
- Implement benefit-sharing mechanisms with key stakeholders—employees, clients, etc.

8.3.7.7 Potential Issues

Typically, organizational reengineering exercises end up with a suboptimal outcome and have to undergo a prolonged revival process to eliminate the issues and then get the benefits from the BPR.

User Satisfaction Survey Form

| *Please mark "X" in the boxes* | *Part #:* | *Customer name:* |

Q1 Overall Experience with DMT

5.Very Satisfisd

4.Satisfied

3.Neutral

2.Dissatisfied

1.Very Dissatisfied

Q4 Clarity of the shipping label on the consignment

5.Very Satisfied

4.Satisfied

3.Neutral

2.Dissatisfied

1.Very Dissatisfied

Q2 Quality of the part against specifications

5.Very Satisfied

4.Satisfied

3.Neutral

2.Dissatisfied

1.Very Dissatisfied

Q5 Speed of shipping the consignment

5.Very Satisfied

4.Satisfied

3.Neutral

2.Dissatisfied

1.Very Dissatisfied

Q3 Quality of packaging of the shipment

5.Very Satisfied

4.Satisfied

3.Neutral

2.Dissatisfied

1.Very Dissatisfied

Q6 Regular information provided by DMT about your consignment

5.Very Satisfied

4.Satisfied

3.Neutral

2.Dissatisfied

1.Very Dissatisfied

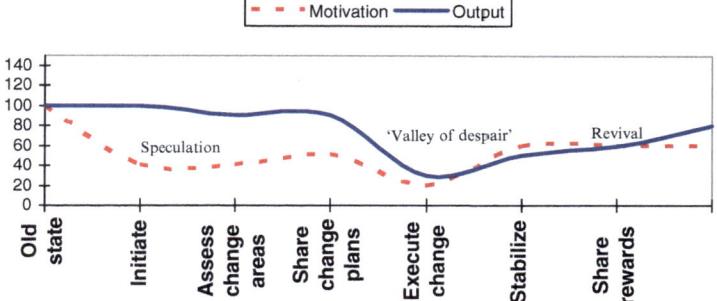

Fig. 8.5 Data collected from clients during the stabilization phase to measure completion of the reengineering exercise

The outcome of a typical BPR cycle along with its impact on employee morale can be seen in Fig. 8.5.

As seen in the above illustration, the organization is struggling to cope with the issues related to change and is unable to clearly complete the stabilization phase. The issues facing the organization are primarily derived from the initial lack of change management and are compounded by subsequent absence of a robust program management office. Some issues that could typically lead organizations to this route are the following:

- During the initial set of communications with employees, key questions were left unanswered leading to speculation and reliance on grapevine in the organization.
- The impacted groups of key employees and managers were not included in the decision-making process; hence the change plan was at best theoretical and not tenable.
- Limited communication and secretive approach ensured that employees do not open up to potential issues and pitfalls that may arise in course of the implementation.
- Unmanaged change, with a purely top-down approach caused loss of workforce, disruption to business, and fire fighting to restore client confidence.
- The stabilization stage could not focus on leading the organization into continuous improvement; instead this phase becomes more of an exercise in meeting pre-transformation SLAs.
- Bad experience with transformation eventually results in loss of key employees, and inability to sustain business at pre-transformation levels.

8.3.7.8   Case: BPR of Inbound Customer Call Center for a Mobile Service Provider

Part 1: Case History

Hawk Telecom (all names changed) is a telecom service provider having GSM service licenses in 18 states across India. The company has been in the business for 10 years and has the third largest customer base in the country.

Hawk operates an inbound customer call center from Faridabad, which is a suburban town close to the Indian capital city of Delhi. All calls to the Hawk customer service helpline from across India are routed to this call center. After every customer call, the customer is sent an SMS text query seeking feedback on the quality of the helpline. The helpline has consistently delivered between 85% and 90% satisfaction rates until about a year ago.

It has been observed that since late 2010 the call satisfaction rates of Hawk have been progressively going down, and are now hovering around 75–80%. Additionally, Hawk's net subscriber addition has been flat or near-zero, despite a telecom market that is growing at 12% per annum. The company's management believed that reducing customer satisfaction is the primary factor for exodus of its existing customers, but was unable to pinpoint the real problem that is resulting in the reduced customer satisfaction ratings. The subscriber base also has a relatively higher average age than many of its competitors, and some people believe that the firm has not been aggressive enough in tapping non-voice VAS (value-added services) and has only been following its competitors in areas of GPRS and 3G.

At this point, the firm decided to undergo a business process reengineering across its various business units, starting with the customer call center to fix the problem of reducing customer satisfaction and to improve net subscriber addition. The BPR exercise was owned by John Peer, who had joined Hawk recently as the chief strategy officer from the second largest mobile service provider in the USA.

Part 2: Assessment

John initiates the project with a high-level assessment of the company's revenue streams and a detailed assessment of the customer call-center operations. He forms a team that interview the CFO and the floor-operations manager of the call center. Some of the data obtained is presented below.

Average Revenue per User (ARPU)

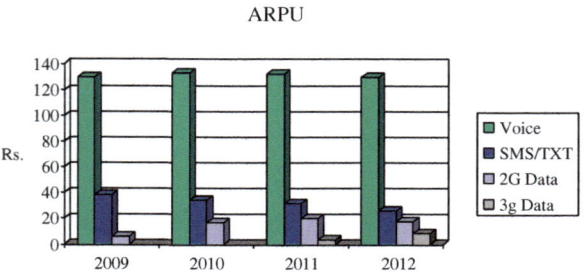

Issue category for which customers are calling the help desk:

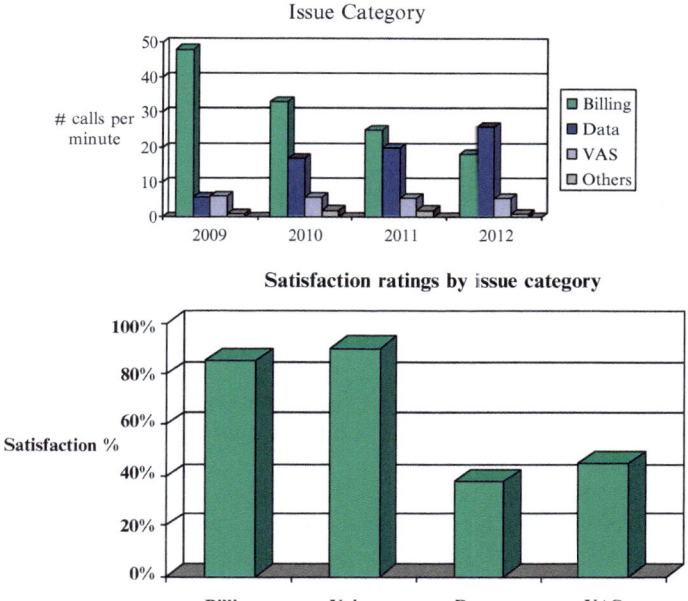

Note: Customer satisfaction ratings have not been stored for previous years so the above data is only for 2012.

Part 3: Analysis

Analysis of the subscribers' spend pattern showed a marked increase in spend on data and related services over the last 3 years. Consequently, the number of data-related issues coming from customers has increased at a disproportionately high rate, and has now surpassed billing-related issues that used to be the primary issue that the call center dealt with. Subsequent analysis of the customer satisfaction ratings showed that customers are least satisfied with the agent's resolution of data-related issues. All the above facts provided ammunition to John to further dig out facts.

A skill profiling of the agents on the floor was conducted. Eighty percent of the agents felt they had only a general understanding of mobile data, and do not consider the training they received sufficient enough to address customer queries. While the same agents felt that they are well equipped to resolve billing- and voice-related issues. Upon deeper inspection, it was observed that most of the agents came from a mathematics or commerce background. But the remaining 20% who were comfortable with mobile-data-related queries are the ones who had joined recently and were from more diverse backgrounds ranging from physical sciences to industrial training.

When a call comes in, it is routed to the agent to the first available agent, with all agents defined in a round-robin sequence. There is a single queue for all calls, and only the complex billing issues are forwarded manually by the agent to the finance department that operates out of an adjacent facility.

Part 3: Recommendation

Industry best practices suggest that calls should be routed to the right agent depending on their skills. And given that data has been picking up market faster than what Hawk has been able to deliver, there is a need to focus more on data-related calls. Consequently, the following recommendations were made:

1. Add capability in the IVR to differentiate between the category of calls—billing, voice, data, and VAS.
2. Create a separate round-robin queue for mobile-data-related calls.
3. Enhance the mobile-data support team by enabling additional members with technical training.
4. Add a second-level support team for mobile-data that would take care of more complex issues, in the lines of finance support team to manage complex billing issues.
5. In steady state, the mobile-data support team and the remaining team should be equal in size, to be in alignment with the actual call volumes.

8.3.8 Managing the Change: People Focus

Conducting BPR involves adopting new processes, adapting to new technology, and accepting new areas of responsibility. For a manager, this environment throws forward a gamut of challenges to manage the expectations of the various stakeholders affected by the change. This section aims at providing different strategies to manage this process of change so as to involve all the users affected by the change and suggests ways to support them throughout this process of change. This can also be viewed as running a *culture change management program* parallel to the BPR implementation.

8.3.8.1 Versatile Engagement: Choosing the Right People Ready to Change for the Change

Here, the focus is on choosing right candidates to spearhead the change. Candidates that are flexible and are ready to accept the challenges put forth by change. The idea is to choose candidates who believe in the process and are ready to champion the cause of BPR in the organization. Only such people should be chosen to represent the employees in the process of change. While choosing the people factors such as age, interests, knowledge areas, and technical aptitude should be taken into consideration. It is also of equal importance to identify the employees who harbor negative feelings towards the change and steps should be taken to alleviate their concerns.

For the purpose of distinction let us call these employees as *pilot employees* and *roadblock employees*. It is important to identify these employees and address separate needs of these users to leverage their capabilities in a better way.

1. *Pilot Employees*
   Distinguishing characteristics of these users are as follows:

   - Want to take lead in BPR initiatives.
   - These users trust the BPR initiative to be a positive and necessary change.
   - Are knowledgeable about existing processes.
   - Knowledge of BPR is an added advantage.

   Action items

   - Give them the responsibility of mentoring other employees and creating a culture of acceptance for change right from the outset.
   - Give responsibility to champion the BPR cause and drive new implementations forward.
   - Select them in the leadership roles while forming the project organization structure.

2. *Roadblock Employees*
   Distinguishing characteristics of these users are as follows:

   - These users do not like the BPR initiative and consider it as a roadblock.
   - Feel ignored in the process of change yet are users of the new processes.
   - Some may remain silent about their feelings, posing a larger threat to the process of identifying pain areas.

   Action items

   - Need to identify their major pain areas and address them as quickly as possible.
   - Need to overcommunicate the need of change to them to solicit their support.
   - Constant support such as training should be given to these employees.
   - Eventually let go of such employees and reassign responsibilities if they do not show characteristics of pilot users even after sustained support.

It is advisable to have a separate team responsible for reaching out to people, identifying issues, alleviating problems, communicating the change, conducting the training, and creating a culture of change acceptance within the organization.

8.3.8.2 Organized Communication: Involving All the Users and Spreading the Right Culture

The objective here is to create a continuous connection with the end users of the processes so that they feel involved with the change and feel that they are an important part of the change. Here, a threefold communication strategy is suggested. The prime objective of following this threefold communication strategy is to make the users aware of the change well before the change occurs. This will help in preparing the users for the change and would lead to a better acceptance of the change.

- *Encouraging Communication*
  This form of communication is informative and is made in order to sensitize the user about impending BPR initiative. This communication should reach the user a few months before the actual change is rolled out. The format may be mass-mailers or charts put up in the common areas of the organization.

Objective: This form of communication is informative and is made in order to sensitize the user about impending BPR changes.

Contents: The contents of the communication should convey the need for change and the advantages of the change in order to create a positive feeling about the change.

Period: During stages 1 and 2 (plan and design) of BPR process. This communication should reach the user a month or two before the actual changes are rolled out.

Format: E-mail to all users or poster put up in common area. Innovative and involving methods like street plays in cafeterias are also being used.

Example: In future while implementing a *manager's dashboard* system, in the requirements gathering phase itself, an e-mail can be sent to all the managers communicating the plan of such a system. This e-mail should carry all the advantages of the system so as to create a positive feel around it so that the managers can look forward to actually using it.

- *Supportive Communication*
  This communication invites the users to seek guidance once the new processes are up and running. This communication is made to guide the users through the process of learning a new system and should contain pointers to using the new system or information about ways to seek guidance.

Objective: This form of communication is made to consolidate the link created between the designers and the end users. The objective is to reach out to the users and help them accept new processes.

Contents: This communication invites the users to seek guidance from support team. This communication is made to guide the users through the process of learning a new system and should contain pointers to using the new system or ways to seek guidance.

Period: When the training is in progress post roll-cut/go live stage.

Format: E-mail to all the users inviting them to raise questions and participate in the trainings. Personalized attention given by mentors to trainees.

Example: Proactive coordination of the user requests
E-mail asking for feedback on new implementation
E-mail asking for queries and doubts regarding the new system

- *Forthright Communication*
  The objective of this communication is to convey to the users the demand to change and make the usage of the new system compulsory. This strong message should be sent out only if usage of the new processes is not up to the mark. This message is sent selectively only to those employees who do perform as pre the set KPIs and fall short of the usage levels that are set as standard for the organization.

Objective: The objective of this communication is to convey to the users the demand to change and make the usage of the system compulsory.

Contents: The contents of this communication convey a strong message for the users as a final ultimatum to accept the new processes. This message should be sent out only if required.

Period: Post roll-out and training if the usage levels of system are still low.
Format: E-mail to the *defaulters* only

8.3.8.6 Learning Through Feedback: Soliciting Participation in the Process of Change

The objective here is to involve the as many people as possible. Feedback should be sought before and after each BPR implementation. Before implementation feedback would give us a broad idea about the expectations of the end users. And after implementation feedback would give us a good opportunity to understand where we fell short of people's expectations and make hence amend our process in a way that suits the end users in a better way. This will also create an impression of a movement where everybody who is involved with the change is a part of the change and makes some contribution to towards the change.

8.3.8.7 Continuous Training: Constant Flow of Knowledge and Experience

It is important therefore to continue the process of training, retraining, and sharing knowledge throughout the BPR implementation phases. Monthly refresher sessions must be organized for users. Apart from this, the manager should also find out the pain areas and learning gaps on a monthly basis and conduct refresher sessions for the same. This will also help in standardizing the usage of new system across the organization.

8.3.8.8 Appraise the Progress: Measureable Targets and Periodic Reviews

It is important to track the usage of new system. Targets in terms of number of users or in terms of number times the system is used or accessed must be set for each business unit. These KPIs must be tracked and reviewed on a regular basis. The managers must also track the usage, link it to employee appraisals, and identify ways to maximize the usage. Apart from maximizing the system usage the manager must identify new ways of leveraging the system or improving the process.

8.3.8.9 Share Your Success: Focus on Cross Business-Unit Standard Practices

It is very essential to have cross business-unit standardization of the usage of the new system. With this objective in mind it is very important to set up a process of constant sharing of knowledge and experience between different business units. Also, users must constantly look for areas of improvement and automation in their work sphere and discuss such breakthroughs in a common forum consisting of representatives from each business unit. This forum can be used to deliberate on the applicability of deploying such successful automations or best practices of one business unit in other business units.

This will enable cross business-unit learning and sharing of best practices and will go a long way in standardizing/increasing the usage of the new system across the organization.

8.3.9 A BPR Case Study

ABC Ltd. is an old company set up in 1954. It is an Indian engineering company in the industrial and manufacturing sector. Based on traditional and age-old policies and methods of functioning the company has recently in the past few years experienced a change in the CEO. Due to its mastery in its area of operation, the company is able to solicit big projects in India and abroad. However, it lacks a technological edge to deliver efficiently and compete in the global market. The new CEO has chalked out a new vision and mission for the organization. To achieve this vision, the company is undergoing massive initiatives to upgrade its technologies and has a new focus on improving productivity and cutting costs using technology.

As part of the new initiatives the company implemented SAP HCM in its HR department to improve productivity of HR team and in turn improve the quality of work–life for other employees. The company was structured as three core business units which in turn had three to four departments. Each department had its own HR team. The SAP HCM system was a completely new technology for the HR department who earlier relied on excel-sheets, e-mails, and manual filing for their daily work. The average age of the HR employees across all departments was closing 45; however as per directives from the new CEO, the company had begun recruiting fresh talent in the HR department of each business unit.

The SAP HCM system was implemented and was completed successfully partnering with a well-known Indian IT consultant. However, the company was not able to achieve its productivity targets that it set before SAP HCM was implemented. In fact the productivity of the HR employees fell drastically. The usage levels of the new SAP HCM system were abysmally low and hence compliance to the HR processes and policies too was on a down slide. When asked for justification, the users constantly complained that the support they received for using the new system was not adequate, their problems were never solved, or when solved they were solved too late. Seeing the experienced employees suffer, the new recruits refrained from using the system.

Traditionally, when the HR employees faced a problem with the excel-sheet-based system they would consult the HR department leader who would solve it or direct them to the in-house technical help. This same support process was retained even for the SAP HCM system. The HR heads faced severe load of SAP HCM support requests which they were unable to handle. This increased their non-value-adding tasks and created pressure on the HR heads to deliver on their day-to-day activities. Due to their lack of expertise on SAP HCM systems, the HR heads hardly ever solved a problem and due to the bulk of requests pending, faced grave difficulties in coordinating these issues with the technical support for SAP HCM. This support process was seen as a major candidate for BPR in the ABC Ltd.

8.3.9.1   Existing Process for ABC Ltd.

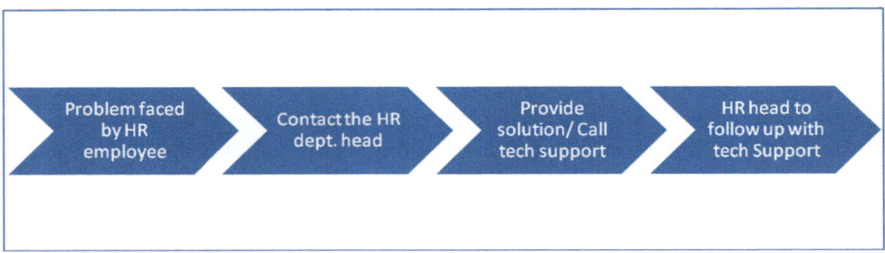

8.3.9.2   Process After BPR

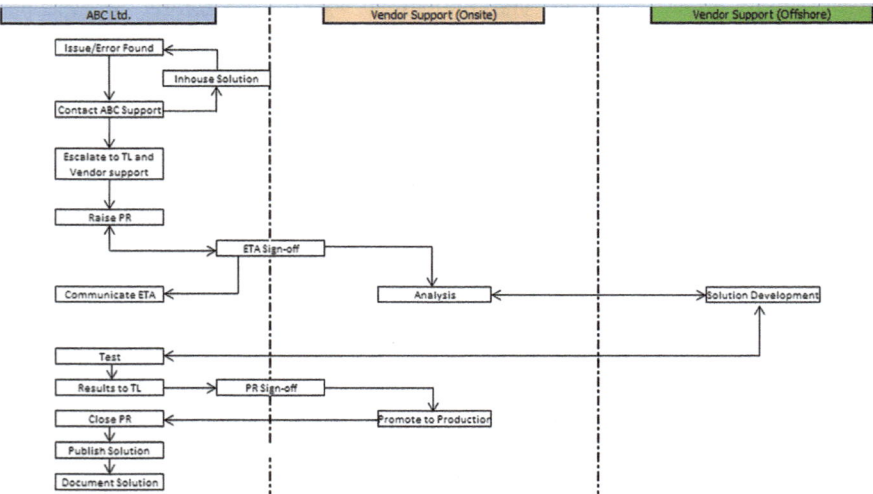

Salient features of new process design:

- New role created for coordinating support requests between users and the SAP HCM support team. This ensured that HR head was relieved the NVA tasks and could focus on core HR activities.
- Formal agreement was made with vendor to support the HR employees from onsite as well as offshore locations. This agreement clearly defined the SLAs for support which ensured that support requests were promptly attended to.
- The entire process was automated using IBM help desk off-the-shelf solution which provided a very simple interface to log support requests. This tool usage was an additional responsibility for the HR employees and they received adequate training for the same.
- Special dashboards were created for department heads to keep track of the ongoing support requests and SLA status.

- The SLA data collected for the support requests was used to check the key performance indicators like SLA missed percentage, tool usage percentage, open request, etc. on a periodic basis.
- Database of common support requests was created which greatly reduced the time to solve queries.

8.3.9.3 Result

Before the BPR initiative was undertaken, the following were the critical success factors:

1. Productivity to increase by 15% within the first 6 months
2. SAP HCM tool usage to increase by 25% within the first year

The actual results as measured after BPR was done were as follows:

1. Productivity increased by 25% in the first 3 months and by 40% within the 1st year.
2. SAP HCM tool usage increased 100% within the 1st year.

8.4 Summary

This chapter titled *BPR Implementation Steps and People View* had three sections. The first section dealt with the business process reengineering implementation. The entire implementation procedure was divided into five steps, namely,

- Initiate strategic change—Planning stage of BPR
- Current process diagnosis—Mapping of current processes
- Process redesign—Selecting the desired end state of the reengineered process
- Plan the implementation and go live—Realization of reengineered process
- Monitor process and feedback—Evaluation of the process performance

The second section of this chapter covered the *people* aspect of BPR initiatives. We termed it the *culture change management program.*

Conducting BPR involves adopting new processes, adapting to new technology, and accepting new areas of responsibility. For a manager, this environment throws forward a gamut of challenges to manage the expectations of the various stakeholders affected by the change. We tried to provide different strategies to manage this process of change so as to involve all the users affected by the change and suggest ways to support them throughout this process of change. The strategies revolve around the following key initiatives:

- Choosing the right people ready for the change to lead the change
- Involving all the users and spreading the right culture
- Soliciting participation in the process of change

- Constant flow of knowledge and experience
- Setting measureable targets and conducting periodic audits
- Focus on cross business-unit standard practices

The final section of the chapter is a case study. The case study is about an old manufacturing organization trying to cope with the challenges for using new technology. The process for technical support to employees underwent BPR to give dramatic results for the company. The productivity and efficiency saw an exponential increase after the BPR initiative.

Bibliography

http://en.wikipedia.org/wiki/Business_process_reengineering
http://www.netlib.com/files/bpr1.pdf
http://en.wikipedia.org/wiki/Business_process
http://unpan1.un.org/intradoc/groups/public/documents/un-dpadm/unpan041436.pdf
http://www.businessdictionary.com/definition/activity-chart.html
http://en.wikipedia.org/wiki/Business_process_mapping

Chapter 9
BPR and Malcolm Baldrige National Quality Program

9.1 Objectives of the Report

1. Understand all the aspects relating to Malcolm Baldrige National Quality Program.
2. Dive in depths into the core value and processes and identify the points where organizational effectiveness is achieved.
3. Do an in-depth study and analysis of all the different criteria that exist within Baldrige framework and identify the most essential and crucial points in each category.
4. Identify the exact point as to where BPR fits in the overall scheme of things.
5. Find out the alignment between strategies—TQM and Baldrige.
6. A case study to highlight our study findings.

9.2 Background Review

The history of Malcolm Baldrige National Quality Award (MBNQA) dates back to 1980s. With the expanding and demanding global market, the competition became intense. The cost and quality focus of Japan emerged as a challenge to American firms. America realized that they need to focus on quality in order to survive in the changed market dynamics.

Malcolm Baldrige was the Secretary of Commerce in mid of 1980s. He was a strong advocate of quality management concepts for the prosperity and sustainability of the USA. After his death in 1987, American congress named the award to acknowledge his contribution in the field of quality management.

Malcolm Baldrige National Quality Improvement Act of 1987 was passed in the US congress. The goal of the act was to increase competitiveness of US firms by recognizing their performance excellence in business.

The award aims to

- Identify and recognize role-model businesses
- Establish criteria for evaluating improvement efforts
- Disseminate and share best practices

MBNQA is managed by National Institute of Standards and Technology (NIST). NIST is a part of the US Department of Commerce. MBNQA comes under the umbrella of Baldrige Performance Excellence Program. The program is a federal change agent for promoting competitiveness, quality, and productivity of US organizations.

9.2.1 What Is MBNQA?

MBNQA is the highest level of national recognition available to US organizations for performance excellence. An organization with role-model organizational management system that fosters continuous improvement in sales and distribution, effective as well as efficient operations, engages and responds to the needs of customers and all stakeholders is qualified to apply for the award. President of the USA traditionally presents this award in a special function held at Washington, DC. Initially the award was designed for manufacturing, service, and small business organizations. Later in 1998 the scope was expanded to cover education and healthcare organizations. In 2007 eligibility for the award was further expanded to nonprofit organizations and government sectors also.

The award is given in each category each year. NIST has no limit on the number of awards that can be awarded to a particular category in each year. However, the total number of awards in a year cannot be more than 18.

9.3 To Improve National Competitiveness Through B Case Study

Baldrige Performance Excellence Program, MBNQA is based on a public–private partnership model. Private sector participates through funds, volunteer efforts, etc.

Table 9.1 details different organizations involved in MBNQA program and their contributions.

It is crucial to bear in mind that the Baldrige Performance Excellence Program is more than an award. It is an outreach and educational program that promotes performance excellence covering a broader base of organizations including the ones that do not even apply for MBNQA.

Organizations headquartered in the USA or its territory can apply for the award. Hence, US subunits of foreign organizations can also apply for the award. While evaluating the applications, achievement and improvements in all categories of the Baldrige criteria for performance excellence are given priority. An organization that clears the initial screening is visited by teams of examiners for verifications and clarifications required. Each applicant is provided a written feedback covering the strengths and areas of improvements in different areas.

Table 9.1   Malcolm Baldrige: organizations involved and their contribution

Organizations	Contribution
Foundation for the Malcolm Baldrige National Quality Award	– Raises fund to endorse the program permanently – Fosters success of the MBNQA program
National Institute of Standards and Technology	– Manages the Baldrige Performance Excellence Program – Promotes innovation and industrial competitiveness
American Society for Quality	– Helps in administering the award program
Board of overseers	– Advisor to Department of Commerce for Baldrige Performance Excellence Program
Award recipients	– Shares information related to practices and nonproprietary successful strategies
The Alliance for performance excellence	– Enhances the success and sustainability of its member Baldrige-based programs – Spreads information and provides significant number of judges and applicants

Organizations in the USA believe that even applying for the MBNQA is a beneficial process. The application process itself provides a lot of scope of improving plans and process alignment, communication protocol, and employee morale. The feedback received after the evaluation by NIST becomes instrumental in strategic planning process of organizations. The objective feedback from a well-recognized knowledgeable source helps organizations to refine and improve their continuous improvement programs.

Baldrige program selects Baldrige examiners through competitive application processes. The examiners have expertise in Baldrige performance criteria, in-depth expertise in different domains and sectors, and proven skills of an examiner. Thus, the examiners not only ensure proper evaluation of the award applications, but also their comments and feedback add value to all the applicants.

Heartland Health, Honeywell Federal Manufacturing & Technologies, LLC, AtlantiCare, Nestlé Purina PetCare Co., Cargill Corn Milling (CCM), US Army Armament Research, Development and Engineering Center (ARDEC), Boeing Mobility (formerly Airlift and Tanker), 3M Dental Products Division, Xerox Business Services, Merrill Lynch Credit Corporation, and Milliken & Company are examples of companies that own MBNQA in different categories.

9.3.1   Why Use MBNQA as a Performance Management Program?

MBNQA helps to build a high-performance, high-integrity organization that can stand out in a competitive market place. Today's market is characterized by dynamic disequilibrium and rapid yet radically changing environment. Survival in such a market requires thinking and acting strategically, alignment of business processes and resources to customer needs, higher degree of workforce, and customer engagement. The Baldrige criteria equip organizations to tackle these crucial issues with effectiveness and efficiency. They provide a validated and valuable framework to plan, perform, and measure results in an environment characterized by uncertainty and dynamic disequilibrium.

MBNQA follows a criteria-based assessment is tailored to the particular organization that is being assessed. The assessment process takes care of the profile, strategic action plans, and customer focus of the organization. As a result, it helps organizations to identify their areas of improvements.

Studies by various academicians and researchers have proved that by using performance excellence, approaches like the Baldrige performance criteria provide multifold benefits to organizations. Productivity, profitability and competitiveness, and customer and employee satisfaction improve after such approaches are implemented. Recipients of MBNQA awards validate that Baldrige criteria help to create a culture of change and excellence within an organization. Employee morale takes upbeat, and a process of continuous learning and improvement is institutionalized in the organization.

Moreover, MBNQA helps organizations to integrate various functions in an effective way providing a holistic view of the organization, its processes, and the business. Baldrige criteria help to link individual components, practices, and processes of organization with one another and with various other processes. Success of organization depends on how the individual components are linked with one another. These sets of linkages form the building block of overall management system of the organization. Some linkages could be

- Link between processes and the corresponding result.
- Link between strategic planning and data requirement from MIS, information and knowledge management.
- Link between organizational decision making and communication protocol followed.
- Link between strategic planning and tactical/operational planning.

Assessing an organization's key processes against the Baldrige criteria helps to define these crucial links of an organization. Once the links are defined, it becomes comparatively easy to monitor that the links are intact at the right place in the right manner. During the process of application and evaluation, an organization manages to identify the gaps between its processes and performance against Baldrige criteria. At the same time organization learns how these gaps can be closed. The external perspective to the entire process of gap identification and gap closure is obtained by the MBNQA process. The journey helps organizations to be more competitive and customer focused. The benefits are reflected in both top line and bottom line of the organization.

Table 9.2   Reasons for choosing Baldrige program for management performance

Reason for choosing Baldrige	Implications for the organization
Framework for improvement without being prescriptive	– Encouragement to development of creative and flexible approaches aligned with organizational goal
	– Demonstration of cause-and-effect linkages between approaches and their results
Inclusive and integrated management framework	– Covers all relevant factors that affect the organization, its processes, and outcomes
Focus on common requirements	– Other efforts like ISO, Six Sigma, and Lean Manufacturing could be integrated with the common requirements
Adaptable criteria	– Can be applied to various organizations with different sizes, sectors, and locations
Leading edge of validated management practices	– Accommodates the specific requirements of an organization
	– Addresses the needs of all stakeholders

The reasons for choosing Baldrige as performance management program are summarized in Table 9.2.

9.3.2   Brief Overview of the Criteria

The requirements for the Baldrige criteria can be grouped in seven categories. The categories for business excellence are

(a) Leadership
(b) Strategic planning
(c) Customer focus
(d) Measurement, analysis, and knowledge management
(e) Workforce focus
(f) Operations focus
(g) Results

Categories 1 through 7 are related to key organizational processes, key plans, goals, and findings. Category 7 focuses on performance in key areas and comparison with competitors.

The criteria for hospital and education sectors are same as business criteria but use languages that are typical to those sectors.

The basic elements of Baldrige criteria and their importance are detailed in Table 9.3. The details of each of the Baldrige criteria are provided in Sect. 9.4.

A typical sample criteria item is provided in Fig. 9.1.

Table 9.3 Elements of performance excellence framework

Element of performance excellence framework	Importance of the element
Organizational profile	– Sets the context and boundaries in which an organization operates
	– Serves as a guide organizational performance management system
Performance system	– Defines organizational processes and results
	– Includes leadership, strategic planning, and customer focus under leadership triad and workforce focus, operations focus, and results under results triad
	– Leadership sets organizational direct and seeks future prospects
	– Overall organizational process accomplishment is achieved the result triad: results though workforce focus and operations focus
System foundation	– Includes measurement, analysis, and knowledge management that serve as a foundation for performance management system
	– Builds fact-based knowledge-driven system for improving performance and competitiveness
Criteria structure	– Item consists of one or more areas to address
	– The seven criteria of leadership, strategic planning, customer focus, workforce focus, operations focus, and results are further subdivided into 17 processed and result items

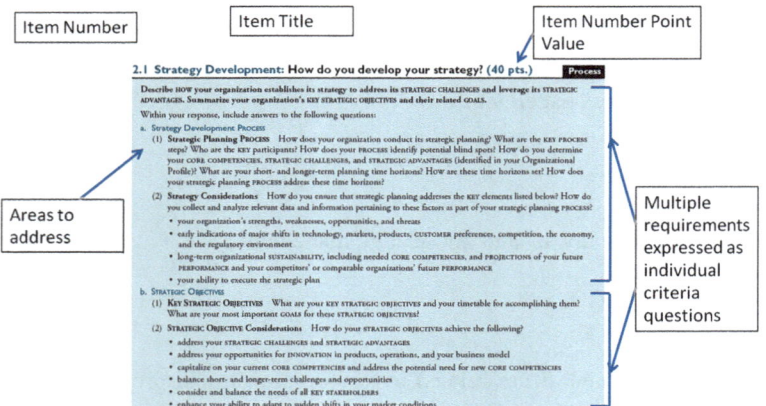

Fig. 9.1 Sample criteria item

9.3.2.1   Criteria in Action

The Baldrige criteria could be made actionable by organizations in three steps.

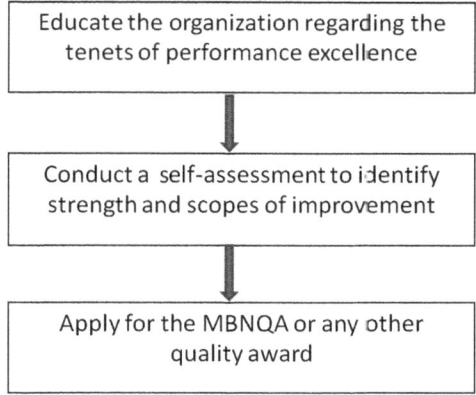

9.4   Baldrige National Quality Program

Baldrige National Quality Program is considered as a huge return on the investment made on the program. Though the number of MBNQA recipients is very less, numerous organizations of the USA and outside the USA have benefited by adhering to the criteria mentioned in the program. In the USA itself, more than 40 states have established Baldrige-type quality programs. Some of the globally respected quality programs similar to Baldrige program are Deming Prize in Japan, European Quality Award Model, Quality Excellence and Prosperity Model of Hong Kong, and Australian Business Excellence Framework. In India, Rajiv Gandhi National Quality Award, Tata Business Excellence Model, and CII-Exim Awards are considered equivalent to Malcolm Baldrige Program and European Quality Award Model.

9.4.1   Self-Assessment Process

Self-assessment process under Baldrige criteria acts as a baseline to diagnose the organizational health and its As-Is processes. Questionnaires are used to collect information related to current organizational processes. The steps of the self-assessment process are as follows.

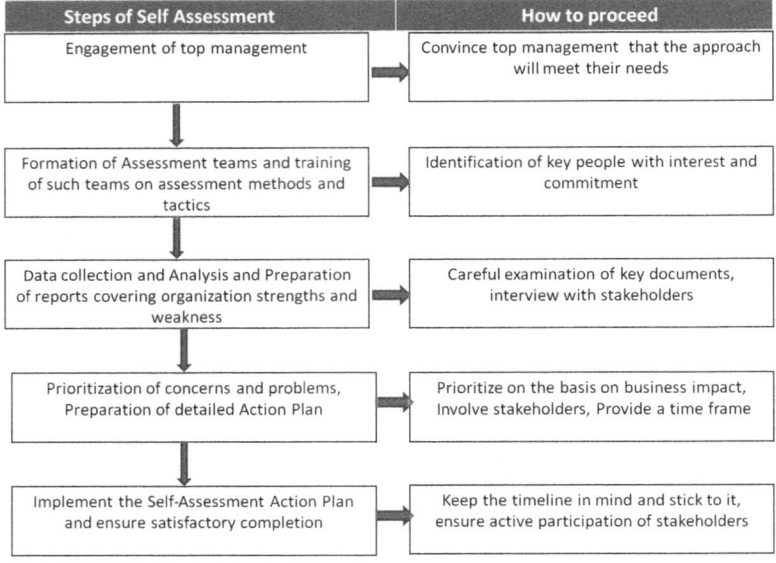

9.4.2   Feedback and Improvement Process

Feedback ensures that the key finding of the self-assessment process is documented in a proper report. This report is understood and internalized by the top management and all concerned stakeholders of the program. The key points of a successful report include

- Actual portrayal of the findings of the assessment team.
- Narrowing down upon the significant issues.
- Findings related to findings and those related to perceptions are separated.
- A strong consensus regarding the key recommendation exists.

In the feedback process, the goals and objective derived from the self-assessment process are communicated to the top management and their support is ensured. The comments and views of leadership could be incorporated before proceeding for planning and implementation.

Improvement process starts with implementation plan, its implementation, and continuous monitoring of the progress. The crucial components of the implementation plan are

- Name of the project
- Objectives of the project
- Measurement metrics to be used for the process

- Key deliverables, tasks involved, milestones
- Methods and approaches of implementation
- Input and exit points, dependencies

9.4.3 Core Values and Concept

Eleven core values and concepts are like 11 pillars of the Baldrige process. They represent the interrelated links of high-performance organizations. Core values and concepts help to integrate the key business processes and create the carving for excellence in the organization's culture.

9.4.3.1 Visionary Leadership

Visionary leadership is imperative to set direction of the entire organization. Leadership decides the future course of actions to be taken by an organization and steers the organization in that direction. Ability of the leadership to align different stakeholders' objective to the organization objective decides the future of the business. The vision needs to be clear and unambiguous. It has to be conceived, understood, and internalized throughout the organization.

Senior leadership also ensures that the strategies employed by the organization are in tune with the vision, mission, and goals of the organization. Leadership must be able to inspire the entire organizational system to work with energy and enthusiasm.

9.4.3.2 Customer-Driven Excellence

Customer satisfaction and perception shapes the future of a company. Baldrige program provides customer focus its due importance. The program and NIST are of the opinion that its customer who decides quality and performance of an organization.

Organizations must understand their customers and the needs and wants of the customers. Customer must be listened, given priority. Complaints must be registered and solved. The customer-centric approach must be embedded in the culture of the organization.

9.4.3.3 Organizational and Personal Learning

Learning and development at personal as well as organizational learning contributes to the overall benefit of the organization. The core value of learning steers the organization to respond to the changing business dynamics and will steer the organization in future days. Learning has to be continuous method, and the outcomes are realized in long-term basis. Various forms of learning include

- Learning through regular job-related activities
- Interacting with coworkers, workers of same or different functions
- Applying problem-solving skills to analyze root causes
- Sharing acquired knowledge with other employees
- Analyzing opportunities of improvement and changes
- Adopting benchmarking approaches industry best practices, etc.

9.4.3.4   Valuing Employees and Partners

Any high-performance organization must value its workforce. Employees must be motivated by organizational mechanism to contribute their best. The organizational environment must be made conducive to promote "out-of-the-box" thinking. Calculated risk taking has to be encouraged.

The reward and recognition scheme must encourage employees to participate in decision-making process. The suggestions, complaints, issues, and career development plans of employees must be taken seriously. Only a spirited employee can come to the organization with positive energy and constructive ideas.

9.4.3.5   Agility

In a market marked by drastic changes in business environment, flexibility and ability to change rapidly counts a lot. This core value of an organization is its agility. Specialists in Baldrige techniques suggest that analysis of workflows, processes, tasks, etc. helps to perform better and faster.

The capacity and product/service mix of the organizations must be flexible enough to adapt any rapid change in market dynamics or customer requirement. The unwanted processes could be eliminated and flexibility must be added in the process. Requirements that add no value to the customer have to be removed.

9.4.3.6   Focus on the Future

Future has its own potentials. Many business decisions require trade-off between short-term benefits and long-term growth. For Baldrige process organizations must have a clear vision of the future and commitment to work in that direction. A clear vision of the future market and industry helps company to visualize its positioning in the future market. The company with a vision for future can identify the resources that will add value to its business in the future, the resources that are redundant, and the resources that the company acquires or develops. In the absence of a clear vision, organizations will fail to take the long-term strategic decisions which in turn can mar the possibility to trap the future business potentials.

9.4.3.7 Managing for Innovation

Innovation decides competitiveness in markets that are highly technology oriented. Managing innovation is a herculean task. Innovation requires right work environment, lots of patience, and managerial support. Many innovations are results of long-term research and development programs.

Culture of innovation requires progressive thinking in the entire organization and its stakeholders. In the USA innovation as a core value will determine the basis existence of companies. Organizations that can innovate will grow and prosper.

9.4.3.8 Managing for Fact

Facts as core value must drive the decision-making processes of an organization. Perceptions and intuitions have their own place, but ignoring, altering, or tweaking facts leads to faulty decisions. Facts reveal the realities of an organization.

There must be a system to measure and analyze performance of people and organizational processes. Performance measurement and analysis helps to analyze the improvements, costs per unit, efficiency, work output, downtime impact, etc. The analysis is critical to judge the overall merit of the functioning of organizational system. With the use of computer software managing organizational performance, analyzing them has become comparatively easier task.

9.4.3.9 Public Responsibility and Citizenship

Both private and public organizations need to understand their responsibility towards common public and larger society. Organizations are part of the larger society. They have certain duties and responsibilities towards the society. Baldrige considers public responsibility and citizenship as a core value of organizations. This ensures that organizations do not conduct any activity that will have negative impact on general public. Organizations must behave as responsible entities that care for common public.

9.4.3.10 Focus on Results and Creating Value

Once the focus shifts from the end result, deficiencies start creeping into the system. The end result drives the process towards the right direction. At the same time customer, the only profit center of an organization is bother about the value she gets. Hence, along with focus on results, organizations must inculcate the habit of creating value for the customer. These two are considered as core values in Baldrige criteria.

Focus on result helps to control undesired process outcomes. It controls waste and ensures efficiency. Focus on creating value adds effectiveness to the system.

The non-value adding activities are trimmed or eliminated. Focus on value adding activities ensures better customer satisfaction.

9.4.3.11   System's Perspective

The Baldrige criteria and core values must not be considered in isolation. These are building blocks of a system that fosters excellence. The system requires proper integration of all the aspects of criteria and values to synthesize an organization that can drive excellence. Proper synthesis requires holistic understanding of the organization, its market, and customers. Designing key business processes with a system's perspective ensures success in the market by linking various requirements and measurement indicators at the right places.

9.4.3.12   Baldrige Criteria: A Detailed Review

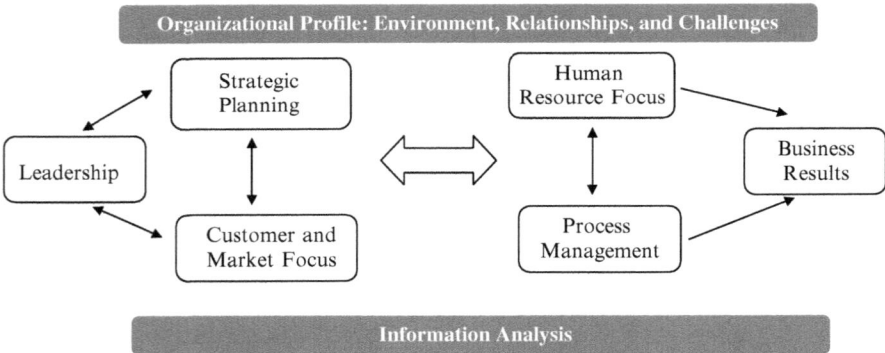

The criteria are a channel for us to focus on the business results. They do so by having focus on customer-focused results, financial and market results, human resource results, and organizational effectiveness results. They have a composite set of indicators which helps us to keep track of the business performance and growth.

Another key feature of the set of criteria is that they are very result oriented and is not prescriptive whether the organization should have an organizational structure or whether it should have segregated departments. The focus is essentially on results and not on process tools or procedures. They are meant to foster incremental and major breakthrough improvements as well as basic change.

The criteria also support and embed a system's perspective to goal alignment. Alignment is tied around measures derived essentially from organizational processes and strategy. The use of measures thus channels different activities in consistent directions with less need for detailed procedures, centralized decision making, or process management. The learning cycle has clearly defined four stages:

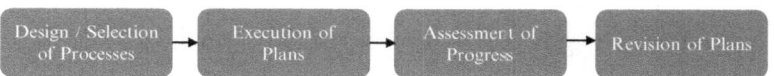

The criteria and the scoring guidelines make up a two-part diagnostic (assessment) system. The criteria are a set of 18 performance-oriented requirements. The scoring guidelines spell out the assessment dimensions—approach, deployment, and results—and the key factors used to assess each dimension.

Organizational Profile:
Looks at the manner how you operate and your relationships with customers, suppliers, and partners.

Part 1 : Organizational Description	**Part 2** : Organizational Challenges
Now under this section we try to find out the answer to some specific questions like what are the organization's main product and services, the VMG framework of your organization, employee profile and diversity, major technologies and facilities, and most importantly the regulatory environment that exists including financial, technical, and environmental regulations.	Now again for the company we need to address a few key questions regarding the challenges faced in terms of what is the competitive environment we are looking at, the size/growth of industry, and the number of competitors that exist. The key factors that play a role in success of the organization. Then we also need to look at the strategic challenges including human, operational, business, and global challenges.
Then we also need to look at the aspects such as which are your key customer group market segments and the profile of your suppliers and how the requirement does vary across different stakeholders.	Finally we need to focus on performance improvement relating to systematic evaluation of key processes and fostering organizational learning and change.

Apart from this the essential points to look at are the differentiators which can be your price, design services, or geographic proximity. Challenges might also include electronic communication with businesses; go to market time and M&A challenges.

Leadership:120 points

The **Leadership** Category examines how your organization's senior leaders address values, directions, and performance expectations, as well as a focus on customers and other stakeholders, empowerment, innovation, and learning. Also examined is how your organization addresses its responsibilities to the public and supports its key communities.

Organizational Leadership and Public Responsibility

The leadership criterion inquires as to the roles and responsibilities of senior management within organizational setup. This basically asks how senior management addresses values, strategic directions, and performance expectations. The criterion also covers senior leader involvement in "focus of customers and stakeholders, innovation, and learning". Essentially this is done by asking five key questions:

1. How do senior leaders institutionalize values and set long-term/short-term directions as well as communicate these values, directions, and expectations.

2. How do senior leaders generate an atmosphere or setting for empowerment, innovation, flexibility, and work-related education or learning.

3. How do senior leaders assess performance and respond to needed changes or performance gaps.

4. How to use resources to close down the gap.

5. How to utilize the findings in order to enhance knowledge skills and abilities.

Apart from these, the senior management is also responsible towards the public and it shows in the manner they anticipate and address the impact of products and services on the society. The onus is on them as to how would they conduct all transactions related to all stakeholders and customers.

How do your organization, your senior leaders, and your employees actively support and strengthen your key communities? Include how you identify key communities and determine areas of emphasis for organizational involvement and support.

Strategic Planning:85 points

The strategic planning criterion examines organization's intentions rather than the actual achievements .It looks into the aspect how the organizations come up with their rules and policies .It also looks into the fact as to how the strategic plans are deployed and then measured.

Strategy development and Strategy deployment

Essentially in the strategy development process we need to address the overall strategy planning process and identify the key participants who are involved.

The analysis of the relevant data should be based on the needs of the customers and requirements, competitive landscape that is prevalent relative to your capabilities, technological and other key changes that might affect your products and services, a basic SWOT analysis along with supplier–partner relationships that is prevalent.

Then we can clearly define the strategic objectives and include key targets and goals and also define a framework to ensure that your key objectives satisfy all stakeholders.

Then in the second stage we move to a point where we need to convert strategic objectives into action plans. We need to bring in key process parameters to measure process performance. Essentially we need to focus on the following factors such as how do you develop and deploy action plans to achieve your key strategic objectives and how you allocate resources and make sure the accomplishment of your action plans. What are your key short- and long-term action plans? What are your key human resource plans that derive from your short- and long-term strategic objectives and action plans? What are your key performance measures/indicators for tracking progress relative to your action plans?

How do you ensure that your overall action plan measurement system achieves organizaional alignment?

Customer and Market Knowledge -   Customer Relationships and Satisfaction

The response of the organization should include the answer to following questions such as how to determine your target customers, how to determine your competition and market segments. It will essentially be important to listen to the market and determine your key customer requirements and their relative importance in influencing the purchase decision of your customer. In this determination how would you use relevant information from former customers, POS, and other historical data in order to improve your business development and lessen your complaints?

The other very vital area that comes into picture is how to build customer relationships. It would essentially answer a few vital questions such as How do you determine key customer contact requirements and how they vary for differing modes of access? How do you ensure that these contact requirements are deployed to all people involved in the response chain? Include a summary of your key access mechanisms for customers to seek information, conduct business, and make complaints. Then it would also focus on your complaint management process whether it's effective or not.

The third vital area is measuring the customer satisfaction. It would ask answers to questions such how would capture actionable information from your customer. What is the procedure of your follow up?

This is basically to answer one question as to how does an organization move ahead, basically think and plan to take into account key customer needs.

Information and Analysis:90 points

The *Information and Analysis* Category examines your organization's information management and performance measurement systems and how your organization analyzes performance data and information

Measurement and Analysis of Organizational Performance – Information Management

Performance Measurement: How to gather and store all the data from varied sources which helps you to take day to day operational decisions. How do you select and align indicators which would help you to achieve overall organizational efficiency. How to ensure and store key competitive data? How to keep your PMS up to date with current business needs.

Performance Analysis: What are the basic analysis that you perform to support your senior leader performance review and organizational strategic planning. How do you communicate the results of organizational-level analysis to work group and/or functional level operations to enable effective support for decision making? How do you achieve the alignment between your key business results and overall organizations strategy.

Data availability and Quality of Hardware and Software: How do you make needed information and data available? How do you ensure the accessibility of the data for all the different stakeholders? How do you ensure data and information integrity, reliability, accuracy, timeliness, security, and confidentiality? How do you keep all your information and data up to mark with the latest business needs and requirements?

Another essential facts to keep in mind is that how does the organization ensure that all the hardware and software are in tune and reliable. Also it is very important that the organization knows the facts as to how to keep the hardware and software up to date with current business needs.

Human Resource Focus: 85 points

The *Human Resource Focus* Category examines how your organization motivates and energizes its employees to work towards their objectives as well as the organizations objective. Also it is very important to build and maintain work environment conducive to the employee and their work .

Employee performance management -Employee Training-   Employee well being and satisfaction

Work systems are a generic category that generally deals with queries about the organization's work processes and jobs and how they are set to promote employee flexibility and innovation. This also focuses on employee motivation as to the addressing the questions regarding the dimensions of compensation, recognition and employee rewards for high performance. It also ask questions as to how to achieve effective communication across business units and work divisions. Also answer questions as to how to motivate employees to utilize their full potential and help them realize and attain their career development and learning objectives. Also how does the employee performance management system work and how does your compensation and R&R scheme reinforce these objectives.

Again moving onto employee education, training and development , it is very important to realize up front as to how your education plans balance short term and long term objectives of the organization. Also how to use the inputs of the supervisors in the overall learning process. How do you evaluate the effectiveness of education and training, taking into account individual and organizational performance?

This is the most crucial aspect and answers questions as to how to improve employee work place satisfaction, health and safety. Then how to determine these factors which would help us to measure the various parameters. How do you support your employees via services, benefits, and policies? How are these tailored to the needs of a diverse workforce and different categories and types of employees, as appropriate?

How to determine formal and informal methods to measure employee satisfaction and well being and try to relate this findings to the business results.

Process Management: 85 points

The *Process Management* Category examines the key aspects of your organization's process management, including customer-focused design, product and service delivery, key business, and support processes. This Category encompasses all key processesandall work units..

Product and Service Processes (45 pts.)

- What are your design processes.
- How to incorporate changing customer requirements.
- How to incorporate new technology,
- How to address design quality and ET.
- What are your key delivery processes and their performance metrics.
- What are your key performance measures/indicators used for the control and improvement of these processes.
- How do you perform inspections, tests, and process/performance audits to minimize warranty and/or rework costs, as appropriate?

Business Processes (20 Pts.)

- What are your key business processes.
- How to design and perform these processes to meet all requirements.
- How do you minimize overall costs associated with inspections, tests, and process/performance audits, as appropriate.
- How do you improve your business processes to achieve better performance and to keep them current with business needs and directions.

Support Processes (15 pts.)

- What are the important processes for delivering your products and services.
- How do you map the internal and external set of support processes.
- How do you design these processes to meet all requirements.
- Include how in-process measures and internal customer feedback are used in managing your support processes, as appropriate.
- How do you improve your support processes to achieve better performance and to keep them current with business needs and directions.

These are some of the questions that can also be asked when you are going for your business management. This Baldrige criterion assesses an organization's or public entity's key management systems and practices. These include the design of customer-focused products and service delivery processes. In addition, the criterion examines process management in terms of future organizational growth. Now the diagram below shows the relationship between the MBNQA and the BPR.

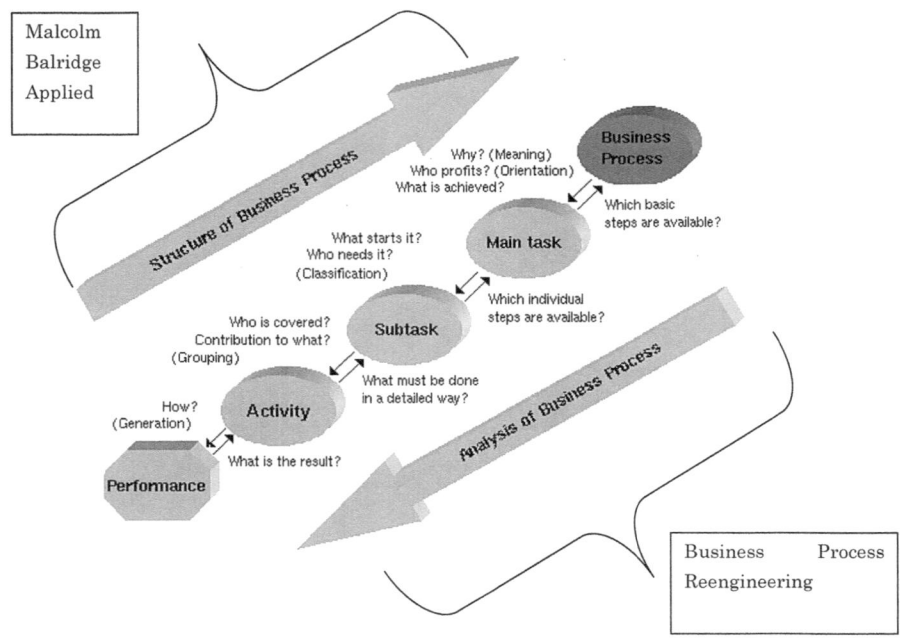

Business Results: 450 points
The results criterion examines an organization's actual or matter-of-fact "outcomes and performance in terms of customer satisfaction, products and services, human resources, and operations" (NIST 2000)

Business Results			
Customer Focused	Financial / Market	Human Resource	Organizational Effectiveness
1.What are the current levels of customer satisfaction relative to competitors. 2.What are the current levels of customer-perceived value again relative to customers. 3. What is the current level of importance that the customer associates with your product.	1.What are the current levels of indicators that suggest your financial and economic value. 2.What are the current levels of metrics which measure your business performance with respect to entry into new markets.	1.What are the current levels of indicators that tell about satisfaction level of your employees. 2.What are the current levels of indicators that tell you about your organizational effectiveness.	1.What are the current levels of your productivity, cycle time, supplier/partner performance, and other appropriate measures of effectiveness and efficiency. 2.What are your results for key measures/indicators of regulatory/legal compliance and citizenship.

9.5   Future Outlook: Alignment of TQM and Balance Scorecard: An Integrated Overview

Now it is very important to understand the relationship between balance scorecards to find out exactly where MBNQA fits in the overall strategy of the firm. The below diagram shows us the relationship between them:

Baldrige results category	Balanced scorecard perspective
7.1 Health care outcomes and service delivery results	Customer
7.2 Patient and other customer-focused results	Customer
7.3 Financial and marker results	Financial
7.4 Staff and work system results	Learning and growth
7.5 Organizational effectiveness results	Internal business processes
7.6 Leadership and social responsibility results	Not addressed

Strategy , Balridge and Six Sigma Alignment		
Management Challenges	**Six Sigma Solution**	**Balridge Alignment**
Lack of linkage and alignment throughout the organization	Linkage and alignment of Six Sigma initiative to the business's "bottom line"	Ba drige Core Value: Focus on Results and Creating Value Baldrige Alignment: Categories 1-6 These "Approach and Deployment" categories must align with Category 7 – Organizational Performance Results. Approach and Deployment processes that don't drive to improved business results contribute very little value to the organization.
An unclear concept, direction, or focus	A leadership-driven, consistent, simple message	Leadership that sets and deploys organizational values, directions, and expectations.
An unclear goal	Strong focus on ambitious, non-ambiguous goals	Item 2.1b Key strategic objectives and timetables for accomplishing them. These objectives are linked to the key challenges faced by the organization. Items 6.1 and 6.2 require the improvement of health care processes and support processes, including the focus on customer/market requirements and the use of key performance measures/indicators to control and improve performance.
Different organizational "silos" with different improvement initiatives	Cross-functional process focus – integration across the organization	The Baldrige Criteria focus on the integrated business system, aligned with strategic objectives and related action plans, not functional "silos," in a way that demands alignment throughout the organization and

9.6 Case Study: A Conclusive End

9.6.1 *Motorola*

In 1988 *Motorola* was recognized for its excellence in manufacturing and business processes and was awarded the Malcolm Baldrige award for excellence. This award is an award based on the successful implementation of a set of criteria and also Six Sigma. The Malcolm Baldrige award is compatible with Six Sigma, Lean Sigma, and ISO 9000. These processes are incorporated for achieving business excellence. The recipients of the award established leadership roles in their community with other business leaders, schools, health-care organizations, or nonprofit agencies. The recipients are national and global role models in the area of business and uphold ethical business practices. In 2002 Motorola won a second Malcolm Baldrige award while implementing excellently the processes of Six Sigma. To qualify for the award, nearly 5,000 public and private sector leaders evaluate the companies based upon a set of criteria. Each applicant to the program receives 300–1,000 h of review prior to receiving the award.

Motorola was one of the first recipients of the Malcolm Baldrige National Quality Award in 1988. They received the award again for manufacturing in 2002. Motorola was chosen for this award because it had a major global role to play. It received recognition because it adopted the Six Sigma program. Under this program, the company was able to yield 3.5 sigma in most of its processes. This translated to 99.73 % process yield. At this time no one else in the manufacturing domain had achieved this. The process that Motorola followed was set as a benchmark and adopted in other companies as well, thus making Motorola a global player in this field.

Motorola brought forward to the world the complexity of manufacturing process. Each company was challenged to improve their processes beyond their current level of success. The company introduced the concept of only 3.4 defects per million products produced. A training center or the Motorola University was also established to impart learning to the Motorola employees. Motorola University has also extended its Six Sigma knowledge and expertise to other companies such as General Electric, Federal Express, Johnson & Johnson, Kodak, NBC, Polaroid, Texas Instruments, Sony, IBM, GM, Toshiba, DuPont, and Black and Decker who desire to adopt the Six Sigma principles of Motorola.

Motorola was also instrumental in bringing lots of process improvement initiatives through proper Six Sigma implementation which helped attain productivity and efficiency at a much higher level than rest of its competitors. Apart from that it also institutionalized processes and systems which are till date one of the best in the entire world.

Bibliography

http://www.nist.gov/baldrige/
http://en.wikipedia.org/wiki/Malcolm_Baldrige_National_Quality_Award   Alignment   of   the   Malcolm Baldrige Criteria for Performance Excellence.pdf. RDYoung—The Baldrige quality process.pdf

Chapter 10
BPR and Automation

10.1 Learning Objectives

- Understanding BPR and evolution of business process automation (BPA)
- Considerations for BPA
- Prioritization criteria for BPA
- BPA into the Future

10.2 Introduction

Thomas Davenport and Michael Hammer working as consultants researched and invented a brand new concept called business process redesign which later gained eminence as business process reengineering or BPR. They stressed on the importance of eliminating "non-value adding work" which the managers all over the world were trying to automate them without assessing the use of them.

BPR, by the mid-1990s, was observed to fall short of its expectations as it failed to deliver consistently across varied industries. Then was introduced the new hot idea, much to the like of process managers, business process management or BPM.

Whereas BPR focused on the elimination of non-value adding processes, BPM aimed at making business processes more efficient with proper utilization of information technology. In spite of BPM having a more balanced focus, critics of BPM have pointed out that it marginalizes the importance of people in knowledge driven companies.

BPA balances both approaches and brings in a whole new concept of holistic and inclusive work methodology by making the processes more efficient without discounting the role of employees. It takes a people-centric approach where it is not solely reliant on technology.

S. Mohapatra, *Business Process Reengineering*, Management for Professionals,
DOI 10.1007/978-1-4614-6067-1_10, © Springer Science+Business Media New York 2013

10.3   Business Process Reengineering

BPR is a management approach aiming at improvements by means of elevating efficiency and effectiveness of the processes that exist within and across organizations. The key to BPR is for organizations to look at their business processes from a "clean slate" perspective and determine how they can best construct these processes to improve business operations and processes.

BPR has been defined as the fundamental rethinking and radical redesign of business processes to achieve dramatic improvements in critical and contemporary measures of performance, such as cost, quality, service, and speed.

Business strategy is the primary driver of BPR initiatives and the other dimensions are governed by strategy's encompassing role. The organization dimension reflects the structural elements of the company, such as hierarchical levels, the composition of organization units, and the distribution of work between them. Technology is concerned with the use of computer systems and other forms of communication technology in the business. In BPR, information technology is generally considered as playing a role as enabler of new forms of organizing and collaborating, rather than supporting existing business functions.

10.3.1   Recommendations for BPR

- BPR must be accompanied by strategic planning, which addresses leveraging IT as a competitive tool.
- Place the customer at the center of the reengineering effort—concentrate on reengineering fragmented processes that lead to delays or other negative impacts on customer service.
- BPR must be "owned" throughout the organization, not driven by a group of outside consultants.
- Case teams must be comprised of both managers as well as those who will actually do the work.
- The IT group should be an integral part of the reengineering team from the start.
- BPR must be sponsored by top executives, who are not about to leave or retire.
- BPR projects must have a timetable.
- BPR must not ignore corporate culture and must emphasize constant communication and feedback.

10.3.2   Business Process Automation

BPA focuses equally on strategy, people, the process for automation, and technology. A continuous business improvement initiative with clearly defined business goals is the right way to adopt for implementing BPA. BPA does not forget the involvement of human intelligence and efforts that go in to make the whole process a success.

Service industries now very much dominate the world economy over product-based industries. It seems pretty clear that the dominance would grow with time. Yet, the recent recessions are proof that these very industries are hit most. The solution may lie in doing more with less, and BPA is the ideal methodology to adopt in these trying times of business competition.

There is no doubt that technology will play even a larger role in the coming years and will determine the efficiencies of knowledge workers, but how technology is going to be used still seems to be seen.

10.3.2.1 Choosing Automation Software

The key to making a quick transition from inefficient, paper-based process to efficient, automated process is selecting the right workflow automation software. There are many to choose from, ranging from low-cost open source tools to all-encompassing high-end suites from the large ERP vendors. The bottom line is to choose that software which best suits the organization's size, budget, and requirements. Key requirements:

- Flexibility. It is a tool that creates the documents and processes needed, rather than one that requires changes in basic processes. For example, does it let its users create, edit, and format their own forms, or does it just provide standard form templates?
- Web Services and Database Integration. It enables seamless transfer of data and can integrate with the database of relevant third-party applications at the form level. Even better are tools that offer pre-built, out-of-the-box integration with the enterprise software packages the business is already using.
- Ease of Use. A workflow automation tool should not require specialist technical skills to operate. A tool that's easy and intuitive to use is preferred as it does not require extensive user training. If it's a Web-based tool, then it should be properly architected for a Web environment, and not just an old client/server package with a Web front end.
- Vendor Reliability. Long-term viability of the vendor is a must. There are many benefits to cloud-based software, for example, but there are also risks: what would happen to workflows and data if the company hosting them in the cloud went under? Open source software provides an implicit guarantee: you can be sure that whatever happens, the code will always be available.

10.3.2.2 Introducing BPA in Small and Medium Scale Organizations

Across the public and private sectors, most organizations are held back by processes that take too long. The reasons for the inefficiency vary.

In reality, many inefficient processes can be streamlined quickly and effectively using inexpensive business process and workflow automation tools. This is particularly true for paper-based processes that involve a lot of human intervention. A common example is expenses reporting, which is still frequently carried out on paper forms that must be passed from person to person for approval and processing. But every industry and organization can cite its own examples too: insurance underwriting, engineering change requests, return merchandise authorization for faulty goods, and many more.

Two steps are recommended to start process automation in an organization. First, one relatively simple process is selected as a pilot project. Second, the scope of the project is properly assessed before starting by writing a comprehensive statement of work that describes in detail how the process is to be automated. This will ensure the automation process runs faster and more smoothly, and it is a necessary step to clarify your organization's thinking about the process itself.

The cost of the process is worked out before automation and compared afterward to gauge the benefits. While the exact benefits will vary depending on the nature of the process addressed, organizations with manual, paper-based processes typically see a reduction of 30–40% in the time taken to complete them after they have been automated—from which they are generally able to extrapolate a measurable cost saving too. Establishing quantifiable benefits from the pilot project is extremely useful if you want to prepare a business case for extending process automation into other areas of the enterprise.

Above all, realize that BPA need not be a difficult, expensive, or time-consuming undertaking. No matter how large or small the business is, or how complex or simple the processes you want to automate, there are tools available that can help you to do the job quickly, efficiently, and inexpensively.

BPA has five key advantages which are:

- Business Goals Alignment: BPA enables real and fast returns on investments by integrating technology and manpower with effective cost cutting techniques. It emphasizes on the fact that cost and revenue objectives may not be mutually exclusive. It allows organizations to produce same output with fewer resources.
- Participation of Right People: BPA involves all internal stakeholders in multiple departments of the organization. With IT support, it aims at driving the business orientation in the right way.
- Identifies Right Processes for Automation: BPA aims at involving people rather than making them just enablers for the process. It has proved a lot beneficial in eliminating highly redundant and multistep processes that rely heavily on communication between people across departments and projects.
- Incremental Approach: BPA works best when applied incrementally to critical processes.
- Ensures Right Technology Selection: BPA helps in the selection of the most suitable technology for a particular firm by aligning its objectives with resources.

10.4   Considerations for Automation

The factors influencing automation processes are:

*   Business impact.
*   BPA should have the full support of top management.
*   Organizational processes too cumbersome to control.
*   Legacy systems bringing the efficiency down.
*   Increase in cross functional transactions.

BPA is defined as computer aided coordination of resources, facilities, and human knowledge to achieve the desired results in a way that the process is optimized. Business process optimization is the ultimate level of automation, where optimum utilization of resources assures superior quality of output consistently.

BPA applies to the whole spectrum of business process tools. It encompasses within it workflow automation, integration of business processes, process control, and improvements concerning intelligence and expert systems. BPA in its simplest form implies to workflow automation by facilitating information flow and integrating it across departments. Throughput is a generic measure for workflow, and workflow automation maximizes it. BPA is not simply computerizing the tasks that are being conducted manually.

It provides a platform to probe and eliminate underlying assumptions in manual transactions. For example, the assumption of purchase order against indents even for general spares can be defeated by the realization that spares can be ordered automatically based on the inventory levels. Automation is an opportunity to simplify workflow and get rid of redundant tasks and non-value adding activities.

BPA deals with lots of delays in business processes arising because of lack of decision-making ability of people and lack of information. Computerized information flows are deployed to make routine tasks and decisions faster. This involves the right people and brings decision making to rightly where it belongs—the frontline.

Automation ensures single point of data entry which eliminates erroneous processing of information. It is most noteworthy to mention here that BPA orients itself around achieving desired results and not just around tasks and transactions—against the popular notion people hold of BPA automating only individual tasks.

BPA believes that speed and efficiency comes not only from automating individual tasks but disseminating error-free information which facilitates to perform faster and take improved decisions.

10.5   Prioritization for Automation

Suitable and practical symptoms for BPA could include any of the following:

*   Repetitive, manual tasks
*   Tasks that are duplicated in other processes

- Inefficient or outdated workflow processes
- Processes that span geographical boundaries
- New businesses or IT initiatives

The next important step is to prioritize the factors keeping in mind their relevance to the outcome of organizational processes and functions. The ability to control any process comes with detailed knowledge of interdependencies and at the appropriate time concerning cost efficiency utilization of available and resources how measured variables are valid and reliable. Control is all about making the right amount of changes.

Optimizing any business process takes much more than just control owing to the complex relationship between different parameters and their impact on the desired results as it requires lot of quality parameters to be simultaneously optimized.

Process optimization is best described as a five-step cycle—*analyze, identify, simulate, validate, and deploy*.

- Analyze: Analysis provides insights to how a process is running.
- Identify: Identify the inefficient processes.
- Simulate: It follows a structured process where situational analysis is done.
- Validate: The simulated results are checked and validated to get intended results before actually enforcing any change.
- Deploy: After verifying the possibility of the changes, BPA is deployed.

The benefits of business process optimization are:

- Higher level of throughput
- Consistent quality of the output
- Optimal utilization of resources
- Elimination of abnormalities

10.6   Conclusion

Properly designed and tested BPA solutions quickly start improving response times and produce more effective and efficient workflow processes throughout the organization, thus reducing costs and improving quality of the offering.

The success of one BPA solution often paves the way for additional automations subsequently which go a long way in making the organization more productive. Choosing the correct BPA platform will ensure that as needs expand, the solution will expand with it.

Relevant usage training of various BPA tools and software should be given to the potential users to acculturate them with the changes in working processes. Without proper training, users who do not understand the new process can quickly derail its success.

Economic or time constraints are likely to limit the process to only a few process cycles. This is often the case when an organization uses the approach for short- to medium-term objectives rather than trying to transform the organizational culture. True iterations are only possible through the collaborative efforts of process participants. In a majority of organizations, complexity will require enabling technology to support the process participants in these daily process management challenges.

Finally, results should be measured against the stated goals and milestones created at the outset. Therefore, a standardized metric should be formulated to determine the success achieved.

10.7 Summary

BPA consists of integrating applications, restructuring labor resources, and using software applications throughout the organization.

The important considerations for BPA to be adopted are:

- Business impact.
- BPA should have the full support of top management.
- Organizational processes too cumbersome to control.
- Legacy systems bringing the efficiency down.
- Increase in cross functional transactions.
- Prioritization for BPA.
- Top management support.
- Available manpower and resources.

Bibliography

www.wisegeek.com, www.alagse.com

Chapter 11
TQM and BPR

11.1 A Brief History

In 1990, Hammer suggested for eliminating non-value-adding activities rather than using technology to automate the processes involved. Till then, technology had been used only for automating the existing processes and not eliminating non-value-adding activities. The focus should be to maximize customer value by minimizing the resources consumed for delivering the product or service. So companies started reviewing their processes and strived for renewed competitive advantage in the limited resources and costs that they could manage. Initially it had to face its share of brickbats, and post-1995, the accusation against reengineering was that it focused only on processes and technology and not on effective change management for the people. Among different product-centric strategies, this kind of reengineering strategy was more a customer-focused initiative. It improved coordination of rate of workflow as well as increased efficiency and responsiveness of supply chain thus increasing customer satisfaction. A more keen focus on the production process rather than an eye on the products would help in further improvement in the company becoming customer focused.

11.2 Definition

There were different definitions given by a lot of experts. Some of the earliest definitions are the following:

Reengineering is the fundamental rethinking and radical redesign of business processes to achieve dramatic improvements in critical, contemporary measures of performance, such as cost, quality, service, and speed.

Hammer and Champy

S. Mohapatra, *Business Process Reengineering*, Management for Professionals,
DOI 10.1007/978-1-4614-6067-1_11, © Springer Science+Business Media New York 2013

Business process reengineering is the fundamental analysis and radical re-design of every process and activity pertaining to a business—business practices, management systems, job definitions, organisational structures and beliefs and behaviours. The goal is dramatic performance improvements to meet contemporary requirements—and IT is seen as a key enabler in this process.

Du Plessis

Some of the key elements that can be interpreted from the above definitions are

- Business process reengineering involves a radical change.
- It involves a change in orientation of the organization.
- It promotes redesign of the business processes involved in the organization.
- It entails an overhaul in the organizational structure.
- It triggers a plethora of technological improvements.

The objective is the improvement of customer service and reduction of costs. Critical success factors are elements that make the strategy of BPR successful. The issues which are important for the operating activities of the organization are dealt by the critical success factors, and the future success is charted.

11.3   Critical Success Factors

Business process reengineering can be successful if only we can identify and define areas where the processes need to be improved. These critical success factors would vary from organization to organization and from industry to industry. These help to focus the efforts of the organization so that efficiency of processes is achieved. Broadly, there can be four categories of CSFs:

1. *Industry CSFs*: These factors depend on the industry in which the organization is operating and differ from organization to organization.
2. *Strategy CSFs*: These factors arise from the different competitive business strategies adopted by organizations. The position of the organization in the industry also is a benchmark for the success factors to be set. So only industry cannot be a yardstick for deciding on the critical success factors. The values and target market will also impact the critical success factors for an organization.
3. *Environmental CSFs*: These factors result from economic and technological changes in the organizations. These factors are out of control of the organization but nevertheless need to be taken care of when deciding on the critical success factors.
4. *Temporal CSFs*: These factors result from internal organizational needs and changes made in the organizations. But these factors are generally short-lived and are related to temporary changes in the organization and are a function of crises that come up as hurdles for the organizations.

A statistical research into CSFs of organizations has shown to have seven primary areas:

1. Training and education
2. Quality data and reporting

3. Management commitment and customer satisfaction
4. Staff orientation
5. Role of the quality department
6. Communication to improve quality
7. Continuous improvement

These were identified when total quality was at its peak. The *critical success factors* can be also categorized as

1. People—availability, skills, and attitude
2. Resources—people, equipment, etc.
3. Innovation—ideas and development
4. Marketing—supplier relation, customer satisfaction, etc.
5. Operations—continuous improvement and quality
6. Finance—cash flow, available investment, etc.

Some critical success factors associated with organizations implementing Six Sigma are

- Executive engagement: aligning the corporate strategy to support Six Sigma implementation and visible consistent support as well as using facts and data to support all levels of decision making and verifying/monitoring results.
- Communications: communicating pertinent facts about Six Sigma and designing human resource policies to support roles and responsibilities laid out by Six Sigma standards.
- Projects: implementing and creating a project inventory having linkages with Six Sigma methodology.

11.4 BPR Methodology

The methodology for business process reengineering consists of the following steps:

1. *Envision new processes*: For this step to be fruitful and help the organization in a positive way, top management support is essential. Also reengineering opportunities need to be identified so that the focus is maintained throughout the revamping of the processes. The technologies that need to be involved, thus enabling the overall improvement and change of the processes involved. But the most important part is that the new processes must be aligned with the organizational strategy.
2. *Initiate change*: This is an important stage in the process of reengineering as in this step, the reengineering team needs to be forged so that they can be the change agents or the champions of the new processes that need to be implemented. This is very important as they need to motivate others to accept change in the organization. In this step, the performance goals need to be outlined.

3. *Process diagnosis*: An assessment is needed to know how IT works as an enabler and is aligned to creating value for the organization. A maturity model related to IT includes five stages:

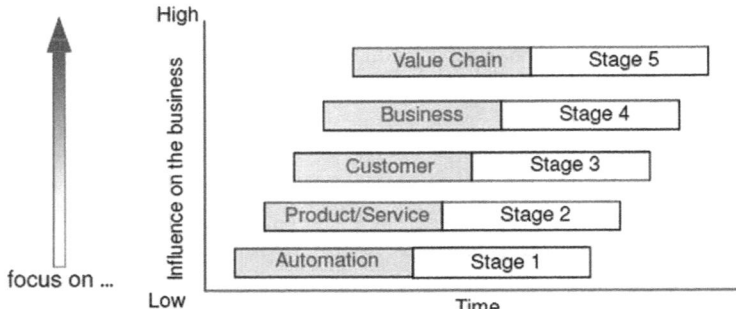

As the above diagram suggests, the five stages of evolving of ITs influence on business with the first stage focusing on automation, the second on the product or service being offered, and then gradually the customer focus and the business focus come in, and also the role of IT as an enabler is more pronounced when it is made part of the value chain through which value is being communicated to the customer. Each stage accompanies with itself changes in skills and competencies of people concerned, a change in the processes, and formation of a steering committee for the goals to be realized and results to be achieved. Also a change in attitude of the way IT behaves towards business and the users. There is also a higher level of interaction between the customer and IT which helps in ice breaking lot of misconceptions on both the parties' levels.

4. *Process redesign*: There is a need to develop alternate process scenarios and a need to develop a new process design. The human resource architecture should also be used to back up the new processes. An IT platform has to be chosen and an overall blueprint of the processes needs to be made and feedback needs to be gathered. Always, it is easier to implement and manage smaller projects and change in processes. Projects attempting large-scale changes will have lower probability of success, and it is difficult to incorporate internal and external changes, namely, political, financial, and technological changes. On the basis of range of business functions to be supported and the level of support needed, there is either an incremental or a modular approach applied to the process redesign.

(a) *Modular approach*

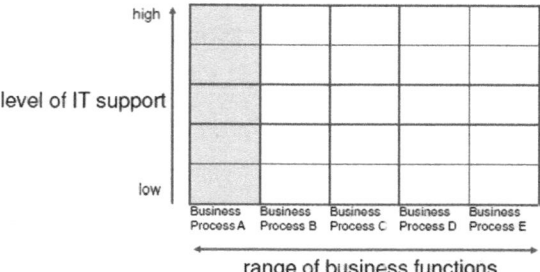

range of business functions

In this case the IT support is in modules supporting a limited set of business requirements. It is devoid of any connection between other modules and it's working is independent of any other conditions or successes of other modules involved in the overall scheme of things.

(b) *Incremental approach*

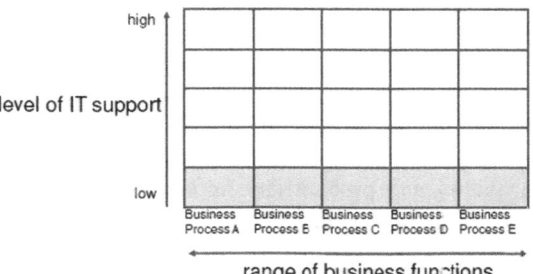

range of business functions

In this kind of approach there is increasing level of support for a series of projects. This kind of approach is helpful when the environmental factors are subject to change and are out of control.

5. *Reconstruction*: Some questions need to be answered in this stage. These are as follows:

   (a) Is the organization ready?
   (b) Is the staff ready?
   (c) Are businesses and/or citizens ready?
   (d) Is contract management in place?
   (e) Is service management in place?
   (f) Is benefits management in place?
   (g) Is performance management in place?
   (h) Are changes ahead been thought through?

6. *Process monitoring*: During the monitoring stage, the clarifications that need to be sought are the following:

   (a) Have changes throughout the project compromise our original intentions?
   (b) Have we done a post-implementation review?

(c) Do we have enough qualified personnel to manage operations including fulfillment contract with third parties?

(d) Are we actively seeking to improve performance?

(e) Are we measuring performance?

(f) Are we setting maturity targets?

11.5 Total Quality Management

11.5.1 Introduction

Total Quality Management (TQM) refers to management methods used to improve quality and productivity in organizations, particularly businesses. TQM is a comprehensive systems approach that works horizontally across an organization, involving all departments and employees and extending backward and forward to include both suppliers and clients/customers. TQM is only one of many acronyms used to label management systems that focus on quality. Other acronyms that have been used to describe similar quality management philosophies and programs include continuous quality improvement (CQI), statistical quality control (SQC), quality function deployment (QFD), quality in daily work (QIDW), total quality control (TQC), etc. Like many of these other systems, TQM provides a framework for implementing effective quality and productivity initiatives that can increase the profitability and competitiveness of organizations.

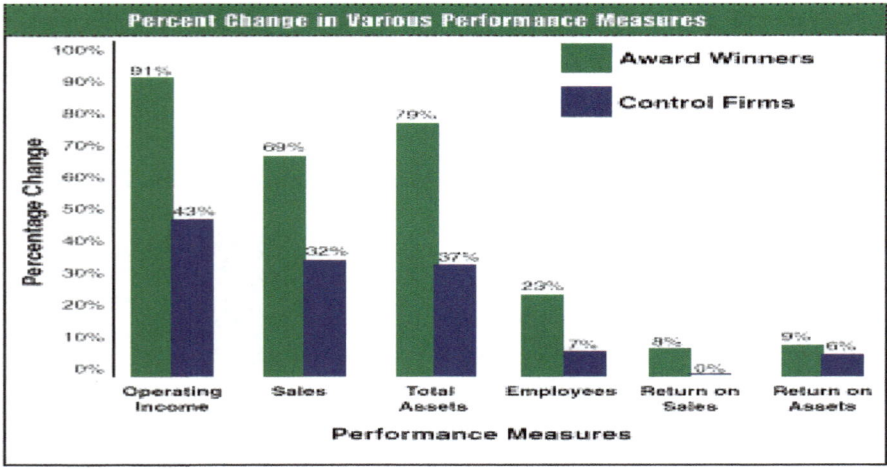

11.5.2   Origins of TQM

Although TQM techniques were adopted prior to World War II by a number of organizations, the creation of the TQM philosophy is generally attributed to Dr. W. Edwards Deming. In the late 1920s, while working as a summer employee at Western Electric Company in Chicago, he found worker motivation systems to be depleting and economically unproductive; all forms of incentives were tied directly to quantity of output, and inefficient inspection systems were used to find flawed goods.

Deming joined hands in the 1930s with Walter A. Shewhart, a Bell Telephone Company statistician whose work convinced Deming that statistical control techniques could be used to supplement traditional management methods. Using Shewhart's theories, Deming formulated a statistically controlled management process that provided managers with a means of deciding when to intervene in an industrial process and when to leave it alone. Deming got an opportunity to put Shewhart's SQC techniques, along with his own management philosophies, to the test during World War II. Government managers found that his techniques could be easily learned by engineers and workers and then quickly implemented in overburdened war production plants.

One of Deming's clients, the US State Department, sent him to Japan in 1947 as part of a national effort to revitalize the war-devastated Japanese economy. Japan was where Deming found a great deal of enthusiasm for his management philosophies. He got complete support in introducing his statistical process control, or SQC, programs into Japan's ailing manufacturing sector. These very techniques brought about a dedication to quality and productivity in the Japanese industrial and service sectors that allowed the country to become a dominant force in the global economy by the 1980s.

While Japan's industrial sector followed on the path of quality in the middle 1900s, most of the American companies were still inclined towards mass production using age-old management techniques. But in spite of this, America prospered as war-ravaged European countries looked to the United States for manufactured goods. This growth of the US markets was fuelled further due to the population boom. However, by the 1970s, some of the traditional industries had lost their sheen and began to be regarded as inferior to their Asian and European counterparts. With increasing globalization happening in the 1980s, helped by stupendous advancement in information technology, the US manufacturing sector started losing out to a host of competitive producers, particularly in Japan.

In response to massive inroads made by the Japanese companies into the US markets, the US producers learned a valuable lesson and began to adopt product quality and productivity techniques into their processes. This brought about industry-wide recognition for Deming's philosophies and techniques in the USA, making him one of the most sought-after academician and author. The "Deming Management model" became the bible for many of the organizations looking to improve. TQM became the new buzzword and a staple for American enterprises wanting to make it big in the 1980s. By the early 1990s, the US manufacturing sector had achieved marked gains in quality and productivity.

11.5.3   TQM Principles

Nitty-gritties related to the framework and implementation of TQM vary from management professional to professional, and the passage of time has brought about changes in the language and emphases of it. But all TQM philosophies point towards the same threads of quality, proactive approach of management, teamwork, and process improvement. As Howard Weiss and Mark Gershon rightly observed, "the terms quality management, quality control, and quality assurance often are used interchangeably. Regardless of the term used within any business, this function is directly responsible for the continual evaluation of the effectiveness of the total quality system." They went on to separate the basic elements of TQM as proposed by the American Society for Quality Control: (1) policy, planning, and administration; (2) product design and design change control; (3) control of purchased material; (4) production quality control; (5) user contact and field performance; (6) corrective action; and (7) employee selection, training, and motivation.

Deming on his part pointed to all these factors as the pillars of his quality philosophies. In his literature, he has contended that the companies need to create an overarching business scenario that prioritized the improvement in products and services offered over short-term financial goals. He went on to specify the benefits that could be accrued in various aspects of the business—ranging from training to system improvement to manager–worker relationships—bringing out a far more healthier and profitable enterprise. Deming was of the view that a well-conceived system of statistical control would prove an invaluable TQM tool for an organization and was deeply contemptuous of companies that emphasized on quantity over quality in their statistical approach. Statistics was the only tool, according to Deming, which would help the managers in knowing exactly what their problems were, learn how to fix them, and gauge the company's progress in achieving quality and organizational objectives.

11.5.4   Deming's Approach

1	Create constancy of purpose	8	Drive out fear
2	Adopt the new philosophy	9	Eliminate boundaries
3	Cease inspection, require evidence	10	Eliminate the use of slogans
4	Improve the quality of supplies	11	Eliminate numerical standards
5	Continuously improve production	12	Let people be proud of their work
6	Train and educate all employees	13	Encourage self-improvement
7	Supervisors must help people	14	Commit to ever-improving quality

- Create constancy of purpose towards improvement of the product and service so as to serve their purpose of becoming competitive, stay in business, and provide jobs.
- Adopt the new philosophy. This is the new economic age. There is no point in living with commonly accepted levels of delay, mistake, defective material, and defective workmanship.
- Forego dependence on mass inspection; look for statistical evidence that quality is inbuilt in the system.
- Improve the quality of incoming materials. Abstain from awarding business on basis of price instead depend on quality along with price as a prerequisite.
- Find the problems; constantly improve the system of production and service. Continual reduction of waste and continual improvement of quality should be strictly adhered to in every activity so as to yield a continual rise in productivity and a decrease in costs.
- Institute modern methods of training and education for all. On the job training, using control charts to determine whether a worker has been properly trained or not should be focused on and more emphasis to be given to statistical methods to find training.
- Institute modern methods of supervision. The emphasis of production supervisors must be to help people to do a better job. Improvement of quality will automatically improve productivity. Immediate action should be taken by the management, in case, reporting of issues related to inherent defects, lack of maintenance of machines, poor tools, or fuzzy operational definitions.
- Fear is a barrier to improvement so drive out fear by encouraging effective two-way communication and other mechanisms that will enable everybody to be part of change and to belong to it. Fear can often be found at all levels in an organization: fear of change, fear of the fact that it may be necessary to learn a

better way of working, and fear that their positions might be usurped frequently affecting middle and higher management, while on the shop floor, workers can also fear the effects of change on their jobs.
- Break down barriers between departments and staff areas. People in different areas such as research, design, sales, administration, and production must work in teams to tackle problems that may be encountered with products or service.
- Eliminate the use of slogans, posters, and exhortations for the workforce, demanding zero defects and new levels of productivity without providing methods. Such exhortations only create adversarial relationships.
- Eliminate work standards that prescribe numerical quotas for the workforce and numerical goals for people in management. Substitute aids and helpful leadership.
- Remove the barriers that rob hourly workers, and people in management, of their right to pride of workmanship. This implies abolition of the annual merit rating (appraisal of performance) and of management by objectives.
- Institute a vigorous program of education and encourage self-improvement for everyone. What an organization needs is not just good people, it needs people that are improving with education.
- Top management's permanent commitment to ever-improving quality and productivity must be clearly defined and a management structure created that will continuously take action to follow the preceding 13 points.

11.6   Making TQM Work

Joseph Jablonski identified three characteristics necessary for TQM to succeed within an organization: participative management, continuous process improvement, and the utilization of teams. A participative management ensures the involvement of all people working at all levels in the management process thus reducing the emphasis of traditional top-down management methods. In other words, the managers take the feedback and guidance of the subordinates who have the responsibility of implementing the directives and set the policies accordingly. This not only brings the top management in sync with the operational details but also motivation to workers who develop a sense of ownership of the processes and feel in control.

Continuous process improvement, the second characteristic, requires the recognition of small, incremental gains towards the goal of total quality. Large gains are accomplished by small, sustainable improvements over a long term. This concept requires a long-term sight on the behalf of the managers and the willingness to invest in the present for benefits which would accrue over the future in the due course. A corollary of continuous improvement is that workers and management develop an appreciation for, and confidence in, TQM over a period of time.

Teamwork, the third necessary ingredient for the success of TQM, involves the organization of cross-functional teams within the company. This multidisciplinary team approach helps workers to share knowledge, identify problems and opportunities, derive a comprehensive understanding of their role in the overall process, and align their work goals with those of the organization.

The six attributes of successful TQM programs as mentioned by him are

- Customer focus (includes internal customers such as other departments and coworkers as well as external customers)
- Process focus keeping in view the future
- Prevention versus inspection engineering of processes that looks to incorporate quality aspects during production, rather than a process which attempts to achieve quality through inspection after the resources have been consumed leading to wastage
- Employee empowerment and compensation
- Fact-based decision making
- Receptiveness to feedback

11.7 Implementing TQM

Jablonski offers a five-phase guideline for implementing TQM: preparation, planning, assessment, implementation, and diversification. Each phase is designed keeping in view the long-term goal of continually increasing quality and productivity. Jablonski's approach is one of many that have been applied to achieve TQM but contains the key elements commonly associated with other popular total quality systems.

- Preparation—Here the decision lies in the management's court whether or not to pursue a TQM program. Training is imparted, the needs are identified whether to go for outside consultants, specific goals and visions are developed, the resources that would be a part of this change process are identified, and communication regarding the exercise is sent across the organization.
- Planning—In the planning stage, a detailed plan of implementation is drafted (including budget and schedule), the support system for the program in terms of the infrastructure is established, and resources who have been earmarked for the process are secured.
- Assessment—In this stage a thorough self-assessment is done—with inputs from the clients/customers—identifying in the process the qualities and characteristics of the various individuals working for the organization as well as the organization as a whole.
- Implementation—At this point, the organization can already begin to determine its return on its investment in TQM. It is during this phase that support personnel are chosen and trained, and managers and the workforce are trained. Training entails raising workers' awareness of exactly what TQM involves and how it can help them and the company. It also explains each worker's role in the program and explains what is expected of all the workers.
- Diversification—In this stage, managers utilize their TQM experiences and successes to bring groups outside the organization (suppliers, distributors, and other companies have impact the business's overall health) into the quality

process. Diversification activities include training, rewarding, supporting, and partnering with groups that are embraced by the organization's TQM initiatives.

11.8 BPR and TQM

Considering the above-mentioned steps for reengineering of the business processes, the first step, being to prepare for reengineering wherein we focus on the vision, mission, and goals of the organization. The second step includes to map and analyze the As-Is processes which brings out the flaws in the present processes and helps in designing the To-Be processes for desirable outcomes. The third step is to design the To-Be process which includes doing a What-If analysis bringing out some To-Be scenarios comparing existing processes with other relevant benchmarked processes for further improvements. The fourth step is to implement the reengineered process which includes aligning the new processes with existing processes and initiate a culture change program. The final step deals with improving the process continuously by constant validation and verification. The TQM philosophy of continuous change should be embedded into the redesigned process. This initiates achieving incremental improvements.

TQM is based on applying continuous change throughout an organization's processes. The important point of TQM is that it approaches its problem in systematic manner and does not demand radical changes. Hans stipulates TQM characteristics; some of them were top-down approach and frame of cultural change; activities of improvement are based on customer satisfaction. BPR and TQM philosophy can work together towards achieving the same goal. As BPR believes in "a gigantic leap" towards success so does TQM if and when possible. There is no superior power or champion that can provide an excellent outcome. Instead, collaboration between these two methodologies produces an efficient and effective process. Hans states "Reengineering should be incorporated within the TQM framework of management as a valuable tool". Firstly, it should be understood that perfection is a process and not a destination and does not appear suddenly and from day one. That is, once a new process is conceived, we need to improve it through continuous improvement. In addition, it is not viable based on the economics of scale to keep on reengineering the redesigned process. Secondly, it facilitates in the smooth transformation from one phase to another. This is achieved by teamwork or individual people efforts. However, to the get full cooperation from participants, a cultural change has to be initiated, and that is where TQM comes in. TQM provides the essential support to enable BPR. This is by initiating the change of people behavior and attitudes creating an amicable environment. Nevertheless, it can be said that TQM approach is dynamic in nature because as customer needs (internal or external) keep on changing, the redesigned process has to be improved in accordance to the required needs. Therefore, embedding continuous improvements into the redesigned process is an excellent approach.

The three principles of TQM are customer focus, continuous improvement, and teamwork. So, all of them hinge on change on changing processes to meet customer needs and expectations in a collaborative manner. The same applies to BPR as well and both methodologies are process based. But for BPR projects, mostly top-down approach is applied, whereas for TQM projects bottom-up approach also works. The major difference though is that TQM is based on the fact that the basic core processes are acceptable; only continuous improvements are required. Whereas, in BPR the aim is to achieve dramatic results by doing a complete overhaul of the processes and totally dismissing the core processes. TQM believes in standardization but BPR is based on flexibility.

	TQM	BPR
Description	Concerned with improving work processes and methods in order to maximize the quality of goods and services	Particular approach concerned with rethinking current systems and processes
Type of change	Planned, continuous	Planned, frame braking
Aim	Keep existing customers by meeting or exceeding their expectations concerning products and services	To redefine existing work methods and processes to improve efficiency
Key driver	Increasingly competitive market and the need to compete for specific customer demands. May also be driven by specific problems such as high costs or poor quality	Competitive pressures and intense need to cut costs
Change agent	External or internal	External consultant
Learning process	Single or double loop	Double loop
Nature of culture change	Customer-focused values	Values objectivity, control, consistency, and hierarchy
Change to team-based work	Often requires a shift to team-based work	Yes. Requires a shift to team-based work because the work is process based rather than task based

The above table summarizes the differences between TQM and BPR, but the basic motive behind both approaches is change in the organization. Where BPR suggests pathbreaking and radical change in the work processes, TQM is more of an incremental change framework. BPR is a one-off event that aims at changing the processes and establishing new systems in place. TQM, being a continuous and incremental change objective, can then be implemented to ensure better customer satisfaction. TQM could then endeavor to fine-tune the new processes that are established as a result of BPR. There is a need for an external consultant in the case of BPR, whereas both internal and external consultants can help in employing the TQM framework.

Single-loop learning is a framework which has faith in the present processes and boundaries of the organization. But double-loop learning refers to challenging present norms, policies, and frameworks and refining them further for increasing efficiencies. TQM and BPR hinge on the basic principle of double-loop learning. A change in culture may take time to implement, but it is fundamental for TQM and BPR along with the double-loop learning framework. TQM is more customer focused and needs the employees to be singularly and positively driven, whereas BPR is a one-off effort and needs objective focus. TQM and BPR taken together can be fathomed as a source of competitive strategy for an organization.

11.9   Quality Function Deployment

QFD can be defined as a systematic approach that forges a series of relationships with customers so that the final product can be desirable. QFD begins at the design stage wherein the customer's needs are identified and then structured into quality attributes, prioritizing them and extracting quality elements from each attribute. But for QFD to be deployed, the organization should possess a quality approach and should be expanding through a vision for optimum quality. So, before QFD, the frameworks for TQM and BPR are essential. So let us use a case for explaining how QFD can be helpful in understanding and improving the processes of the organization.

11.9.1   QFDs and the Voice of Clients

Science and Technology Parks (STP) tenants; demands have increased also because they need a change and also the inability of competitors to come to terms with the tastes of the customer. STPs have responded to this increased demand by offering high-value, low-cost alternatives which are efficiency driven, but often with a cost to service effectiveness. An alternative response by some STPs is also to try to move up the customer value chain and to provide higher-quality premium services which can be customized to meet changing tenant needs.

   QFD is a planning tool which helps to fulfill customer expectations by translating customer expectations into procedures of STP. QFD can help STP clients to maintain their competitive advantage in the market by providing right data in the right time at a right place. QFD helps to identify latest technology and job descriptions to carry out operations and minimize design errors. In other words, QFD is a way to capture, organize, and deploy the voice of STPs' tenants. QFD has often been associated with product development activities, but it is equally useful in the service industry as well. The QFD concepts and tools are useful in a plethora of fields and help in providing services in its long-run and short-run applications. An important QFD tool, the house of quality, when applied as a simple cause-and-effect matrix, shows the process' input–output relationships with the varying strengths between the different inputs and outputs. This structure analyzes a process map and makes it conducive for further improvement efforts in STP processes and better control over the processes.

STP needs to be all ears for its clients' problems and worries. A successful STP should be able to route the customers to the correct service providers, who should be in turn able to serve the customers according to their changing needs. It is more important also to know what the customers don't want, and apart from that, the suppliers have now been considered as tenants as well as suppliers. So for having a fruitful relationship, the STPs need to introduce new methodologies in collaboration with these suppliers, and the new and innovative processes employed by the service providers need to be monitored and implemented for the benefit of every stakeholder involved. The methodologies for controlling quality as well as improving the processes, TQM, BPR, and QFD can be used in this case for implementing quality standards and at the same time also reengineering the processes which do not add value to the organization.

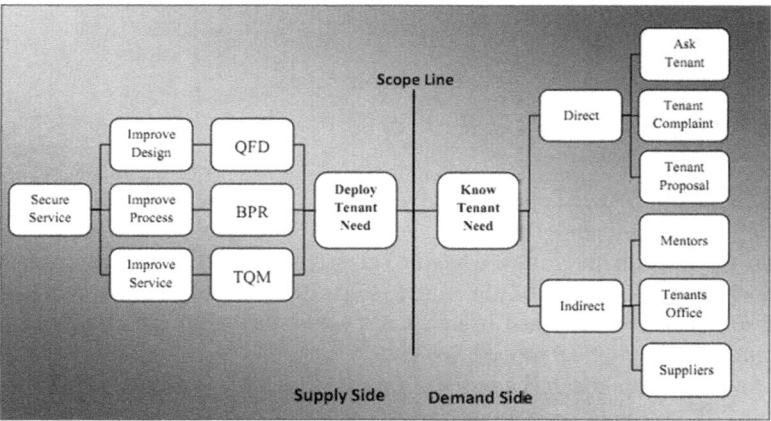

This kind of a supply–demand process can help in bridging the tenants' offerings and the customer's needs.

11.9.2   The Quality Focus

STP is a service provider for its clients, which are in turn service providers for the end customers. So for an STP, skilled staff and different service providers are the most important assets which are very difficult to quantify as these are mostly services that are being offered. Due to these intangible aspects of STP services, it is very difficult to assess the quality as well as production of these services. The primary factors for better STP management are human resources, client management, and service providers. Mostly here we are dealing with human capital which is not easily quantified, and it needs assessment based on assumptions. It is the ability to manage these intangibles that differentiates good STPs from others. The interaction between STP staffs, service providers, and STP clients is so dynamic that it cannot be valued by any metrics or be predicted. STP processes and procedures which could be derived from strategic planning can be depicted as follows:

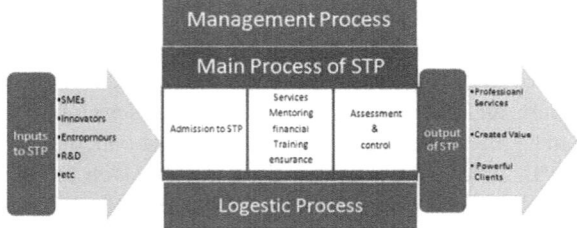

When the requirements of customers are dynamic, the internal procedures also need to be responsive and prone to change to map client requirements onto the STP procedures.

11.9.3 Methodology Used

A questionnaire survey is posed to all customers to gauge their needs and requirements. This method not only gets the voice of STP tenants but also tries to measure clients' satisfaction in terms of what the enterprise can deliver to its customer based on client feedbacks to the STP. In order to sense the needs of STP clients and respond to these, an STP should ask itself some critical questions which would help in morphing these into STP processes well.

A four-phase approach is a series of four matrices that is used to map the requirements of the customers postconducting the survey. These start with high-level client wants and requirements and finish with well-defined service requirements that should be considered by service providers. The first matrix called the service planning matrix takes the input from the voice of the client tables—the most prioritized needs. Service planning changes the client-defined requirements into quality characteristics, which quantify the client requirements and help in defining and designing targets. The second matrix takes this as the input and defines the components or parts of the system. The third matrix deals with the process layout, and the fourth matrix gives the metrics and monitors the supply of assured service processes. According to this framework, seven steps are designed to shape requirement matrices to design service processes and the standards for services to be provided by suppliers, which are as follows:

1. Define the customers' expectations from the service.
2. Analyze the expectations of clients as normal, expected, and exciting.
3. Prioritize clients' requirement.
4. Translate these "voices" into technical objectives. (This is where QFD bridges a major gap between the users of the services and the suppliers. This step gives the providers specifics on which design efforts have the most value to the clients and to be focused upon.)

5. Based on the previous transformation of voices into technical objectives, there is a need to determine how each of the clients' expectations can best be satisfied.
6. Plan for services. The objectives for the concept and design are focused upon to drive the manner of production. These in turn help us in predicting demands; thus, operations have a much better chance of supplying consistent product quickly because of the guidance from QFD.
7. Update the original client expectation QFD matrices as the services ages and the client requirement changes. If the original QFD matrices are updated as new information becomes available, services' launch time can be further reduced, and new services can be introduced in progressively shorter cycles.

The most important step being step 4, we'll elaborate on how voices can be translated into technical objectives. Implementing QFD on an STP needs two types of committees, new services and improving existing services. These committees are composed of members from marketing, planning, finance, and client office. QFD committee will develop a clear vision and set long-term goals. Output of QFD committee must be utilized in two ways:

1. Including QFD committee outputs in STP business plan or strategic plan.
2. Reengineering the existing procedures in STP to serve new services.

House of quality would be formed for the first and foremost prioritized services. This house will be formed for other services too.

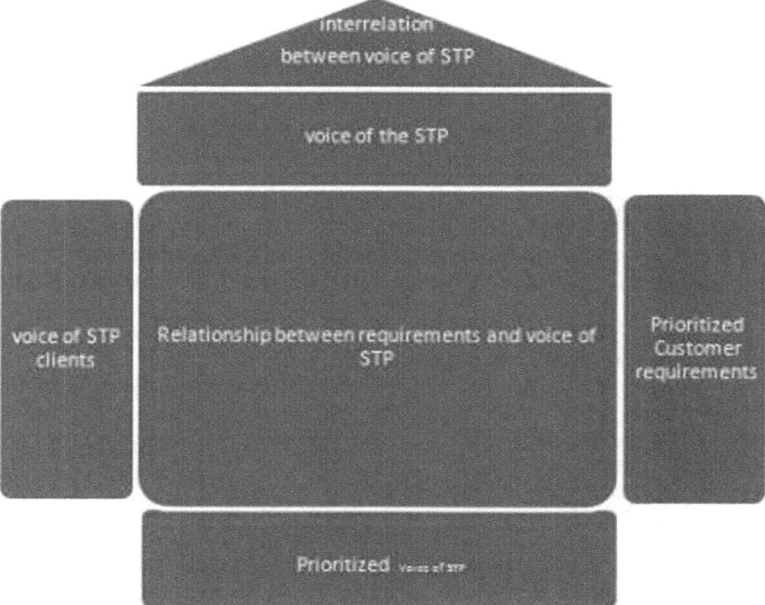

The house of quality converts the voice of customer into design requirements that meet specific target values and are an indicator as to how STP will meet those new requirements. By building house of quality for STP, everyday changing customer expectations are used to drive the design process of new services and improve existing services.

Voice of STP clients was fed to the house of quality matrices, and technical attribute of prioritized service (synergy among clients through exchange of experiences) was extracted from the first matrix. Technical attributes fed to the second matrix to achieve service process features, and finally its outcome was used as an input to the last matrix to form control mechanism features.

11.10 Conclusion

TQM and BPR though ultimately aim to achieve operational efficiencies attempt to do so through different means. BPR is the most divergent and suitable for an organization seeking dramatic changes; though it is widely used by organizations on the brink of collapse, it can also be used as a means to stimulate innovation.TQM is the preferred path when the quality of the product is the major concern. To conclude, none of these approaches can be used as off-the-shelf solutions, rather they offer a variety of options for managers and should be used judiciously to achieve the outcome most desired by the organization. QFD as well being a tool for planning towards achieving customer focus through collaboration is an efficient way to streamline processes once a quality focus is achieved through reengineering and by implementing TQM.

Bibliography

http://home.pacific.net.hk/~williamw/compare_tqm_and_bpr.htm
http://webs.twsu.edu/enteng/papers/sinha1.pdf
http://unpan1.un.org/intradoc/groups/public/documents/un-dpadm/unpan041436.pdf
http://www.usq.edu.au/extrafiles/business/journals/HRMJournal/AJMOBarticles/OD-TQM-BPR.pdf
http://www.isixsigma.com/index.php?option=com_k2&view=item&id=1300&Itemid=156
http://rapidbi.com/management/criticalsuccessfactors/
http://www.articlesbase.com/management-articles/total-quality-management-an-introduction-685318.html
Joseph JR (1992) Implementing TQM, 2nd edn. Technical Management Consortium, Inc., Albuquerque
http://www.qualitydigest.com/nov98/html/tqm.html
http://www.johnstark.com/fwtqm.html
http://www.referenceforbusiness.com/small/Sm-Z/Total-Quality-Management-TQM.html
"Implementing Quality Function Deployment (QFD) in STPs; Higher Competitiveness through Understanding the Voice of Clients"- an article by Shahram shookuhi (Technology Vice President of Yazd Science and Technology Park), Dariush Poorsarrajian (Planning manager of Yazd Science and Technology Park), Mohammad Saleh Owlia (Associate Professor of Yazd University)
http://www.wizdom.com/Documents/glossary.html

Chapter 12
Case Study: AEGON Religare

12.1 Introduction

AEGON Religare Life Insurance is a joint venture between Dutch insurance major AEGON, Bennett, Coleman and Company, and Religare Enterprises one of the leading integrated financial services groups in India. After the insurer launched operations in July 2008, as a late entrant in the market, AEGON Religare faced huge competition from other well-grounded players.

AEGON Religare had quite high aspirations. It aspired to launch operations across 25 locations at once. It realized enabling the processes with IT can help them reach such lofty aspirations. Thus the IT team had to deliver three systems within 5 months. Hence Srinivasan Iyengar, director of IT and change management, AEGON Religare, saw a need to build agility and adaptability into both process and technology in the company. "We wanted a business process management (BPM) solution to streamline our sales management process and the dissemination of information on the agency and customer portals," says Iyengar.

However, implementation of the BPM project was not an easy task. It was the first time that such a thing was being done in the industry. Moreover the vendor did not have a prior experience of implementing this solution in the Indian life insurance industry. Also this was for the first time in the industry that select peripheral systems like sales management system and procurement management system were being automated.

And the project was scheduled to be delivered within a very tight time frame. It was stipulated that three systems need to be deployed within 5 months.

The first project that was to be implemented was the sales management system which would increase sales productivity and track all agents. The second project was creating an agency portal, which would serve as a single window for all agents' activities including tracking new business proposals, placing alerts and information regarding policy servicing, etc.

S. Mohapatra, *Business Process Reengineering*, Management for Professionals, 239
DOI 10.1007/978-1-4614-6067-1_12, © Springer Science+Business Media New York 2013

The incidence management system, the third project, was devised with the aim of increasing ROI using a single system to monitor all user complaints, helpdesk support, and queries.

The projects helped business alliance partners keep track of the latest status of proposals, thus allowing them to get their work done without having to do follow-up with the company. The collection window, which used to close by 5 PM so that staff could reconcile accounts, now can stay open for an additional 2 h every day. These extra 2 h could make the company over Rs 6 lakhs a year. And as all agency-related requirements are now met from the portal, a total saving of Rs 12–15 lakhs could be done.

12.2 Objective

AEGON Religare needed a solution that could meet the following objectives within an aggressive time to market:

- Enable technology to be the key driver for superior customer service
- Support multiple sales channels and a pan-India launch on the first day
- Provide a portal to act as the core information source for the sales channel
- Provide a single view front-end—independent of multiple back-end systems
- Improve productivity and drive faster speed to market

Hence to achieve the above objectives, a user-friendly solution is required that could automate existing business processes and also provide seamless integration and process execution across a number of independent systems. Moreover the type of solution that was needed should also enable agility and adaptability to be built into the processes and the technology to ensure a future-proof and responsive business process model, thus enabling AEGON Religare to deliver on its promise of superior customer service and providing need-based solutions.

12.3 Challenges

The company had launched its pan-India multichannel operations in July 2008 with over 25 branches spread across India. Its core business philosophy was to help people to plan their life better. So providing high-quality advice to customers and ensuring superior customer service are its top priorities. So it attempted to offer policy servicing on the phone via Interactive Voice Response (IVR) System by issuing the customer a T-Pin for authentication. They were the first company to include the customer's medical report in the policy kit. So in such a service company where customer orientation was the main focus, it was necessary to automate its other processes. As opined by Srinivasan Iyengar, director of information technology and change management, AEGON Religare, "With faster, automated processes within the new system, employees can spend more time building customer loyalty."

Thus, the company identified that lead management and case management are the two areas in which this company has to concentrate so as to make itself different from others and thus gain majority market share. But in order to realize this vision, the company needed to surpass the challenges which are

- Servicing city mapping for assignment of lead
- Auto assignment of lead to direct agency or tied agency as per-defined logic
- PIN code mapping for assignment of lead to business manager or agent
- Escalation of mails of multiple leads
- Mapping department with assignment and escalation of the case
- Incorporating non-CRM users in a case
- Auto assigning cases to non-CRM user
- Sending alerts to user

12.4   Solution

Explaining the need for customer management solution, Srinivasan Iyengar, director of information technology and change management, AEGON Religare, said that customer-focused strategies essentially require CRM solution to help acquire customers thorough various touch points and thus shall help in translating operational data into actionable insights for proactively serving customers. Thus, the company decided to opt for a solution that would help it achieve competitive advantage.

After considering a number of options AEGON Religare decided to implement Microsoft® Dynamics™ CRM 4.0, supported by Religare Technova, a Microsoft® Certified Gold Partner. Srinivasan Iyengar, the pioneer for such a change, opined that the industry faces unique, multiple challenges such as high levels of customer attrition, selling more new products to existing customers to improve profitability and getting net growth in customer base every year. Religare Technova which has in-depth understanding of the financial services industry and its demands is best suited to partner with AEGON Religare in its endeavor to streamline.

Thus, the two modules automated by this solution are

- Lead management system
- Case management system

12.4.1   Lead Management System

As already stated this area is the most important aspect for the company. To have better control, better accountability, prompt action, and outstanding service to the customer, a special logic is introduced in the lead management system. First a lead is generated which can be by any of the following ways like through Web, internal portal, e-mail, SMS, phone, or direct walk-in. The logic then facilitates automatic allocation of nearest agent for each lead. After the agent is automatically allocated, then the system sends an allocation SMS alert to the agent to whom the lead is allotted. Simultaneously other relevant details like client information are also sent to him.

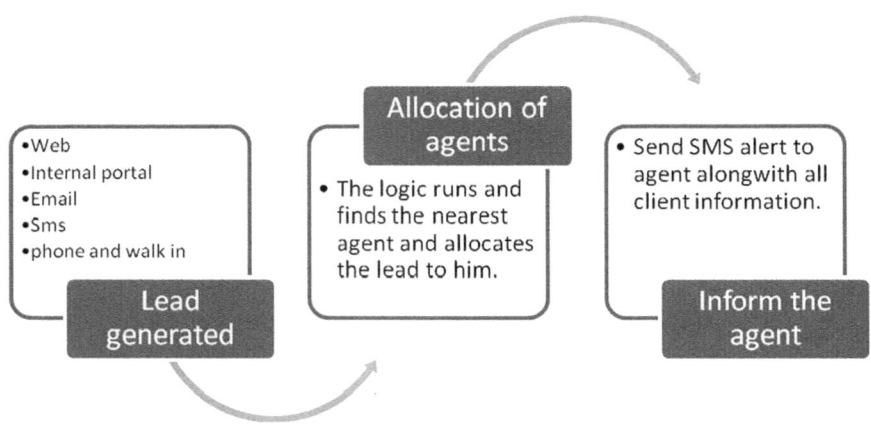

•Web
•Internal portal
•Email
•Sms
•phone and walk in

Lead
generated

Allocation of
agents

• The logic runs and
finds the nearest
agent and allocates
the lead to him.

• Send SMS alert to
agent alongwith all
client information.

Inform the
agent

Lead management module

12.4.2   Case Management System

Cases of complaints can be raised by phone, e-mail, Web, or internal portal. The cases then get automatically assigned based on the reason type and severity. A log is maintained for all the case-related activities under CRM activities. This is used for future reference when a similar problem would have arisen. From this log, the cases are selected for escalation process. This system facilitates quick service to customer complaints and is thus instrumental in retaining the client base and also procuring new customers.

The above modules were supported by three projects where AEGON Religare undertook. They partnered with Cordys for its implementation. These were

- *Sales management system*: which aimed to increase sales productivity and track all agents
- *Agency portal*: which aimed to create a single window for all agents' activities that would include tracking new business proposals, alerts, and information regarding policy servicing
- *Incidence management*: which aimed of extending ROI using a single system to monitor all user complaints, helpdesk support, and queries

Cordys is known for its expertise in BPM, rapid application development (RAD), and superior software integration capabilities. Thus, it was chosen to automate the business processes at AEGON Religare. With the inherent flexibility, scalability, and reusability of the Cordys Business Operations Platform (BOP), AEGON Religare can

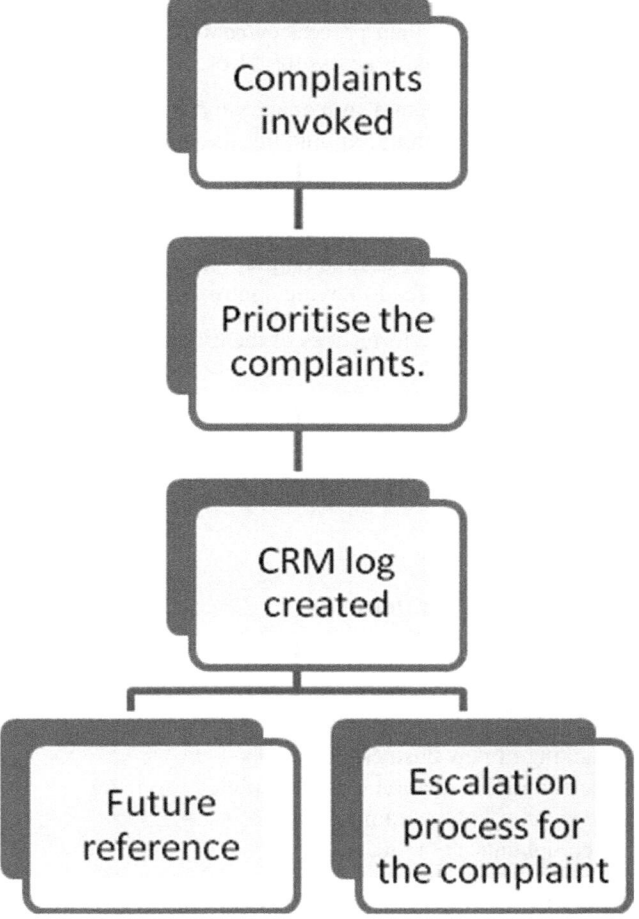

Case management module

implement process innovation quickly and cost-effectively. Additionally, the platform is standards based and offers an easy-to-use model-driven approach to development requiring a single skillset and a faster time to market than any other offering.

12.4.3   Sales Management System

AEGON Religare deployed Cordys BOP to orchestrate its sales management process and the broadcasting of information on agency and customer portals. The following steps were undertaken during implementation:

- Identifying all existing business processes.
- Mapping these processes to their process owners.
- Streamlining all these processes across the 51 branches of the company.

The sales management system also manages and tracks agent on-boarding and productivity automatically, thereby eliminating the traditional manual tracking of processes. It could do so by implementing end-to-end management and visibility of inputs and processes. Cordys interfaces with the already existing underlying infrastructure of AEGON Religare. This interfacing allows the business to manage the input processes and thus drive the desired output. The end result of this implementation was significant as it made the following contributions:

- Achieving consistency of performances of the processes.
- Improving speed of delivery.
- Creating a single view of the business.

The sales management system is completely integrated with core systems, enabling AEGON Religare to effectively manage and monitor sales operations, in real time.

12.4.4   Agency Portal System

Now in the agency portal, Cordys aimed to provide a single self-serving window to all its agents. The numerous functions of this window are

- Including tracking of new business proposals.
- Providing alerts and information regarding policy servicing.
- Keeping a track on agents' commissions.
- Registering complaints and requests.

The platform is fully integrated with back-office systems including a CRM system, that is, the case management system for tracking and resolving of issues and complaints and management of information systems for report generation.

12.4.5   Incidence Management System

The incidence management system was designed to increase ROI using a single platform to monitor all user complaints, helpdesk support, and queries, as well as all kind of problems related to tracking and service requests. The Cordys implementation included first the automation of complaint and issues logging system and tracking system; then it accordingly allowed issues reports to be routed automatically. The system can also track the time it takes to resolve a query, and depending on the delay, the system can automatically escalate the issue.

The three projects which spanned for a 5 month period aimed to automate the processes which could give a competitive advantage to AEGON Religare.

These three projects had a strong cohesive bond between them and were seamlessly integrated across all the 51 branches of the company. These projects gave support to the lead management and case management module of the company.

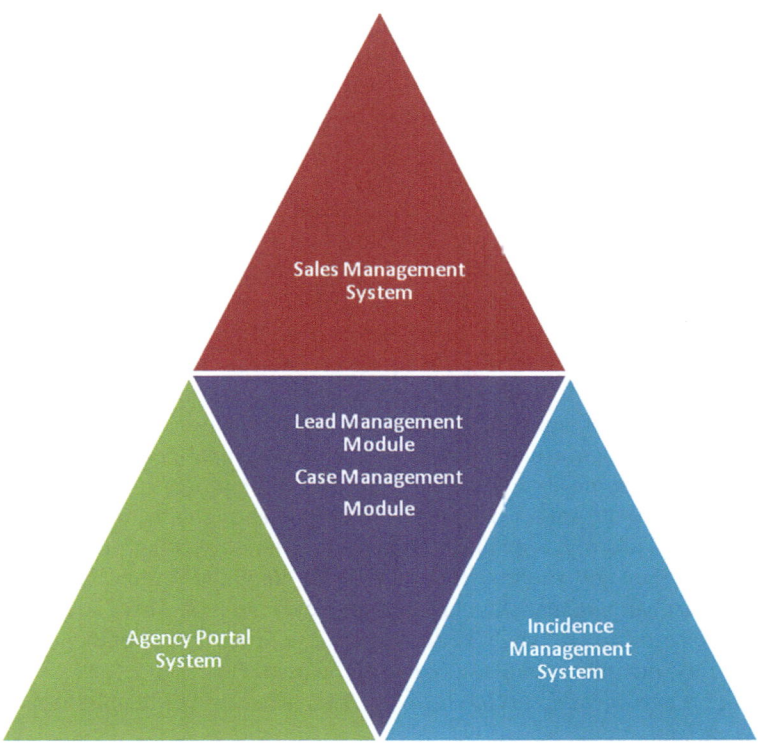

Current system

12.5   Business Benefits

Microsoft® Dynamics™ CRM 4.0 and Cordys allowed AEGON Religare to have a granular view of its customers, helping the company to design better products, improve service levels, and reduce operational costs significantly. Thus the business benefits which are derived from this automation are as follows:

- *Improving efficiency across branches*: AEGON Religare has more than 50 branches across India where leads are assigned and cases are used. So now because of Microsoft® Dynamics™ CRM 4.0, all leads are assigned automatically, and every lead is attended based on the assignment matrix. Additionally the agents also get assignment alerts along with relevant client information which ensures optimal utilization of all available resources. Srinivasan Iyengar, director of information technology and change management, AEGON Religare, says, "With faster, automated processes on systems, employees can spend more time building customer loyalty. As a result, productivity has improved." This increase in productivity of employees has also increased the efficiency of all the branches.

- *Enhancing customer satisfaction*: With a combination of easy-to-use customer interfaces and robust functionality, the system delivers quick and easy access to customer information. Clients can also reach the company by all possible ways like direct walk-in, phone, e-mail, and SMS. This spontaneous access has improved both employee and customer satisfaction. The solution creates an efficient working environment for employees, which is resulting in more satisfied and successful customers.
- *Providing greater customization*: The solution can also improve campaign management for AEGON Religare. It captures all promotional-related activities of the company. For instance, a custom-made campaign, KILB—Kum Insurance Lene Ki Bimari—was introduced by AEGON Religare, and all leads were mapped with this promotion management tool. The response of the campaign was carefully captured through Microsoft® Dynamics™ CRM 4.0. This information could be useful to the company, as by this, the company will able to know the impact of the promotion. Additionally, all leads will be attached with the latest active campaign which will help company take monitory calls.
- *Leveraging first-mover advantages*: Cordys BOP provides AEGON Religare with a single platform for designing, executing, and monitoring business operations. The platform has enabled the orchestration of existing investments while creating a strategic solution that allows the company to continue to respond quickly to changing market conditions and leverage first-mover advantage.
- *Faster time to market*: AEGON Religare enjoys faster time to market through the reusability, flexibility, and ease of use of the platform.
- *Total cost of ownership (TCO) is lower*: This is because of the platform.

  - Can leverage existing IT investments
  - Is completely Web based and therefore highly scalable, without the need for additional IT investments or maintenance and installation costs.

- *Improved operational efficiency*: The operational efficiency of the branches has increased and so have productivity and cost savings. For example, faster and more effective reconciliation and cash collection have led to reduced time to process payments with conservatively 2–3 man hours per day which can be used for other activities in each of the 51 branches.
- *Single self-serving window*: The agency portal system has already resulted in a 20 % reduction in the number of calls from agents. It has transformed the way the company communicates with agents and other sales groups, providing online access to real-time information on clients, their policies, and premiums, as well as commissions paid to sales agents.
- *Faster issue resolution*: The new incidence management system has resulted in a larger number of issues being closed within the agreed service level agreements (SLAs), with at least 10 % faster closure of cases to date. Previously this was not measurable.

12.6 Summary

As an insurance company, AEGON Religare's main objective was to automate its sales force, customer service, and reporting systems. So the company was also looking towards auto assignment of lead to direct agency or tied agency as per-defined logic, finding city for assignment of lead, sending alerts to users and agents, incorporating non-CRM users in a case when there is any complaint, and mapping department with respect to assignment and escalation of the case. To solve all these issues, the company decided to adopt Microsoft Dynamics CRM 4.0. It provided a granular view of its customers which in turn helped the company to design better products, improve service levels, and reduce operational costs significantly. At the branches, since now all the leads are assigned automatically and every lead is attended based on the assignment matrix, the employees can cater to more serious issues like building customer loyalty. As agents get the assignment alerts along with client information, this ensures proper utilization of the services of all agents across India. The software has user-friendly customer interfaces and robust functionality, thus delivering quick and easy access to customer information. Also, clients can reach the company through all possible means like direct walk-in, phone, e-mail, and SMS. This spontaneous access has improved both employee and customer satisfaction. The automated sales management system, agency portal system, and incidence management system facilitated CRM to be built on the two most important modules of the company, namely, lead management and case management module. Thus with faster automated processes on systems, employees can now spend more time building customer loyalty, resulting in improved productivity.

Bibliography

http://www.ciol.com/SMB/SMB/Case-Study/Aegon-Religare-deploys-CRM/145257/0/
http://www.computerworld.in/articles/aegon-religare-implements-bpm-automates-systems-0
http://www.cio.in/node/3839#
http://www.religaretech.com/pdf/Casestudy/CaseStudy1.pdf
http://docs.google.com/viewer?a=v&q=cache:vtjYRb53w3cJ.www.cordys.com/cordyscms_sites/objects/01d264da3b09fbc3bfe179e1c141c5d6/aegon_case_study20091109.pdf+Aegonreligare+cordyscase+study&hl=en&gl=in&pid=bl&srcid=ADGEESgugEL2BX6B7lvmMjeNgXAqJckBTrMnx3vicwWRofNu3Mi7htr6Zu9A7MTc1EewZDUeEAhAaFZYpqpFOTa-sRRfgjLwyN74wlQwADlioMdUgDYnG4ufennftGUmUVj57ufi2SZp&sig=AHIEtbS2jOidthrTqewoRFDMvt56JFS7WQ

Glossary

Action Plans The term refers to specific activities or tasks that a company performs keeping in mind the short term and long term objectives.

Activity The steps involved in a process that produce and consume artifacts that are owned by stakeholders.

Alignment Alignment refers to the basic consistency among various objectives and processes which support those. Effective alignment requires a common understanding of purposes and goals and use of complementary measures.

Artifact Anything that is consumed or produced by a process or activity.

As-Is It is the condition or method in which the existing processes are working in an organization.

> **As-Is Model** A model that represents the current stage of the organization without any specific improvements included.

Baseline It is a line that serves as a basis for calculation or measurement or standard for processes.

Business process Management The co-ordination and management of a business process which will invariably involve some business process modeling.

Business Process Modeling Any process modeling exercise that is performed in order to enhance overall operations of a business.

Business Process Reengineering (BPR) A fundamental reconsideration and radical redesign of the organizational process in order to achieve drastic improvement of current performance in cost, service, and speed

Business process Re-engineering It is used specifically when business process modeling is applied to existing processes as a part of process improvement exercise.

Continuous Process Improvement A policy which encourages employees to find ways to improve process and product performance based on the metrics specified, on an ongoing basis.

Data Repository A specialized database containing information and also metadata (data about data) and relationships between them. It is used to provide a common resource for standard data elements and models.

DMAIC Define, measure, analyze, improve, control (A Six Sigma Framework)

Indicators It is refers to a numerical value that quantifies the input output of a process or service.

Innovation Innovation involves the adoption of an idea, process, technology, or product that is either new or new to its proposed application.

Iteration A self contained set of process executions within a process.

Knowledge Management The use of inferences drawn from the knowledge repositories which helps in increasing responsiveness and innovation.

Metrics The quantifiable portion of a company's performance is gauged using these set of measurements.

Optimization It is the process of making something as efficient or as perfect as possible.

PDCA Plan–Do–Check–Act (A TQM Framework)

PDCA Plan Do Check Act.

Performance Measure An indicator that can be used to measure quality, cost, or cycle time characteristics of an activity or process usually against a benchmarked value.

Performance "Performance" refers to output results obtained from processes, products, and services that permit evaluation and comparison relative to goals, standards, past results, and other organizations.

Pitfall It is a hidden danger or a source of some trouble.

Process An approach to doing something that consists of a number of activities.

Process Improvement Process (PIP) A method to introduce process changes to improve quality, reduce costs, or accelerate schedules.

Process mapping Refers to relating different processes to one and another to form an integrated view of the business function.

Process Process is a series of activities that takes an input and provides an output which can be used with a business bent of mind.

Productivity It basically refers to the efficiency of the resource under consideration.

Quality Function Deployment (QFD) It focuses on quality and communication to transform customer needs into product-and-process-design specifics. Also known as the "house of quality".

Repository It is a place or storage where things like data can be deposited for safekeeping.

ROI Return on investment. It is a measure of the profitability of a project or even can be that of a company.

Role Part played by a person, place or thing that has an interest in the system or project.

Simulation It is a process or act of imitation of the functioning of some system or a real life condition.

Six Sigma Six Sigma a business management strategy developed by Motorola for achieving 3.4 defects per million parts produced.

Six Sigma Quality A process is said to have achieved Six Sigma Quality when it produces no more than 3.4 defects per a million opportunities

Stakeholders The term "stakeholders" refers to al. groups that are or might be affected by an organization's actions and success.

Standardization The process of setting of a technical standard which acts as a guideline.

Swim Lane An area on an activity with defined border, the content of which are associated with a stakeholder.

System It is an entity or collection of entities that collaborate in some way to meet a set of requirements.

Total Quality Management (TQM) A comprehensive and structured approach to organizational management that seeks to improve the quality of products and services through ongoing refinements in response to continuous feedback

To-Be It is the state which the company aims to reach after implementing a certain plan.

To-Be Model Models that are the result of applying improvement opportunities to the current (As-Is) business environment.

Transaction It is the act of transferring or exchanging of goods, services etc.

Validation Refers to something which meets its original requirements.

Verification Refers to something that works correctly and without errors.

Workflow Management System Integrated software tools for supporting the modeling, analysis, and implementation of business processes.

Workflow A system whose elements are activities related to each other by a trigger relation and triggered by external events that represent a business process starting with a commitment and ending with the termination of the same.

Index

S. Mohapatra, *Business Process Reengineering*, Management for Professionals,   253
DOI 10.1007/978-1-4614-6067-1, © Springer Science+Business Media New York 2013